Enlightenment
in SUBURBIA

Enrica Mallard

BALBOA.
PRESS
A DIVISION OF HAY HOUSE

Balboa Press books may be ordered through booksellers or by contacting:

Balboa Press
A Division of Hay House
1663 Liberty Drive
Bloomington, IN 47403
www.balboapress.com.au
1 (877) 407-4847

Because of the dynamic nature of the Internet, any web addresses or links contained in this book may have changed since publication and may no longer be valid. The views expressed in this work are solely those of the author and do not necessarily reflect the views of the publisher, and the publisher hereby disclaims any responsibility for them.

The author of this book does not dispense medical advice or prescribe the use of any technique as a form of treatment for physical, emotional, or medical problems without the advice of a physician, either directly or indirectly. The intent of the author is only to offer information of a general nature to help you in your quest for emotional and spiritual well-being. In the event you use any of the information in this book for yourself, which is your constitutional right, the author and the publisher assume no responsibility for your actions.

Any people depicted in stock imagery provided by Getty Images are models, and such images are being used for illustrative purposes only. Certain stock imagery © Getty Images.

Print information available on the last page.

ISBN: 978-1-5043-1356-8 (sc)
ISBN: 978-1-5043-1355-1 (e)

Balboa Press rev. date: 06/14/2018

Contents

Acknowledgements

To all who have taught me, including all the beautiful clients who have crossed my path, thank you for sharing your knowing and facilitating the awakening of my knowing.

To my dear family and friends, thank you for your encouragement and for facilitating me in writing this book even when I wore the cloak of fear within the world.

To my editor Leah Szanto, thank you for being so reassuring and brilliant and for guiding me through this process.

To my husband David, thank you for your loving allowance of me as I dedicated myself to writing this book.

To my son Patrick, thank you for your open-hearted innocence and unconditional love and beauty. You remind me every day what is possible.

To my son Sean, thank you for your wisdom, clarity and insight. I am so grateful for all our deep conversations in Consciousness.

To my Guru Paramahansa Yogananda and others of the spiritual lineage of the Self-Realisation Fellowship, Jesus Christ, Bhagavan Krishna, Mahavatar Babaji, Lahiri Mahasaya and Swami Sri Yuteswar, thank You. All searching ceased when I found my way to You, fear dissolved in a Love beyond measure. Words alone can never express my Infinite Gratitude and Love for You and God. As I wrote this book Your Presence was never far. I asked to be shown and I watched as it all unfolded. Thank You.

Introduction

WHAT I KNOW IS that we are all Magnificent beyond description. We are all Unique aspects of Divinity that will never Present the same. You Being You is what you are here for.

I lost access to much of this knowing when I incarnated. I was clouded by the density of matter. I bought the story I was born into as real, as who I was. It was all foreign to me and I could not see past the fear that arose being in that reality, so I chose to remain in the formless reality of my internal reflections and knowing.

I perpetually reflected and contemplated Who We Are and what impedes us Being Who We Are in the world. For the most part, I even questioned incarnation.

It was when I stopped rejecting the notion of incarnation and stepped into an allowance of my body that the awareness to write arose. I did not set out to write a book. I was expressing externally and grounding on the page my private and personal reflections.

Soon I realised that the information was not for me alone. I began expressing the knowing and developed a series of classes. Those classes soon translated into the chapters of this book.

This book feels like a coming out for me. For 55 years I have lived a private life reflecting and contemplating Who We Are, sharing only with close friends and clients in the past 20 years. Now it is out there to read, if you choose.

Do not consider this book prescriptive. It is knowing that has projected through Who I Am. Consider it more a conversation and an invitation to bring more of your own knowing to Light.

I hope it inspires you to know what you know. I hope it invites you to expand your scope of thinking and perceiving. Mostly, I hope that it facilitates, even in a small way, you knowing Who You Are and for you to Be that in the world, whichever world you frequent.

Consciousness has expanded sufficiently on the planet that Who We Are can be received wherever in the story we choose to Be, even in suburbia.

At times, I have used terminology that articulates the energy I am perceiving. You may not have used those word labels in the same context, stay with me as we share the awareness.

As you progress through the book, I have included a few practical exercises. Choose for yourself if you wish to undertake them or a variation that comes to your awareness.

The book itself is a process, and you may choose to journal your observations and awareness as you read the book. My target is for you to know and acknowledge the Magnificence of You.

Thank you for choosing this book. It has been a joy to write. There are an infinite number of possibilities to receive this information and it honours me that this book has crossed your path.

In Gratitude,
Enrica

Chapter

One

MY STORY

I WAS BORN ON 12ᵀᴴ February 1963, one of twin girls. Two girls had already been born into the family, all within 2 years and 3 months. My parents, like many others, were Italian migrants who came to Melbourne, Australia for a 'better life' after World War II. They adopted a strict parenting approach and focused on 'putting food in our mouths and shoes on our feet'. They demonstrated their love by providing for us. This was the most valuable thing for them, having come from the experience of the frontline.

The facts of my story are not extraordinary, they are quite common. However, it is not the facts and figures of my story that define the story, but rather it is how I experienced it that is my story. We each have a unique story in the way we experience it, a uniqueness that cannot be invalidated. No one can say to you that you didn't experience what you experienced. Even if the world judges it as insanity, it does not alter what you consider to be your reality. The sharing of a story bears witness to another being. It is an acknowledgement and an allowance: I see you, I hear you and I receive you.

When we have been *seen* and *heard*, we are often freed from the attachment to our identifications; we are freed from the character we act out in the stage of our lives and we can become open to the

1

possibility of unveiling Who We Really Are. This unveiling can occur as we detach from the facts and figures and shift to perceiving from our hearts and Souls. Bearing witness from this place will change this world of ours.

So here it goes…

There was much anguish. If he stayed, we would all die. If he died the two of us would live. As an act of pure and unconditional love, he chose to die so that we could live. This brother, I would later know as my own son, left the planet for the sake of me and my twin.

From that moment, I vowed to protect my sister forever. I would never let anything happen to her. I had vowed it on the death of our brother.

In each moment, my resolve strengthened. I had also confined myself and felt that this was it. There was no other place, there was nothing else to do. I didn't allow myself to know that I was here to be born into this world. This world was foreign to me and the cloud of its density had already veiled me from remembering Who I Really Was. I had created separation and I did not acknowledge the body I was incarnating in.

When things started to move, I was in shock, and desperation overtook me. The words for the feelings were, 'What is happening? I have no control over what is happening to me'. I was being swept up in a force greater than my will. I had vowed to stay with my twin forever yet something was driving me away from her and she was not coming with me.

The journey was treacherous and painful but the deepest pain was the separation from my twin, the one I had vowed to never part from, the only thing I was here to do.

Suddenly I found myself sliding out of what I later realised was my mother. A sudden gush and I was out. I had failed. The one thing I had to do, I failed at. I left my sister behind!! I did not protect her. I did not keep my promise. The feelings were so strong.

I didn't know that my sister would be born soon. There was no concept of time. There was only this stationery moment in which I was a failure, something that I then felt could never be changed.

I screamed and screamed. Not from the physical journey. I was grabbed. 'Put me back! You don't understand, I don't belong here.' Twenty minutes later (after being manually rotated) my sister was born.

My father didn't come to the hospital after receiving the news that he had another two girls. He stayed at work. My pattern of failure strengthened: 'I was not good enough, I was not a boy'. His desperate need to perpetuate his name had failed. My mother had failed, again.

The shutdown showed up in full force. I realised that survival rested on maintaining my isolation. Any sense of protecting my twin was overtaken by the dread of surviving this foreign place. I took comfort in sucking my thumb and hiding under the security of my baby blanket. My mother would say I was a 'good baby', not demanding at all. A quiet baby was a Godsend. She didn't look beyond survival.

I felt I didn't belong here. I found no one that knew me. I didn't recognise anything. This sense of isolation presented itself in the world as shyness and quietness. I could not interface with this world. One clear characteristic was my silence. In particular, I couldn't speak or interact with boys. Within, I continued to experience dread and terror, a frigidity in being in this world. This continued throughout my early years and into adulthood. Fear was my constant companion. In any moment if I checked in with myself, I always wanted 'out'. I never felt I belonged in the world and deep within I continually questioned why I had to be here. This certainly didn't feel familiar or safe. I had no relationship with my body, the only feeling was an intensity of fear.

We all attended a Catholic primary school. I shadowed my twin and it helped that we were placed in classes together. She was outgoing and social, so I hid behind her, literally! Being physically taller than her I began to develop poor posture as I perpetually tried to shrink myself, to hide.

We lived virtually across the road from school. Being very strict, my parents required us to go home for lunch everyday (there were rare exceptions when we stayed at school). I didn't mind as it provided safety. It certainly didn't assist my social ineptitude!

In 6th grade my first glimmer of hope appeared. There was something else in the world that could support me other than the shadow of my twin and being shrouded in the rigidity of my family environment.

The hope came in the form of my 6th grade teacher. She was a tall, loving and beautiful teacher and she cared about me. I sat in the back of the classroom and felt her caring. It was a feeling I remembered as familiar. For the first time, someone outside the construct of my family provided some safety. I secretly cherished her, I recognised true love in her and from then on, I began yearning to be loved in the world. I didn't understand it then, but the love I was yearning for was the Love that was Who I Am, that was my Nature. The separation I had created did not give me access to my Self. Her unconditional love revealed a glimpse of it to me. It would console me at night while seeking protection in my bed. I would rock myself to sleep, often rocking for hours as I retreated from this world into my internal world. This is where I lived more truly as my Self. It was such a relief to no longer reside in this world. When I got to a place of bliss I would sleep in its embrace. Much later in life I would recognise that feeling as Being and connecting back Home.

Being the last year in primary school, it was inevitable that I would part from my teacher but I didn't really conceive this in a reasonable way. The day she left, I, with my twin and a small group of her friends, escorted her to her car. I was quiet as usual. When it came to saying goodbye, a grief overtook me and I began to sob. I remember noticing the shock in the girls nearby, looking bewilderingly at my overreaction. I grasped her with both arms. I only reached the top of her legs. I didn't want to let go. My hope was leaving my life. I felt stranded in the world again. I had heard a hope in a song but she was real and in my life. After that day, I shut down further. I was incredibly overwhelmed as soon I would also be starting secondary school.

The hope in a song came in the 6th grade also. Every week the Education Department broadcast programmes that we would listen to during a free lesson. For a time, they would broadcast Bob Dylan's *Blowin' in the Wind* (Dylan, 1962). I didn't understand what the words meant but I experienced a knowing, a familiar resonance of what I was yearning. It was a promise of what was possible and what was more truly real for me and that too gave me much comfort. I remember later in life reflecting back to these moments, being so grateful to that person in the Education Department who broadcast that song week after week. In my mind, I had that person pegged as a rebellious male teacher who needed to get the word out. To whoever that was, thank you. As they say, you never know where the ripples of your actions will reach. Bob Dylan's lyrics and later Van Morrison's, would provide me much solace and inspiration, capturing the resonance of what I was 'trying' to both articulate in my mind and express from my heart and Soul.

In the year that followed, I moved to an all-girls Catholic Secondary School run by the nuns of the Convent of Mercy. My teacher was a strangely attractive man and I liked him. He created a nurturing environment that cradled both my insecurity and my naivety.

My twin, being stronger in the world, began to rebel. She bleached her hair and began to smoke. I couldn't summons the strength to follow.

My teacher was also gay. I had never known someone who was gay. I envied his rebellion and my assumption of his freedom, such was my naivety.

In that class I met a student who changed my life. We didn't interact much, between her absence and my shyness we may have shared five words.

The reason for her absence was because she had leukaemia and she was dying.

Looking past her bad wig and her pale, unwell appearance, there was something different about her. I couldn't put my finger on it, but I was drawn to her. I would long for her to be at school each day but that didn't happen very often.

When she did come, she didn't do much. I would glance at her continually as she sat quietly at the back of the room. I couldn't resist.

By this stage, my internal reflections and experiences were my real life. Her energy matched something I recognised and then I realised its' substance. She was angelic, maybe even literally. There I was, stuck in fear and dread and she had no semblance of those feelings. She was pure and clear. She was grace. I was drawn like a moth to a flame. This girl was dying yet she was not afraid, nor did she concern herself with the 'living in this world' that brought such fear to me. I was resisting this world while she was purely Being.

I continued to wish to see her, I felt blessed when she was there. Then came the news. The beautiful angel had died.

It was the first time in my life that someone I knew had died. I became more numb than usual. Everything felt surreal. What was this grief?

The class attended the funeral. I sobbed and sobbed, but why? I didn't know her well, as I said, we may have exchanged five words.

I sobbed because I now knew. I sobbed because I had been in the presence of someone who had shed this 'mortal coil'. I had been in the presence of a Conscious Being in this reality and I was not isolated when I was near her. I felt deep grief over the loss of this angelic presence in my life, something that I recognised as familiar to me.

That day was also the start of something new. Without knowing consciously what I was doing, I continued to speak to this dear angel and even task her! Every time someone died I would ask her to greet them and escort them over. Where did that come from? I didn't know and I also didn't know if it was real, it didn't matter to me; it felt right, it felt like I was being of service to the person who was passing. My thinking then was that I wasn't able to assist from my current position, but she was. Calling on her came naturally to me. These days I call on others in both the angelic and astral realms to support those crossing, but more on that later.

During the remainder of my time at that school, I plunged myself into study, something that didn't come easily, even reading was difficult as I am dyslexic. I had to learn everything by rote, reciting over and over to get the content firmly enough in my head to pass my tests. I became interested in boys, but only from afar. I never had a boyfriend, I could barely sustain girlfriends. I was really only friends with my sister's friends. They got a package deal being friends with my sister. I felt like the girl that never got picked for anything. I didn't consider how others received my frigidity. My sense of isolation limited what I allowed myself to notice and to Be.

I continued to go to church on Sundays, mostly on my own. I didn't question the teachings of the Catholic Church, I just felt comfortable as I contemplated while attending mass. I do have to admit, however, that another part of me checked off going to mass so that I didn't go to 'hell'.

What did begin to show up was a distinction between the routine of reciting prayers and mass and the warmth and comfort of communing with the energy of Jesus and God. I didn't fully grasp the connection then, but I recognised the same familiarity that I experienced with those that crossed my path and 'touched my heart'. These were the incidents that provided glimpses of Home.

This different experience of God was reinforced one day when I arrived at school only to be told that a bus was waiting for me to go to an Italian poetry recital competition where I was expected to recite a lengthy Italian poem. I went into shock and the situation became surreal (an out-of-body sensation). I never failed my scholastic obligations. What was this? I was totally unaware of the commitment, let alone knew the poem!! But then I felt rescued. I had no voice, literally. I woke up that morning as usual but without a voice. I wasn't unwell, I just couldn't speak. What were the chances? The day I was expected to do something I couldn't deliver, I had no voice. After my teacher's initial skepticism, she realised I was telling the truth and my twin took my place. She was not fearful; I think she relished the chance to get out of normal school work. I realised that day that God had my back and the communion I was finding comfort in was showing up in my life.

Living like this continued into college. God had my back again when I met my husband. We both were undertaking an undergraduate degree in accounting. I still could not interact well socially and lived life in a numb existence. He looked past all of that, took me by the hand and we were married a few years later. I am so grateful, for he is an amazing, loving and beautiful man and father whom I love deeply.

Things changed dramatically with the birth of our first child in 1992, a boy. We nearly lost him at birth. He was delivered with a vacuum suction that caused internal haemorrhaging in his right frontal lobe. He was resuscitated at birth.

Sixteen months later our second child, another boy, was born. I recognised this son as the brother that left my mother's womb so that my sister and I could live. He has been a gift in so many ways and continues to share his own awareness and knowing with me and the world.

During this whole time, I fell into a depression deeper than the numbing I had previously experienced. Functioning was difficult. My husband would be at work and with no other help I felt both inadequate and overwhelmed. I loved my children but the daily functioning was physically draining me. I would count the seconds until my husband would return home.

I knew my first son was not developing as expected. When I began noticing that my second child was doing things that my first child could not do, I began to panic. Assurances from others that each child is individual and that he would develop in his own time didn't 'cut it' anymore. I needed to act.

This realisation was the shock I needed to break through my depression, numbness and frigidity. I had to do something for my son. I began 'snapping out' of the numbness. I had a task to do, I needed to 'fix' my son. I began educating myself about what was happening to him, about intervention programmes. While I did this, it became clear that the person who was in greater need of help was me. This 'wakeup call' with my son's health was really my 'wakeup call'. I finally began to awaken in this reality and when I came to the point where western medicine could not offer any further help for my son, my journey to alternative therapies began. Before too long, while experiencing some of the energy and Consciousness work I was participating in, I began to recognise the familiarity of what I knew coming into this reality. I began consciously to 'seek' in this world, yearning for the match to what I knew already and had not found very often. I continued to hide, but underneath the covers, I was slowly emerging from within.

During this period, it became clear what was stopping me from functioning, and preventing what was familiar to me from showing up. I had found the words to describe it. The familiar feeling was Who I Am and 'stuff' was clouding my access to Being Who I Am. I couldn't find it in this reality because I bought this reality as real, and allowed it to be a buffer from me experiencing Who I Am. I remembered Who I Am before incarnating, and now I was choosing to Be that while incarnated. I totally committed myself to shedding what I could perceive was buffering me from Who I Am. I trained and practiced in various energetic and Consciousness modalities, attended and facilitated in personal growth workshops and events and even began seeing clients, as I was beginning to 'see' clearly what was stopping others from Being Themselves. My years of living internally had honed an ability to perceive energy and retrieve information beyond the five senses and I began utilising this capacity to facilitate others.

I continue to hone these skills while incarnated. This may sound odd, but I knew it was my 'physicality' that I had to learn to commune with in order to access more fully what I knew and what arose instantly when I didn't have a body.

A tremendous shift on this journey occurred during the process of my father's passing. My father passed at age 79 on the 30th April 2005.

Six months before this date, what seemed like a regular lunch at my mum and dad's place, turned out to be a pivotal moment for our family. My eldest sister and I independently became aware of an energy in the room and we instantly looked at each other. I, being more visual, had a knowing that this was my father's brother who had passed at the age of five from an ear infection (my father was a few years older than him), however, standing before me now was a handsome man in his thirties. My sister, being more auditory, heard him speak calling my father by the nickname he used to call my dad. He also told my sister that he was waiting for his brother. I did not hear the words literally, but knew it without needing to hear the words. I also knew that because there was no time/space where his brother was, we would be uncertain of a timeframe but I knew, despite my father not being diagnosed with any serious illness, that he would pass over in the foreseeable future.

Instantly we shared that dad's brother was present and had called out to dad. We did not share anything further. When my father heard the nickname he turned white, for no one called him that name except his brother and he never shared it with anyone else. Dad left the room in fear. He did not typically share anything personal with his family, so this was too intense for him to experience in front of his daughters.

A few months later my father had his own experience with his brother. As recounted by my mother, he saw a young man at the foot of his bed and yelled out in fear 'Who is this man in my room?' Once again this drained the colour out of him (from my mother's observation). He did not discuss his experience with his daughters and we respected that.

I continued to check-in with my uncle and as time moved on, I continued to sense his presence, waiting for his brother. I knew that I did not need to do anything.

A few months later came the diagnosis, my father had oesophageal cancer and 'there was nothing that could be done'. It was picked up after my mother's doctor observed that dad didn't look well.

My father then began the painful and fearful period of knowing about the diagnosis. He never accepted death. He continued to put his faith in doctors even though they did not treat the cancer.

It was during this period that my father asked me to help with the energy work I did. Thankfully, I was aware enough to be detached, being very conscious of the bigger picture that was unfolding. With immense vulnerability, my father shared some of his story with me. I felt so honoured. His story of abuse from his own father was shed as was my father's belief that he contributed to the death of his brother. He believed that because he hit his brother the week before he died, he contributed to him dying. He carried this weight with him. I shared my insight that that was not the case and that his brother held nothing but love for him. I know that this 'work' was facilitating my father's transition. It wasn't about healing his cancer, it was about healing what covered his Soul.

We chose to care for my father at home, something that he asked for and we did voluntarily to ease his anxiety about what was happening to him.

The day before dad passed he became very restless and relentlessly uncomfortable, requiring sedation. His doctor admitted him into a palliative ward at the local hospital.

That final day, all his immediate family came to say goodbye. Mum, my sisters and I remained. I continued to perceive the situation moment by moment. It was clear that dad wanted us all there. We offered Reiki and prayers, then we became aware that his passing was close. A shift was felt by all of us. We gathered around the bed and all placed our hands on him. Like a veil had been lifted I began to see very clearly. I saw my uncle waiting for dad. His mother and father and a group of relatives and others my father had known were in the distance. But principally, I knew that I had been preparing my father at this end and that I would be handing over to his brother any moment now and he was ready and waiting to receive him.

I then saw two Light Beings flanking my father's bed. Another sister would later recount that she saw a flash of light at about this moment. I wasn't fully in this world so I didn't experience the flash but saw these two Beings. I had a sense that they were attendants to help escort my father over. Within seconds of them attending, I felt my father leave his body and I literally saw his Light and Soul exit and move together with these attendants. I knew that they were going to his brother. The handover had occurred.

Whilst in awe of what I had just experienced, my attention turned to my father's body. I felt a tremendous responsibility to complete this process for my father and ensure his body was taken care of.

We all stayed for a time, but I needed to hand over the body to those that would prepare him for burial, so I stayed a while longer. I helped prepare him, I covered my father's face and I helped slide him onto the gurney. I did not leave until the hearse was out of sight.

The day of the funeral, I chose to be a pall bearer for my father, despite others saying it wasn't necessary or appropriate (being female). They didn't feel the sense of responsibility I felt to care for my father's body. I carried my father that day and I placed my father in the ground. The sense of honour and completeness was immense. What started six months ago in that kitchen was now complete.

The experience with my father unlocked a capacity to perceive freely between the worlds. It had always been present, but now the increased clarity stood out to me. What had shown up in the past as uncertain was now beyond doubt and became part of my everyday experience and reality.

Since then I have found myself supporting, informing and sometimes facilitating transitions, each with their own Unique Presentations. Each transition reveals a beauty and richness of the passing process and it provides me much honour and joy to contribute to and sometimes participate in such a loving process. What happens in the story with someone passing is quite different to what shows up when perceived at energetic vibrations. I continue to be amazed at the glory of our Being at the time we shed our incarnation.

Now my relationship with my father is so beautiful. I have had many sojourns with him. He has shown me where he usually is, once giving me a guided tour. He has been present during many sessions I have undertaken with clients. I love him deeply and I am grateful.

The gift of my father's passing was also a training in trust. All that I perceived could very well be imaginings. The world would certainly judge it so. But for me it was knowing, often bundles of information that could not be verbalised. Having others perceive the same information certainly helped to build that trust. When I had the trust, I realised I didn't need trust, that trust was a crutch until I acknowledged my knowing.

The years that have passed since have been devoted to Consciousness and have been both a roller-coaster ride and a blessing. I have been led by the hand and received intuitively the teachers who would facilitate the shedding of my unconsciousness.

For example, during meditation one day, quite a few years ago now, a man sat next to me. I didn't recognise the man but the next day as I was browsing the New Age section of a local bookstore I turned the cover of a book and saw a picture of that man looking back at me. It was Eckhart Tolle, and I had picked up *The Power of Now* (Tolle, 2004). I then knew I was meant to read this. The book became a source of insight and aided me to recognise truth within myself. Thank you.

A few years later, on that same bench within my meditation, another man appeared, a holy man. This holy man stayed for approximately six months. He did not speak and I would sit quietly with him. The sense of relief and feeling of Home was so complete, reassuring and comforting. In the day to day world, I sought to find out who this holy man was. It took six months. The day I came across *The Autobiography of a Yogi* by Paramahansa Yogananda (Yogananda, 2016), the holy man left my meditations. In the book I saw his picture. It was Lahiri Mahasaya, one of the Gurus of the Self-Realisation Fellowship. The holy man stayed in my meditation until I found my way to him, Paramahansa Yogananda and the other Gurus of the Self-Realisation Fellowship (SRF). One of these Gurus, Jesus, had already been in my life. These teachers showed me that no separation exists, and any separation we experience is not truth. They came to show us all Who We Are and what is possible, even while incarnated.

It was with the teachings and practices of the SRF that I finally felt I stopped running towards Consciousness, the illusive future 'event' that never arrives. My deep yearning eased, and I stopped searching. I recognised Home and experienced joy and communion with this familiarity of Home.

I knew I wasn't fully 'There', though even saying this is a contradiction, and a reflection of apparent time/space. I knew I was having experiences rather than an Isness of Communion.

My day to day life was certainly changing. I left behind much of the social 'chit-chat'. Previously, I had wanted to participate but now I recognised the distractions and deviations from Who I Really Was.

What still remained was a disconnect with my body. I knew something else was possible and continued to ask for awareness.

It was probably about five years ago that I made a conscious choice to stay here in my body. At that time, I still didn't have awareness of why I needed to incarnate. I figured that if I was here, there must be a reason and I chose to stay to receive the awareness.

I know now that we are all here to return Home to Oneness. The feeling of seeking the familiarity of Home that I experienced during my life was not unique to me, it exists for all of us. Most of us, however, are misidentifying things of this world as those things that are familiar, and Home cannot be found there.

Whether you allow yourself to know it or not, we are all incarnating to 'know Thyself' and return to God. I now know that incarnation is not separate from any other Presentation of existence, we have just made it so within our ego/minds. I certainly made it so in my ego/mind. I had created separateness between Who I Am and my body.

Then came another pivotal moment, not that long ago, on my 54th birthday. I experienced Communion with my body. It did not commence as a pleasant experience. I sobbed for two days, finding comfort only in foetal position.

I was experiencing the profound judgement which I had bought as real and stored in my body. There was so much judgement of the wrongness of my form, of how I looked, how I was in the world, and I allowed it to be so real that I decided that incarnating was like a grotesqueness.

When the tears subsided, I began to experience a deep caring for my body. I was in allowance of my body no matter how it showed up. I beheld the Beauty and Miraculous Presentation of my body, the same as when I received nature and the earth, and the cosmos. I experienced the familiarity of Being and now my body was included. Actually, I couldn't find a beginning or an end. I was more genuinely experiencing the Infiniteness We All Be. I was so surprised with the ease and simplicity of it All. It was my resistance to my body and incarnation that created the gap, the division.

My body without judgement wanted to show up with the introverted disposition, the autistic tendencies, auditory sensitivities, OCD and dyslexia that I experienced during my life and had made so wrong. I resisted my physicality from being revealed and consequently I presented as fearful and rigid.

In communion with All That Is, the diversity of this Presentation was just that, a diversity of Presentation, no different to the diversity of Presentation within nature and all things. We marvel at the richness and exhilarating diversity of nature, yet not the diversity with which our bodies show up, with which We All show up.

What would our world Be like if we all knew Who We Are and began to Be that in the world? We would begin to experience the diversity and Magnificence of all the Unique Presentations of Oneness with no judgement of more or less, only different.

A New World has already come into form where this is showing up. I perceive it, some days more than others. This is not a race in which some win and others lose. We Are One and until We All Commune in Oneness, not just as an experience but as an Alwaysness, an Isness, we will all continue expanding Consciousness for without All, Oneness is not complete.

Two

WHO ARE YOU?

SHARING MY STORY WITH you in Chapter One is useful to illustrate the distinction between what unfolds in your life and how you experience it, the unique experiencing that cannot be invalidated. So, who is having the experience? Why is it unique?

The awareness around these questions comes back to one question: Who Are You – really? Who provides these unique experiences and expressions in the world? Is that You? Does anything colour who you think You are?

When I ask the question, 'Who Are You?', where does your mind take you?

Do you commence a process of retrieving bundles of information that define 'Who You Are'? Do you access what already exists in your mind as 'Who You Are'? Do you retrieve the facts and figures that make up your life journey so far? Do you include an assessment of how you think others see you? How the world sees you? Is there a satisfaction in being able to articulate 'Who You Are'?

Most of us, when asked this question, react by accessing the information within our ego/minds and begin to retrieve lists of identifications of who we think we are. We begin to identify all the characteristics that appear in our stories, which define us, and represent our uniqueness.

This uniqueness as individuals is often defined by our diverse cultures, race, society, religion, appearance, physical conditions, gender, preferences, conclusions, assumptions, opinions, etc. Many pride themselves on these aspects. Our societies have criteria for these, often contrary criteria from one society to another, and we can choose to adopt or rebel against them. A few people within these societies establish new criteria.

There are those of us that do not look beyond the labels of these identifications and enjoy the sense of belonging that it creates at the level of ego/mind. Even though experience provides a unique perspective, this is often ignored for the sake of fitting in and feeling accepted.

For others, they notice the difference between the identifications, how those identifications are experienced and the level to which there is compliance with criteria that is adopted as objective, but can never be, as identifications always originate from someone's perspective.

So, is that all we are? A bunch of identifications, judgement and expectation both inwardly and outwardly? If we had no identifications, who would we be?

I was born knowing that we are much more than any list of identifications. However, with the process of incarnating into an apparent realm of dense matter, I lost that clarity, most of us lost that clarity. I was in a foreign place. I accepted my environment as something I needed to fit into. It was through getting back to what I knew before incarnating, that I began freeing myself and clearing the fog.

I resisted this world, which showed up as a fear of living in it. I created an illusion of separation. I labelled myself as wrong for not matching the identifications required of me in the story. It was only when I began buying out of it all, that the information I already knew came through cognitively.

So, Who Are You?

You are an incarnation of a Unique aspect of Cosmic Consciousness, The Universe, Divine Mother, God[1]. This Uniqueness is Your Soul. Your Soul is literally a Divine Spark or Flame of God. Your Soul is the apparent individuation that is 'out of this world' and Infinite. It is this apparent individuation that shows up as Your Unique Being. Even the term 'incarnation' literally means 'into flesh', implying that 'some thing' is coming into flesh. Your Soul is the 'some thing' that is coming into flesh. While the Soul is also an individuation of Oneness, it is the closest to Our Infiniteness that we Be whilst we continue to exist.

When I speak of 'Self' or 'You', I am referring to the Expression or Presence of Your Soul in the world and in existence. When I refer to 'you', I am referring to you as reflected from the ego/mind which contains a library of references from story: past, present and future, including any other lifetime, and which gets reflected back to you when triggered/recalled.

Each provides a unique experience and cannot be invalidated. The Uniqueness received from Being 'You' is a reflection of Your Essential Nature and the unique expression of 'you' is informed by all the content of your ego/mind, and all the charge and point of view we have on that content, resulting in a clear Unique perception (from 'You') being translated into a unique perspective (from 'you').

Even if you have no experience of Your Soul, please stay with me and be open to experiencing what comes to your awareness from the discussion.

'Who You Are' does not evolve.

There is absolutely no need to evolve Your Self. You Are Perfect; You Are a Unique Presentation; You Are Infinite; You Are an aspect of God Re-Presented as Your Soul. When you Be Your Self in the

---

[1]   I use the word label of God at times, however, this is also interchangeable with the word labels of Cosmic Consciousness, Divine Consciousness, Source, The Universe, The One, The All (among many other word labels). If you have a loading with the word label 'God' due to its use within your own and/ or other societies including religions, then please add it to the identifications you will be listing later in this chapter.

world there is no distinction between 'you' (the ego/mind) or 'You' (The Soul, Who You Are). When this shows up consistently, or more accurately, as an Isness (as the construct of time/space is no longer a consideration or relevant), the ego will have been dismantled sufficiently so that the information You receive from the perception of Your Soul is also received by the mind and there is no longer a separation or distortion of the information. It is a balanced state where there is 'no charge' in the body/mind complex, thus there is no interference with the knowing of You coming into cognitive awareness. This can be called 'Enlightenment'.

Whilst You exist, this will continue to Present as a Unique Expression. There is no 'need' for it to Be any particular way. It will reflect as Your Essential Nature.

The evolution that is spoken of in the personal development arena refers to changes in perspective. It is when we work to bridge the gap between 'you' and 'You' that we experience changes in our perspective, often feeling more freedom, lightness and less constrained by identifications. Some call this evolving but it isn't evolution. It is the shedding of what is buffering you from the fullest Expression of Your Self in the world and in existence.

The only purpose of incarnation is to know Self, to return to what is innately familiar (family) to You and return Home; to come to the awareness of that aspect of God that is You, and Be that in the world. This is the communing with God, Cosmic Consciousness, Allness that is the origin of religions. Once You return Home, the toggling between incarnation and not and even existence and non-existence may occur with no charge or position.

Whether you are cognitively aware of it or not, you are here to return Home and the way to begin is by asking 'Who Am I?' and experience the communion of what unfolds as you Be that question.

This chapter is the beginning of a process that began for me as I worked with clients and reflected on my own 'wake up' process. It is about getting clear on the content of your identifications, the sum total of which appear as your current perspective. What your perspective is of the question 'Who Am I?', is more accurately where we will begin.

For most of us, the ego/mind is still in place and we function predominantly from the ego/mind. When this shows up, there is a discrepancy between the perception of Our Soul and the translation of that information by the ego/mind. This is what provides us with our unique perspective on the happenings in our lives and in the world. This discrepancy is literally what is buffering each of us from Enlightenment – it's that simple!!

I like to use the analogy of the Michelin Man[2]. All the content and charge of the ego/mind creates a buffering that energetically shows up as you wearing a cloak like a Michelin Man. This cloak also represents how our bodies show up as a deviation from our potentiality. It also contributes to the brain function we utilise in any moment. It is the charge we have on all that content of the ego/mind that directly reflects how thick your Michelin Man suit is and consequently what is buffering 'you' from 'You'. The buffer is not You, but the story will judge it as you, you will judge it as you. It is not You, it is far from Being You, yet it is how you show up in the world.

Depending on how clearly or how foggily your perception is relayed by the ego/mind, your responses to questions in life and of life will be different to the original awareness received by You and, most certainly, your perspective of 'Who You Are' will be different.

No one outside of you can tell you 'Who You Are'; not your parents, your teachers, your peers, your religious leaders, your governments, your society or anyone else's society. However, for many of us, our perspective of who we are is still defined by all of these factors outside ourselves. The benchmarks imposed on us from outside ourselves are adopted and stored in the ego/mind as reference points.

Most of us play out a lifetime within the context of the story and live somewhere along the spectrum (reform, compliance and rebellion) of the boundaries, judgements, conclusions, etc. of that

---

[2]   Bibendum, commonly referred to as the Michelin Man, is the symbol of the Michelin tyre company.

environment. Buying into that reality, we are caught within the same confines of the story.

The story of the world (history) at a macro level is the sum total of all of our individual stories set on the stage of the planet, together with all the systems and frameworks around such things as government, economics and currency, health and social status. It is all a bigger version of identifications at the micro level. Observations and studies are made but all within the context of the world of cause and effect, good and bad, right and wrong, the story of the ego/mind: the dualistic reality. Judgement, expectations, assumptions and conclusions are an accepted and welcomed system of management and control.

Some societies speak of realities beyond this dualistic reality, often in the context of religion and spirituality. For most, the dualistic reality is all that exists and any suggestion otherwise is considered lunacy. Then, call me a lunatic because I know beyond doubt that Who We Are is much more than that, so much vaster than our ego/minds could possibly conceive of.

So, let us continue to look at "story" and what is happening for all of us, not just those of us who label ourselves as being on a spiritual path (which is simply another identification by the way).

We each have a unique story. I shared some of my own experiences and personal story in the previous chapter. I revealed that it is not the facts and figures which define my story, but rather how I experienced it. Consequently, no one can invalidate my story because it is my own unique perspective even if it was coloured by my identifications. Additionally, by observing beyond the facts and figures, we are already beginning a process of dismantling the rigidity of our identifications.

Every single person who is living, has lived and who will live has their unique story and no one can invalidate it. We are each having unique experiences within the content of our environments.

We are relating to one another; we are declaring our position on every identification, those we have adopted, and those we have not. We share common interests, pleasures, objectives. We share our disagreements, conflicts, opinions of injustice and intolerances.

Some belong, others don't. Some are outcasts, others are placed above the other. Some are deemed criminals, others are angels. It is all in relation to another and we all have our position in relation to it all: it is your unique perspective.

There is little or no sense of yourself being anything other than the content of your environment, your physical body, and how you relate to each aspect of that environment. Your sense of self is held by the ego/mind which orchestrates the happenings within a day. As you grow, the content of your ego/mind expands, storing information from parents and other family members, teachers, society, etc. You build links of consequences of actions and inactions both cognitively and unconsciously. The reservoir of who you are from the ego/mind perspective continues to build and change. Your body continues to reflect this content also. You also have little or no awareness beyond the body and think of yourself as your body. You are the person named on your birth certificate, you are who your family is, what you do, where you are from both geographically and socially, you are what you believe, stand for, etc.

Your ego/mind also has access to all previous lifetimes and thus all the stories you have ever participated in and created identifications in. Even though you have no or little cognitive memory of these, all of the content is available in the library of the ego/mind and all the charges (emotional, mental, physical and spiritual) that existed then are still in place in any specific moment unless it has been transmuted, that is, you have removed the charge on it. In addition, all the patterns and commitments previously locked in often play a role in attracting those same experiences. It is all in the vibration of like attracting like, even if it is unconscious. But much more on this later, including how the information appears to be carried forward lifetime after lifetime.

In the dualistic reality, life is the cycle of birth and death within the environment we are born into and which few break free from. We task ourselves to behave somewhere along the spectrum of the polarised reality, for example, 'I aim to be a good person' or 'the world hates me and I hate it'. Accordingly, this justifies the need to govern and attempt balance within this reality. So every society that considered itself separate to another, built their own value systems, judgements and consequences. The result was innumerably diverse and contradictory systems of management and control, all vibrating at varying levels of Consciousness and all believing that their systems are preferred and resolve the balance they determined is required for their reality.

Success is measured by the judgements established within the environment you are born into, often based on 'doingness'. For example, getting an education, getting a great job, rate of pay, amount of money, looking a certain way, behaving a certain way, representing your family adequately and appropriately.

We will discuss Right Action in much more detail later but it is relevant to mention it here. In the story, organisations, religions, governments, cultures, societies, advocate certain appropriate behaviours and, with some, ideal behaviour and service to others. Where those behaviours or outcomes of behaviours mimic what occurs naturally when we Be Our Selves, Our Essential Nature, I call these Right Actions. Not all recommended behaviours are Right Actions as there is a need to distinguish those recommendations which are heavily clouded by ego/mind, even at the macro level. That is, like at the micro level, the knowing of Being does not filter through and the recommendations bear no resemblance to the originating awareness or Our Essential Nature.

Right Actions can be useful while you are still functioning from the ego/mind as these behaviours mimic how You would show up if you Be You. However, Right Actions alone will always be a crutch to give you a glimpse of You. It is not the same as Being You, and thinking that you are a 'good person' because you do Right Actions is another filter that buffers 'you' from 'You'.

The greatest use of Right Actions is in reducing the significance of you and indirectly dropping your buffers whilst you experience a sense of Who You Really Are. This is the true purpose of service to others: putting aside the significance of you and your story with the bonus effect of transmuting ego/mind content. The result can be the opening of the heart and accessing Soul and Being, Who You Are, even if only temporarily. Once you have a glimpse, the seeking of that feeling of Home may really begin in earnest.

Every experience you have within this world provides an opportunity for you to check-in with Your Self and notice if you feel a resonance with You or not. Religious teachings sometimes refer to this as 'your conscience'. It can be termed as your 'gut feeling' and awareness. It can also be termed 'intuition'. Even though in the story the labels themselves have much judgement and limitation, these are all labels for the knowing of Your Soul and is Your Soul attempting to get through your ego/mind to reveal knowing to you.

What if the knowing Presented as Your Soul and Being are the true Nature we as Beings are seeking to return to? Our Essential Nature, when unhindered by the buffers of the ego/mind, shows up as true caring, loving and complete allowance of diversity. There is a knowing of Oneness with all no matter how it is revealed. What if societies are trying to mimic what occurs naturally and, having forgotten the origin, install benchmarks in an attempt to reclaim access to Our Selves?

When someone is lost in their ego/mind they cannot relate to others in what society may define as 'a healthy manner'. This is a product of an ego/mind that is so 'foggy' with content that virtually none of the knowing of the Soul can filter through. The intensity of this experience is often what leads some to numbing and addictive behaviours and can be a trigger for mental illness developing. In these cases, the Divine Love and access to knowing and awareness that reflects in the Essential Nature of the Soul becomes inaccessible. This is truly the definition of the 'Lost Soul' as the knowing and awareness of the Soul literally cannot get through.

The story will judge this person and would establish a system of justice for any behaviour considered by that society to be unacceptable. In the context of the journey to Enlightenment, judgement is futile.

This happens identically at the macro level. One society establishes a system of justice for any behaviour of another society considered to be unacceptable. It is all in the context of story.

For others, their perspective of 'who they are' in the story (and their society) is deemed overwhelming, insufficient, undesirable and/or imperfect and they chase another perspective even if for a short time. For example, rebellion, numbing, 'losing themselves' while watching TV, a movie or reading/fantasising over a magazine, taking a break from their story and perspective and wishing that it were different. The society they find themselves in establishes benchmarks, judgements and positions for every aspect of the story and whilst trapped within its confines we each judge ourselves based on those criteria.

We define happiness by the level to which we achieve and maintain the meeting of these criteria. It is not sustainable and can prove fatal when so much significance is placed on maintaining expectations. We are looking in the wrong place for happiness. Happiness is Being You irrespective of any doing. It is Being without needing to do, with any doing coming from what you choose to do, not need to do. Even in situations where you find yourself with responsibilities, for instance, at home with children or at work, if you choose to respond and take action rather than feeling obligation and no choice, then happiness is possible even when the story may tell you there is no choice. It is all in the potency of choosing rather than the impotence of being told what to do.

Staying within the confines of the ego/mind also both exposes and confines you to judgement according to the society you are in. For those who have begun to awaken to the knowing that they are more than that which their society defines them as, limiting the search for Self within the confines of story will also prove futile.

Despite all of the above, even without you cognitively knowing it or giving attention to it, You are guiding yourself out of those confines into the broader and Infinite scope of Your Soul and Who You Are. Sometimes this occurs with intense emotional events and trauma. It is occurring continuously for all of us, in this lifetime, as well as past and future lifetimes. For most of us, it is what is required to bypass the conclusion that the ego/mind has the answers for everything in our lives.

As an aside, teachers can also show up in our lives. Teachers that show us Who We Are and guide us back Home. If a teacher is not facilitating your knowing that You Are Infinite and Magnificent then they too are a hindrance to you Being You. I often say 'If a teacher puts themselves above you, on a pedestal, run away, fast.'

Let us go further. We can observe that having a unique perspective is a reaction (charge) to the already subjective content of your ego/mind. Your story is your experience of the content including the charge you have on that triggered content. Much of your content has been stored, prejudiced by indoctrination, family, government, society, religions, media, etc. and this includes the significance of it all.

So let us look at the content. What is the content of our ego/minds, prejudiced or not? What is this content that is the buffer that does not allow the clear perception of the Soul to be received by the mind? What hinders you Being You in the world?

In short, all the identifications we have taken on or bought into and consequently stored (cognitively and unconsciously) within the ego/mind. It is not dissimilar to a library; a resource of identifications; their relationship to each other; their significance and consequences; their conclusions and assumptions as determined by your unique and subjective perspective, both cognitively and unconsciously.

Here is a list of some common identifications:

☐ Your name;

☐ Your address;

☐ Where you were born;

☐ Your immediate and extended family;

☐ Your pets;

☐ Your pride;

☐ Your ancestral line;

☐ Your genetics;

☐ Your social status;

- ☐ Your traditions;
- ☐ Your nationality;
- ☐ Your roles;
- ☐ Your preferences;
- ☐ Your religion;
- ☐ Your appearance including your size and weight;
- ☐ The schools you attended;
- ☐ Your beliefs;
- ☐ Your behavioural patterns;
- ☐ Your manners;
- ☐ Your job, if you have one or if you don't;
- ☐ How much you earn;
- ☐ Your memberships – professionally, socially, health-wise and recreationally – including sporting teams;
- ☐ Your musical taste;
- ☐ Your sexual orientation, preferences and judgements;
- ☐ Your behaviour;
- ☐ Your emotions at any given moment;
- ☐ Your loyalties;
- ☐ Your style and/or trends you follow/don't follow;
- ☐ Your traumas or accidents;
- ☐ Your language;
- ☐ Your diagnosis;
- ☐ Your masks (short-term to long-term);
- ☐ Your judgements;
- ☐ Your values;
- ☐ Your expectations;
- ☐ Your dreams and aspirations;

☐ Your conclusions;

☐ Your assumptions;

☐ Your commitments; and

☐ Your likes/dislikes.

Both cognitively and unconsciously we have all chosen and established innumerable interconnections and relationships with identifications that are accessible by our ego/minds.

Exercise One

Using the identifications listed above (and any others you may be aware of) create a list and/or map of the content of your story. Record these in a journal or notebook as it may be useful to reflect back on them as your perspective changes.

I am not here to judge good or bad, it just is. What I hope is that you simply begin to observe and notice those identifications you are wearing. Just notice what you notice, adopting an impersonal approach, as though you are conducting a case study on yourself. Notice what interesting information you can reveal.

If you were to approach it from a position of significance (charge), we would be perpetuating the same rather than observing what is.

You may notice that you gain further awareness as you continue reflecting on this. I know for myself, it was interesting to observe what came up for me earlier in the exercise and observe changes in perspective. Remember that 'Who You Are' can only be perceived by You and is an Isness, it is your perspective which changes.

Spend time to scan for as many identifications as you can. Ask a friend to help. Have fun with it. Stay open to it for a few days as you may get a few more in the early hours of the morning when your ego/mind is less active.

There is no need to do anything with your information other than gathering it.

After you feel you have captured a full picture of you in your story, ask yourself:

- ☐ Are these all the identifications I am cognitive of?
- ☐ Are there any I am not cognitive of?
- ☐ Are there any I have dropped or changed?
- ☐ Does this reflect 100% of me?
- ☐ If not, what or who else am I?
- ☐ If over 100%, how does that show up?
- ☐ What else is there?

Write your information in your journal.

The objective of these later questions is to come from a different angle and uncover more that have not been 'flushed' out, perhaps from deeper within the subconscious. As your awareness grows, please add to your list or strike through any that no longer have a charge, that is, they no longer illicit a reaction or personal response or position in you but rather prompt no reaction at all; the true 'flat-lining'. When we 'flat-line' on all our identifications, that is more truly our death, the death/dismantling of the ego/mind, where there is no position or charge on anything, and consequently a freedom to choose whatever you choose. This also can be described as Enlightenment.

Now let us look at story from the perspective of vibration.

Everything that is manifested has a level of vibration ranging from the vibrational sound of 'Aum' ('the Word of God') to the varying vibrations of density that can be received by the physical senses and translated using the brain and the subjective ego/mind. This is anything that can be seen, heard, tasted, felt or smelt. Some emotions also exist at roughly this vibration even though they are not 'solid'. What is solid are the intensities they can produce.

I discuss this from my own observation and knowing, rather than a scientific perspective. 'Scientist' is not one of my identifications.

When you buy into this reality as all that exists, you lock out your ability to receive the vast majority of what is available at vibrations that are 'not solid'.

Just like Wi-Fi, radio and satellite signals, all vibrations are present and full of information, your access is simply dependent on whether or not you can attune to the vibration and receive it. Most people are only cognitive of using the physical five senses as receiving tools, yet much more is going on beyond those senses.

Incarnating can certainly hinder our capacity to pick up all vibrations, but the greatest obstacles to picking up the information are the identifications we choose to wear as 'cloaks' and which block or alter what is perceived by The Soul. This can also be called your karma (which we will discuss later). The Soul has the capacity to receive all vibrations, at all vibrational levels. It is certainly not limited to the five senses.

Our identifications also include conclusions with regard to physical incarnation, thus, most of us lose access to the deeper information beyond the physical. The ego/mind has content declaring that we are only what we can see, hear, taste, touch, smell. The ego/mind even buffers the notion that there is anything else beyond what its contents are.

Let's get back to manifestation and how it shows up for me.

The beginning of apparent matter is the vibration of the 'Aum' sound. This is the arising of existence from the Unfathomable All/No-thing of the Unmanifested. 'Aum' 'condenses' to form Consciousness which is experienced as space. Up to this point there is no content. When I check in, there is No-Thing other than the form of Consciousness. There are no positions, no individuation, only Manifested Oneness and what can be called the Manifested God. The 'Aum' vibration then shows up at the level of form as Consciousness, experienced as space.

When I ask myself: 'What is Light?' I see Light as a transporter, a channel, a connector, a carrier. It is like a vehicle of communication. As a vehicle, it of itself, has no content. Water in our dualistic reality reflects a similar nature. What Light can carry and relay and connect is the content. It is made from the fabric called Consciousness. It is like the 'doing' word of Consciousness.

Energy is also made from the fabric called Consciousness, and at this point, energy has content. Differentiation has begun to show up. Creation in Infinite forms begins. Though not in physical form that can be easily observed, energy has characteristics.

At the level of story, where there is much density as well as All There Is, we have 'Aum', Consciousness, energy and matter. There is no separation in Oneness. There is no away. It is all an Isness. It is all projections of Light from Oneness. The level to which it can be received depends on your perspective.

Let us play with this notion that energy has characteristics. Let's do another exercise.

Exercise Two

Draw, write, indicate in your journal, however you choose, your description of the different energies I am suggesting below:

☐ What is the difference between being at the shoreline of a beautiful sandy beach on a sunny day, versus being at a bar where a fight just occurred and someone was fatally stabbed?

☐ What is the difference between sitting on the floor of a forest next to a 100-year-old tree versus sitting on your couch watching an episode of The Simpsons?

Reading these comparisons alone arises in you an awareness of the diverse energy of each situation, and again, it arises as an experience unique to you, due to your perspective.

Don't judge the content of where the words have taken you, notice only the energy that meets you. The energy has content and it is useful to notice it, differentiate it and receive the information.

I have used about thirty words in each comparison and due to all our reference points they illicit a response. Notice also the charges we have implanted on words.

If you did judge it, note down what identifications you used to create the judgement. Can you clarify what the individual identifications are? Or does it feel like it is coming from a 'concoction' of identifications?

The value and purpose of this exercise is to continue to build your muscle of observation which contributes to and facilitates the dismantling of the ego/mind. It also expands the scope of your life beyond your current confines. Continue to play with this yourself. Notice energy and notice how your capacity to receive information that is 'not solid' will expand.

Let us get back to manifestation:

For me, energy seems to condense, forming molecules, atoms and so on. Matter becomes denser and denser as it apparently compacts until we can see, hear, taste, touch and smell it. This is all part of the manifested. Beyond manifestation or existence is the All/Nothing from which 'Aum' is created, 'Aum' is God in action.

Trying to understand beyond manifestation, at the level of mind, can only be glimpsed whilst also seeming unattainable. This is sometimes spoken of as the Unfathomable, the Unnameable and the Unspeakable, as any level of definition creates form and separation and any attempt at Beholding It is futile.

Know that You are not separate from 'It', and You are part of Oneness, and until you know this and return Home, Oneness perceives an incompleteness. Oneness awaits Your return Home. You are missed in Oneness, that is Who You Are. Until each of us, individuated from Oneness, returns Home, Oneness is incomplete. You are not who you are in the story or how you are judged in the story. You are an inseparable part of the Magnificence and Infinity of Oneness.

The analogy I often use for this is a mother dog who has given birth to puppies. We are all like the puppies. We go off and explore the world, the narrow world that we think is all that is. We focus on ourselves. When the yearning for safety and nourishment comes, we seek to return to our Mother. Coming Home is like the lost puppy that has wandered off and then finds its way back to suckle its mother for milk. All yearnings are dissipated, all needs are satisfied. That warm, safe, nurturing place is what it feels like to return Home and even for us, all yearnings dissipate and all needs are satisfied. The Mothers' job does not feel complete until all her puppies have returned to Her and she can offer the nourishment and warmth that is given freely. Everything is about returning to Mother. There isn't anything else. Until all the 'puppies' are no longer lost and have returned Home, Mother will continue to await their return.

In the story, at the dense level of vibration, this is not recognised but mimicked in the foundations we create for ourselves. The notion of Being and toggling between existence and non-existence with no position cannot be tolerated. Non-existence arouses a sense of annihilation rather than the sense of Divine Love, Joy and a feeling of returning Home, which is what truly shows up.

For many, existence itself can be a perspective in relation to story, maybe in relation to being incarnated in a body. The existence I speak of here, is the coming into form from No-Thingness. The individuation of the All/No-Thingness into Oneness. At the level of Oneness, there is existence, existence of All of Us. We appear as individuated but that is not real. An analogy often used, and used by Paramahansa Yogananda, is that of a movie (Yogananda, 2016). This reality is merely a projection of Light containing the information of the individuation of You into apparent form. In reality, Light beams/transports/projects the information and, with the content of your ego/mind, you translate it as solid matter. If you didn't have an ego/mind and You communed in Oneness, you would perceive the content purely as a projection of Oneness and existence and You would not have a point of view about existence or non-existence.

Matter shows up as dense because we expect it to based on the content of the ego/mind. We continue to show up as we do because the content remains the same.

The ego/mind has no comprehension of or tolerance to non-existence. It locks in the information that unless the density of its contents are complied with, you will die. Ironically, it is in letting go the charge on the content of the ego/mind that living can truly and expansively Be. At the dense level of vibration this is not conceivable let alone received as a possibility.

To illustrate, imagine that you are a ball within a ball. At the level of dense vibration as interpreted by the ego/mind, the matter of both balls appear compressed to the point that they are solid. Being the ball inside the ball you would not even know that there is a bigger ball. You have no means of experiencing the larger ball. You think your universe is you as this solid smaller ball. As you begin to receive information from lighter vibrations, the apparent compaction of matter begins to show up as less dense and you can notice less of a compaction of you as the smaller ball and that there exists something beyond the smaller ball, maybe even to experience what is beyond even the larger ball. This is similar to our Universe. If our Universe is the larger ball, and each one of us is a ball within the larger ball, as we receive lighter vibrations, we perceive the other balls within the larger ball. The lighter and less condensed the vibration, the more we experience a lack of any structure forming any of the balls and we begin to feel Oneness with everything – even beyond the larger ball which can also be perceived as formless. The other interesting thing is that the balls did not evolve or change form, the information was received differently based on the perspective. When the vibration received is light and formless enough to see clearly, the perception and the perspective provide the same information – there are no balls.

Let's get back to your story, now, from a vibrational perspective. Your story is the 'stuff' that makes your 'ball' solid.

When you incarnate into a body and enter the family and society you are born into, this is received and interpreted as very dense vibrationally; you are in a realm of form. Your body presents as a solid object. Your family, where you live, structures, trees, ground, the earth, the sky, sun, moon, etc. can all be observed by the five senses.

Your life centres around doingness with mostly physical objects, matter. From a vibrational point of view this is labelled 'dense': an apparent compaction of Consciousness forming matter to a level that can be processed and interpreted by the five senses.

This level also includes non-physical matter such as emotions and thoughts. Emotions and thoughts fit into this end of the spectrum because they are a solidifying of reactions and charge by the ego/mind. At the other end of the vibrational spectrum there is no position, charge or significance and not even words to create a thought. We can slip out of duality into non-duality. Information is perceived and not compressed, collapsed, reduced or funnelled into the density of thoughts and emotions.

At the dense end of the vibrational frequencies we are in a dualistic or polarised reality. The reality of cause and effect: yin/yang, dark/light, good/bad, right/wrong.

As matter appears compressed, in order to know and recognise something, our ego/minds require us to know and recognise what is not.

We can observe a table, for example. We notice its shape, design, dimensions, where the legs are and where the table is situated. Whilst functioning at this level of density we see, taste, touch, hear and feel the table and where the table is not.

Bypassing duality, there is no table and we would be able to move through the space where those that buy into the existence of the table see, taste, touch, hear and feel the table.

This analogy reminds me of the scene in *The Matrix* movie (Wachowski, 1999) when the young boy in the Oracle's waiting room was bending the spoon. Neo asked how he did it. Someone functioning in a dense vibrational reality will try to bend the spoon as a doingness. The boy responds: 'Do not try and bend the spoon. That's impossible... Instead... only try to realise the truth...There is no spoon. Then you'll see, that it is not the spoon that bends, it is yourself.'

You cannot try to convince yourself that there is no spoon. It is simply what arises as awareness as you drop all that clouds you from receiving awareness, the knowing of Your Soul.

Where to start?

We have begun already. All the identifications you have listed about yourself are characteristics of 'your spoon' and what makes 'your spoon' solid; consequently, while you maintain those characteristics 'your spoon' stays solid.

Your perception of 'Who You Are' is heavily coloured by the content of the ego/mind, your story and your perspective of the significance of that story. This is common to most people. What makes our stories unique is the content itself and how we experience them. No two stories are experienced the same way. We may share similarities which contribute to our perspective of belonging somewhere, but no story is experienced the same as another.

Even in the news we hear reports of stories. For example, we relate to a misfortune or tragedy and open ourselves to it or we disapprove of a behaviour and call to gather arms or government action to stop the behaviour.

None of this is 'Who We Are' but until we do experience 'Who We Are', maintaining stability and control in our lives and in the world through our perspective of stories, is the closest thing we have to feeling at home.

We have forgotten and so we strive to feel at home somewhere. With our ego/minds confining us to story, both at micro and macro levels of the world, we seek to find that feeling (a mimicking of Home).

Notice what happens when a tragedy occurs both at a local level or on the world stage. We drop all the significance around identification and our hearts open. Our ego/minds have lost control and the buffer that is normally in place is absent with the confusion of lack of normality and stability. Some build further buffers and buy into fear whilst others feel no differentiation and automatically the ego/mind is bypassed. The Soul's non-position on identifications is accessed and experienced and we feel a non-polarised Love for those affected. It could be a mass shooting, 9/11, tsunami, refugees, the starving, fatal bushfires or earthquakes. When the level of control of the ego/mind is shattered by such events, the heart opens and the Soul is accessed. Unfortunately, with the ego/mind in place both at the micro level and the macro level, it takes something of magnitude for the ego/mind to be bypassed when we are relying on something outside ourselves to bypass the ego/mind. It literally depends on the level required by the ego/mind to maintain control and normality.

Notice also, when 'things get back to normal' or when the media coverage stops, the ego/mind regains control and confines you back into your story and relief with normality is experienced. This is the confines, the prison of the ego/mind, which we think is our safety and our home. It is not, but until we begin to know 'Who We Are' this is a crutch that functions to mimic Home although it bears little resemblance to Home. Home is more like the communion and Oneness that is heartfelt when a disaster occurs. When the ego/mind dismantles, this is what shows up all the time, no need for a disaster to bypass the ego/mind. We do not experience it as confusion, rather, as nurturing and Love for all. Once it Is, we perceive relief and a returning Home.

Interestingly, bearing witness to another's story can be useful in the dismantling of the significance of our own story, even if not cognitively chosen. This can be one of the first Expressions of Being. This is a contribution to Enlightenment, however, whilst within the confines of the ego/mind, Enlightenment is unattainable.

Additionally, when we focus on story, we are misidentifying the yearning to know Self and to commune with God, as belonging in the story. We don't remember Who We Are and are blindly seeking the feeling of Home in the story. Unfortunately, what occurs is more attachment to the contents of story and more separation and buffering rather than getting closer to what we are truly yearning for.

So let's start to uncover more about the unique composition of your story.

The composition of your story is made up of the content of innumerable identifications both cognitive and unconscious that you have chosen to 'wear'. The exercise we are about to undertake will provide an opportunity to change your perspective of your story. You may have experienced your story as providing a level of security and stability, a strong foundation from which to 'jump off' into the world. For others their story is the polar opposite. They are lost and lack foundation in the world.

When we begin to list the content of your story, you may begin a process of observation that seems a type of separation between You and your story. Don't panic. It is all OK. We are energetically taking a few steps back to look at what is there for you, in the same way you may take a step back to observe the beautiful and colourful selection of cakes within a patisserie display cabinet.

Exercise Three

Spontaneously respond to the following questions. Don't think too much, allow information to come even if it doesn't make sense. There is also no need to justify what arises, make it significant or judge it; play with what comes:

- ☐ Are you what you do in the world?
- ☐ Who are you to the world?
- ☐ What do you think of yourself?
- ☐ What does the world think of you? Is that important to you?
- ☐ What do your friends and family think of you? Does that matter to you?
- ☐ Do you take that personally?
- ☐ Do you belong in the world?
- ☐ How successful are you in the world?
- ☐ Do you have control over your life?

Again, spend time writing what you receive to each of these questions. It will give you a further sense of yourself within the broader story of the world. For now, sit with what you receive, practice not to judge it or draw conclusions – remember it is simply a gathering of information. At the denser end of the spectrum you may not be conscious of judging and drawing conclusions. Begin to notice if you do. I find it helpful to observe how interesting the information is rather than assigning any level of significance to it.

There is an analogy that is often used with perspective that comes to mind now. It is the analogy of a group of people gathered in a circle around a chair and each is asked what they see. They are each looking at the same chair but due to their different perspectives they see something different.

This is the same for all of us. Your perspective of others in their story and their perspective of you in your story will differ. Consider the identification of culture, this one identification alone will totally change someone's perspective of you, and that is only one identification we each hold in our ego/minds. What is interesting is that your perspective of you and others perspective of you are both valid within the context of the story. Everything is coloured by our identifications. There is no right or wrong even though the story will go to war to prove there is!!

Knowing more about the ego/mind can also facilitate the loosening of its control as 'captain of the ship', a role the ego/mind holds on to tightly. Again, the ego/mind holds the point of view that if you do not follow its direction, you will literally die. It tricks you to thinking you are the character you are playing. What is interesting is that this confinement to the ego/mind can itself be fatal. For those that function totally from the ego/mind and who have intense trauma or debilitating experiences, it can show up as no way out of the confinement and suicide can sometimes be seen as the only option. These are 'Lost Soul' experiences and the only relief can be found in the knowing of the Soul. In the story, religion and spiritually provide a doorway to exit the ego/mind confinement, a crutch that whilst one is still functioning from the ego/mind, can provide some relief. This relief is temporary until Being You is chosen as your reality.

Let's look at ego/mind in more detail.

This section is not a textbook definition of the ego/mind. I am not a psychiatrist or psychologist or a doctor of any kind, again not my identifications. I have awareness and what is clear to me is that the ego/mind playing out in our humanness and beyond (that is, the dualistic reality continues to play out vibrationally even after we leave our bodies) creates the buffer between how we show up in the world and Who We Are.

If we were all egoless we would all be Enlightened. We would be happy in our non-position on anything. Some may say this would be boring. The concept of boring only appears when we are trying to do, whilst adopting criteria for what is interesting or not, and judging ourselves, or being judged from outside, in relation to that criteria. It is all more layers and buffers rather than fewer. In reality, it would not show up that way as our Divinity would show up in an Infinite Rainbow of Presentations and possibilities, just like nature and the cosmos which have no position; nothing is personal. What an array of Magnificence, and those are the aspects we are currently aware of. We are that Magnificence. We have not yet dismantled the limited perspective of the ego/mind to know it and Be it.

Let us get back to the ego/mind as defined from my perspective: The ego/mind:

☐ Is the 'I' or 'self' that distinguishes itself from other 'selves';

☐ Defines your self-importance or lack thereof;

☐ Defines your self-image or lack thereof;

☐ Defines your self-esteem or lack thereof;

☐ Is the benchmark upon which you experience and/or react to the outside world (that is, anything outside of your self);

☐ Is the sum total of all your identifications, attachments to experiences and judgements. Everything you identified in Exercise One and everything else you are not currently aware of;

- ☐ Is what you refer to as 'me', 'my', 'mine';
- ☐ Is only partially cognitive. Most of it is unconscious and emerges when events (actions, words, inputs from the five senses) trigger and access the unconscious information and stored consequences;
- ☐ Does not allow a direct connection/communion with You, being a buffer to Being You, creating an apparent separation;
- ☐ Provides a response/reaction, based on its contents and charge, to every experience you have both with yourself and outside yourself. This is how you show up in the world.

The ego/mind is a construct of the apparent individuation of you at the dense level of vibration. This is where significance, importance and separation take many forms as defined by the identifications we have already explored and that you have begun listing.

The ego/mind defines why you are different to anybody else. It creates definition, justification, conclusion, assumption and significance around self-importance and self-image. It defines your self-esteem. It creates a profile of you and how you relate to the world. It does not always provide positive views of these, often it can show quite negative views of you.

Here are a few examples:

- ☐ 'I am so fantastic, everyone should be honoured to be in my presence'
- ☐ 'I hate myself so much and blame my parents for how I turned out'
- ☐ 'I love myself'
- ☐ 'I can't get past what happened to me, I have no control'
- ☐ 'Get out of my way, I have arrived'

- ☐ 'I know so much more than you'
- ☐ 'I am stupid'
- ☐ 'I wouldn't be caught dead with that person'
- ☐ 'I don't belong here'
- ☐ 'I am the best'

The perceptions of the Soul are always Present.

When we begin to be aware of the ego/mind and to observe the interesting dynamics that unfold because of it, we have then regained some ability to choose consciously rather than be driven by the effect of the ego/mind.

An analogy that is often used is that of being in a flowing river, the flowing river representing your life. If your ego/mind is 'captain of the ship', that is, has total control over your body/mind complex and your life, you will be buffered down the river without a paddle, not conscious of the obstacles and rocks, no control of the speed, depth or direction in which you flow down that river. Your ego/mind is in charge of your life. Everything is referenced by what already exists and is stored within the ego/mind.

When You begin to take charge of Your Self, it is like You are a Giant in the River of Your Life and You consciously choose where to step and whether to step. You don't need a paddle outside of Your Self to guide You or support You, yet You may use any tool You choose. You are bigger than any obstacle in Your way. You are potent, in charge and choosing for You. Whilst the ego/mind is still in place to some degree, you will have both awareness from You and content from the ego/mind, that will inform you. The more you observe and the more you 'wake up' to what is showing up and 'Who You Are', the more conscious you Be. References to the content of the ego/mind are made as a tool, together with all Infinite awareness of Consciousness.

Interestingly, the New Age arena often recommends 'going with the flow'. This is the notion of not making anything significant and practicing detachment. However, there is a missing ingredient:

conscious choice. With conscious choice, the passive activity of 'going with the flow' transforms into potent choosing and action and you Be that Giant in the River of Your Life, referenced by Your Own Divinity. Truly, this is the unfolding of your own awakening.

As long as the ego/mind has the satisfaction of being in charge, it doesn't care that the information it is 'spewing' out is not real.

The ego/mind will tell you anything to maintain its position as 'captain of the ship'. I often see that when people are at a challenging point in their lives and/or are beginning to question the meaning of it all or are on the cusp of dropping the significance around their content, there is a massive and desperate surge from the ego/mind. It is an example of what I call 'the Cornered Animal Syndrome'. The ego/mind comes out in full force, for example, showing up as uncontrolled behaviours, anger and rage, illness, destructive thoughts, total confusion and total doubt. The ego/mind fights to maintain control.

This also occurs at the macro level, as we are seeing play out on the world stage. The 'Cornered Animal Syndrome' is out in full force. This is occurring because of the expansion of Consciousness showing up. Actually, a New World has already begun instituting. The Old World will fight until it too will be dismantled (more on this later in Chapter Nine on the New World).

The content of the ego/mind is both cognitive and unconscious. You only know about the cognitive part of your ego/mind. The subconscious ego/mind content comes to the surface when events and experiences trigger a response/reaction from the library of associations, consequences and conclusions stored in the subconscious ego/mind. The cognitive ego/mind is only a small percentage of the ego/mind. The analogy often used is that of the iceberg, where we only see what is above the surface, the tip of the iceberg, however, the vast majority of the iceberg is submerged.

Here are a few examples to illustrate:

☐ You and your friends are out at the pub after a soccer match. Your team lost and you are drowning your sorrows. In come a group from the rival team, chanting their victory song.

You have had a few drinks so already you have lost access to some of the awareness you may have otherwise received. Something triggers in you and you begin a physical fight. You have reacted to associations and judgements in your ego/mind, most likely also including a reptilian brain reaction. Your ego/mind doesn't care, it is joining the dots of all the information stored and you become more unconscious and not thinking, have reacted. Your ego/mind is 'captain of the ship'. When the incident is over, you wonder why you reacted or the degree to which you reacted, maybe even in disbelief that it was you who did it. The story will have its system of justice for the behaviour. From a Consciousness perspective, You were not accessed, but clouded by the ego/mind.

☐ You are listening to a piece of music that your father used to listen to. When he played that piece of music he would sing along and be happy and jovial. When you hear the music now, decades later, even when the first few notes are heard, you automatically feel happy and think of your dad. Your ego/mind accessed the 'happy' and 'dad' charges, having stored the correlation with those notes of music.

☐ You hear a loud screech from a car outside. You immediately have a panic attack, unable to catch your breath. The sound was interpreted by the ego/mind which then retrieved information about a car accident you had as a child whilst in the back seat of a car. As a consequence, messages are sent to your body in this moment, alerting you that you are in danger.

☐ Ever since you can remember you have been terrified of water. Even having water touch you initiates cries of terror. What you are not cognitive of is that stored in your subconscious ego/mind is a memory of a past life where you and your children died having been swept away in a flood. Water in this lifetime triggers the recall of the information stored and, whilst not cognitive of the memory, produces extreme fear in your current body.

When you become aware of the ego/mind as it is present in you and you know that You are not that, the journey of awakening is recognised cognitively as having begun. We are all on the journey of awakening (even though in truth it is not linear in any way) and it is at this stage that seeking begins in earnest, as you are not totally blinded by unconsciousness and have some degree of conscious choosing. You begin to recognise the resonance that shows up as something familiar to You and you choose what matches that vibration or contributes to it showing up.

In fact, seeking began the moment you came into existence, however, until you are sufficiently 'awake in the dream' you just don't know it cognitively, but having the experience of knowing it, is labelled the presentation of 'the seeker'.

Sometimes the expression 'asleep in the dream' is used to describe the state where you think that you are your story and nothing else exists. I will reference the movie *The Matrix* again (Wachowski, 1999). Can you tell I think it is an awesome movie? It portrayed this concept of 'asleep in the dream' superbly. In the movie, as in this reality, the world showed up as it was programmed, as the ego/mind. It showed up as real but was not actually real. The real world only showed up when you bought out of it as a reality. In the movie it was taking the red pill. In our lives it is bypassing or dismantling the ego/mind to access Self. In the same way, anything is possible once you buy out of the story. The laws of this reality will no longer apply and we too can dodge bullets like Neo, all from the awareness which arise from Self.

This is not science fiction, this is real and is already showing up, though you may not know it yet. Unlike the movie, the reality I know as real is Magnificent and Infinitely Beautiful and it is this reality we will all become aware of, that we will awaken to. As we each awaken to Who We Are this will show up more and more, and while some remain to be awakened, to commune again in Oneness, our 'job' is incomplete, We Are incomplete.

Chapter

Three

OUR SOULS AND OUR
ESSENTIAL NATURE

IN THE STORY OF our lives and in the societies we find Our Selves in, there is little spoken in regard to Who We Are beyond the identifications that we choose to wear.

As we discussed in Chapter Two, a confinement is created within the story and societies and it is all content and positioning in relation to that content.

This 'stuff' has nothing to do with Who We Are. It is the stage We have chosen to Be Our Selves in, the stage of this world and incarnation.

It provides us with opportunities to know Our Selves, yet these opportunities, for the vast majority of us, get lost or diverted by the significance of the stage and roles we are each playing out. The Being who is the actor is neglected.

Let me expand on this by broadening the scope of the stages We choose to frequent. For those confined to functioning within the ego/mind, the stages of this world are the only stages. Often our roles play out on a different stage, for example, a home stage, a work stage, a community stage.

My awareness expands beyond this scope of stage. While we will examine this in much more detail later, there are many realms which exist and which we all choose to play in. The only difference is the vibration at which they resonate. They are not here or there, they are all Present, all with varying vibrational frequencies, just like Wi-Fi or radio signals. Note, however, that the only reason we observe them as distinct frequencies and realms is because we are observing them.

For me, the dualistic reality goes beyond this world to realms which most of us frequent after we transition from our physical bodies. The content we wear in this world continues to be held vibrationally. Anything other than Oneness is dualistic in nature, even after we transition from our physical bodies.

The discussion of Enlightenment is, therefore, always in the scope of the bigger picture of what buffers you from Being You, when You are incarnate and when You are not. There is no away.

I shared my awareness that Who We Are is an individuation of Oneness Re-Presented as Our Souls. In this chapter we will explore this in depth. Again, notice what you notice rather than adopting my awareness as absolute.

You come into apparent form from Oneness, a projection from Oneness. Your Soul is a Unique individuation of Oneness, the Manifested God, and this shows up as Your Being. It is Your Soul that animates the body/mind complex (the Soul is also called Anima, same as animates).

I have used and will continue to use the term 'apparent'. I have found it useful to describe a knowing that it is simply because we are observing Our Selves, that the individuation appears, context appears. If we returned to Our Oneness state, You know the individuation of You is a projection from Oneness. You appear separate but are not. You remain reflecting You while communing in Oneness, until even that form and context dissolve. You do not have a point of view about it.

Beyond Oneness, there is the All/No-Thing and non-existence, which is often termed as the Unfathomable, Inconceivable, Unnameable, the Unmanifested to which You are not separate, however, our minds cannot conceive Being non-separate from non-existence.

In existence, the more we receive information from higher levels of vibration and Consciousness, a lessening of form shows up around the information we receive.

When we receive vibrations at the level of Oneness, we perceive past the illusion of form and know it to Be Consciousness and 'Aum' vibration. It is only because we expect form to show up and are looking for form to show up, that it shows up, thus I call this 'apparent form', like an apparition.

You show up as form because you are looking for You. This is a product of the apparent/projected individuation of You from Oneness. Context now exists. So, let us look at You.

You are from the fabric Consciousness, which has no position or charge, however, You have some content. You have no charge or position on that content which I call 'Your Essential Nature'; it is Your Spirit; it is an Isness and it comes with Breath.

Until You awaken fully and remerge with the Unmanifested, the All/No-Thing, Your Soul, Being and Your Essential Nature/Your Spirit will show up in all lifetimes, between lifetimes and when not choosing lifetimes. Your Soul is also like a homing pigeon. It will yearn and experience the pull Home. Like birds know the migration route even through storms and lack of stillness, You too, know Your way Home. The storms and lack of stillness for us are our ego/minds, and without you being cognitively aware, You are guiding Yourself Home. A pigeon doesn't believe itself to be the storms and lack of stillness, however, we often judge ourselves so. This is the lie of the ego/mind.

Like energy, which has characteristics, You also have characteristics, Your Essential Nature. This can also be called Your Spirit. These individuated characteristics are projected by Light and Breathed to life with the Soul in the body/mind complex. The information of Your Essential Nature, which is the only content of the Soul, is projected in that Light and shows up as You. It is like the Unique Breath of God Breathing Your Unique Spirit (Respiro) to Be that as You Be. It is this Expression that is Inspiration, even in the story, as literally you imbue 'In Spirit' into Your Being and doing. It is God in action.

The Soul has no content of identifications other than the characteristics of Being. It has no position on these characteristics, it just Is. There is no judgement or benchmarking, it just Is.

Our Souls are also known as

- ☐ A Spark or Flame of the Divine
- ☐ Your Essence
- ☐ Anima
- ☐ Your Light
- ☐ Superconsciousness
- ☐ Your Higher Self

It reflects Your Being characterised as Your Essential Nature, Your Spirit.

As it can be difficult to grasp this Infiniteness of which I speak, I will again use an analogy.

Consider the Infinite Oneness of existence as an Infinitely-Faceted Diamond reflecting and projecting Light. This is the high vibration where Light is eternally created and generated.

Each Facet of that Diamond is Unique and the rays of Light communicating the Uniqueness of each Facet of that Infinite Diamond are so Spectacular, their Greatness and Magnificence is beyond words.

Each Facet is not separate from every other Infinite number of Facets. You cannot separate one Facet from the Diamond. Even if you were to attempt to separate or block out the rays of Light, that would merely change the direction of the Light or cover the Light. You cannot put out the Light. At the vibration that Light is created, You would only perceive one Infinite Light. It is when we receive the information at denser vibrations, while incarnated or not, that the individuation can be observed, even the individuated rays of Light projecting content.

Functioning from the ego/mind, you would not be open to receive this information.

Equally, the Diamond is not whole without each and every Facet, and the Diamond is not fully Who It Is until all the Facets Shine brightly as Their Essential Nature, Their Unique Being, Their Spirit.

Each Facet reflects and projects a Unique aspect of the Diamond. No Facet is more or less significant than another and each is indispensable for the Diamond to Know Itself and Be.

You are a Facet of the Infinite Diamond that is Oneness, the Manifested God. Your Soul is literally the reflection and projection of Light from the Infinite Diamond. It is a Unique Presentation of Oneness that does not and will not ever again appear the same in existence. Your Soul reflects the characteristics of Oneness, projected by the Light from the Facet of the Diamond that is You. Your Being is how Your Soul shows up and Your Essential Nature is the characteristics of that Being, the Spirit of that Being, the Breath of God, God in action. This is the Unique Presentation of the Being of You; Unique as Yourself. This is Your Essential Nature and it will never ever be duplicated.

While we are here to Know We Are the Facet of the Whole, the Light reflecting and projecting from that Facet can take us back to the Source of that Facet and Oneness, to Home. At any moment, we can Be Oneness, access is eternally available.

Oneness is incomplete and not fully reflected and projected until You Shine as You. Once You Know that and realise the individuation of this reflection and projection of Light, You can return Home and remerge in the All/Nothing (existence and non-existence). Ease, relief, joy and peace arise, and all yearnings dissipate.

Know that Your Soul, as projected by this beam of Light, will take you to Oneness.

Being You as Your Soul communes in Oneness and is the gateway to Oneness beyond any content. While You are not separate from Oneness the individuation does appear as a beam of Light projecting the information of You. It is the beam of Light projecting You that incarnates a body and chooses a lifetime. It is not separate from Oneness though it appears so.

The Light beam carries vibrational signatures full of information projecting You and information about karma and any other information about your existence, experiences, etc. No terabytes necessary here, we are in the realm of Infinite energy and resources. Maybe one day we will not only be using The Infinite Cloud to store data, we will also be using Infinite power, freely given, to facilitate our Being here. I perceive that 'value' will be redefined as 'what is Infinite' rather than 'what is rare or scarce'.

Deity and teachers who are fully Enlightened re-emerge from the Unmanifested into Manifested Oneness, not requiring to incarnate, though they may choose to, projecting the form they are recognised as and which is useful in guiding all of us back Home. They do not differentiate 'Them Selves'. It is only in denser vibrations where form is differentiated that significance arises. This is even in thought form. We have the point of view of who we call on, pray to. 'They' do not, only 'appearing' in a particular form to facilitate You returning to God.

Let us now take a moment to come back to this reality, this world. While there is no away in Oneness, you may feel a sense of familiarity with where we are going next, purely because you recognise it from references within your ego/mind. Having said that, with regard to all that I speak of, please check in with Your Self as to what resonates with You. It is not about adopting my awareness as your own truth unless it is your truth, otherwise, it risks becoming more layers and more buffering which prevents You from Being You.

Exercise Four

Part 1:

Here is a simple exercise to perceive Your Essential Nature, Your Spirit.

Think back to an event when you were young, something fun maybe. Think about what happened. Notice how it felt and observe the experience.

Ask yourself:

Does the You that is watching that past event in this moment feel the same as the You that experienced the event?

Do you feel the same age as the You from the past?

Do you feel the internal nature of your reflection?

Write, draw or detail in whatever form you choose, your observations in your journal.

You are ageless, timeless and not subject to time/space. You are not from this reality of identifications and content, however, You can observe it all. You are the One observing the event.

If You choose, You could bring Your attention to anything, in any past, present or future reference point, gather the information and You will feel like the same You no matter what (literally – no matter of the matter!) You can also do this beyond all references points, in the Infinite Field of the Universe.

Even in the story, the observation is often made that inside we feel the same but looking in the mirror as we age, we do not recognise ourselves. That is because it is not You in the mirror. What you see is a product of buying into the dualistic reality and consequently the ego/mind and its definitions and conclusions of a lifetime. You are observing the projection in front of You.

For some, the experiences of life may have been too traumatic or intolerable and consequently they feel they have lost Their Spirit. It is never lost; it is shrouded by the content of what occurred, adding to the content of the ego/mind. Go back to when you could feel Your Spirit, use your imagination if you have to, reflect and write what you discover. Please know that it is not lost, only covered up, and returning to Our Spirits, Our Essential Natures and Home to Oneness will provide relief and is why we are all here - yearning dissipates only 'There'.

Now let us take your observation of You a step further:

Part 2: What are the characteristics, traits and attributes that would describe You, Your Essential Nature, Your Spirit, that shows up as Being You?

The purpose of this exercise is to continue the observation of how You show up. There is no right or wrong. It is what You notice.

What You may begin to notice are traits and characteristics and we will use words to label them, words that have associations within the ego/mind but these traits and characteristics are of a different class. They are not the product of the ego/mind which shows up as content, and add further buffering, rather they are like a Nature. We use the words to help us describe what shows up, even though of itself, this is limiting.

While Being You, You would perceive these characteristics more like a bundle of energy full of information and You could say, 'I show up like that', pointing to the bundle of energy. You would not need to funnel it down into denser vibrations and try to capture it to gather the information.

In this reality, we will be funnelling the information down, thus the use of words in an attempt to articulate these characteristics of how You show up. It can never capture it as Your Essential Nature is Infinite in Nature, but it is useful in building the muscle of observation.

It is like a personality, but it is not the personality that is the product of the ego/mind. It has no content, rather a Nature of how it shows up, Your Essential Nature.

Your Essential Nature shows up when the ego/mind loading is gone or low or when you are Present in the Now. Ego/mind characteristics show up when the ego/mind is in place and are the filters and buffers that hide You from you.

I first began noticing the Essential Nature whilst working with clients. I would observe how they showed up when they first arrived in the room, as they shared the reason they had come to see me, to seek facilitation for. As I began to observe the information Presenting, I noticed that each client Presented in their Being in a Unique way, different to how they showed up while functioning from their ego/minds. This was when I began perceiving the buffer between how they showed up in the world and Who They Really Were.

When I work with clients, I am facilitating the bridging of this gap between how they are showing up in the world and how they would show up when Being Them-Selves. Everything that we seek is a yearning to remove this buffer. With no buffer, there are no needs or seeking; there is Being and Oneness.

Most of us have made an assessment, based on our perspective, of how we show up in the world. This exercise is about beginning to observe for yourself how You show up.

Notice:

☐ How do you show up when you are alone in nature? How do You show up when You are alone in nature? Is there a difference?

☐ How do you show up when you see a puppy smiling and wagging its whole body? How do You show up when You see a puppy smiling and wagging its whole body? Is there a difference?

☐ How do you show up when you are alone? How do You show up when you are alone? Is there a difference?

☐ How do you show up when you are around family? How do You show up when You are around family? Is there a difference?

☐ How do you show up when You Know there is nothing wrong with you? How do You show up when You Know there is nothing wrong with you? Is there a difference?

☐ How do you show up when there is nothing you need to do? How do You show up when there is nothing You need to do? Is there a difference?

☐ How do you show up when you think you have made a mistake? How do You show up when you think you have made a mistake? Is there a difference?

☐ How do you show up when it doesn't matter and no one is looking? How do You show up when it doesn't matter and no one is looking? Is there a difference?

If, in this moment, you cannot receive any information on a distinction between 'you' and 'You', that's OK. Suffice to recognise that I am making a distinction. Asking other people may not help as they are more likely to list identifications e.g. you are nice, you are gentle, you are a leader, than attributes of You beyond your ego/mind and their ego/minds, even though those same word labels may be labels you would use to describe Your Essential Nature, Your Spirit. The difference is that from the ego/mind the word labels are full of judgement, expectation and conclusions. As a description of You, the words articulate, in a limited way, a Nature of You, more like an archetype. The words are used to gather a bundle of energy to experience You.

Write, draw or record your observations in your journal in whichever way you choose. If you can't make a distinction, write 'The characteristics of the Essential Nature of Who I Am are different to the personality that shows up from the ego/mind. The Essential Nature is clear of content and does not judge me. No one else will ever show up as Who I Am. I Am a Unique aspect of Oneness and Oneness is incomplete without me awakening to Who I Am. Oneness awaits my return Home. I Am a Unique Breath of God reflected as My Spirit.'

Re-read what you have recorded and if there are any further characteristics of You that remain to be 'captured' record these in your journal in whichever form you choose.

Remember, we are beginning this process of observing the characteristics of You. I got the information from my clients after a lot of practice. If you begin to practice receiving information, if you choose to receive the information, your observation muscle will strengthen and you will open to receive information. This is where it is great to note that the less significance you put on the information, the more accurate the information you receive. As soon as you put any level of significance on the information you are noticing, you have just shifted from Being to the ego/mind, and the information is no longer clear. It will instantaneously reflect the content of your ego/mind. See everything as merely information and you will receive it all.

Part 3: How do you turn up when you are empowered?

In the story, empowerment within a particular society is the same for everyone. In western society, it is expected to show up as: assertive, superior, outgoing, standing up like a lion, being 'ballsy', not taking any nonsense, belongs, looks like other empowered people, looks wealthy, has a masculine energy, loves and/or aspires to have followers and to be up on a pedestal for others to see them, to hail them.

The expectation is static and standard. Very few people meet the expectation. Some do periodically or in particular circumstances. We judge these people as being successful and 'having made it'. Most people never feel empowered. They judge themselves as not being able to meet the heavy expectations and, thus, diminish themselves to always show up lesser, smaller, a follower, never belonging. This shows up as the opposite of empowerment, an outcome of the dualistic reality from which this empowerment structure originates.

Even those who in particular environments do show up as empowered, for example, a CEO of an organisation that is intimidating and/or feared by his or her employees, may not show up as empowered in a different environment. If you witness that person in another setting, on another stage, in most cases, their empowerment will not show up, or they would have to install further filters to maintain what they have decided is the persona they need to portray to the outside world.

There are some people functioning from this ego/mind empowerment and, having become so practiced at it, cognitively fuel their empowerment with the energy of those they drain around them. They can also drain the planet. They are very aware that they have people in their grasp, and, taking advantage of this, thrive on the energy they source from being energetically plugged into them. Watch out if you are plugged into someone like this, you will be drained to the core!

For the majority, ego/mind empowerment is all such hard work, whether you are maintaining a façade or judging yourself as not successfully maintaining a façade. Even those tapping into others for their energy are still maintaining a huge buffer from accessing Self, and they are totally misidentifying this as power and potency, whereas it is actually abuse.

The common result of ego/mind empowerment both for those maintaining it and those receiving it, and which I see frequently with clients, is a total draining of energy, often a cause of chronic fatigue. This is what exhausts us and is one of the major contributors to stress in our lives, particularly work-related stress.

This ego/mind empowerment is not true empowerment. It is more judgement within the dualistic reality of right and wrong, good and bad. Those that succeed today will be failures tomorrow, all the while trying desperately to maintain 'success'. While within the confines of the ego/mind, this has and will continue to prove fatal. Just follow the celebrity news and unfortunately you will see it often.

This is not empowerment. This is full of content and to sustain it is exhausting. Have you noticed that even this conversation is exhausting! More and more identifications are required to keep it going or to convince yourself that you are OK. Alternatively, you create other identifications to reassure yourself that you don't comply to the standards of empowerment, and then you feel OK because you have 'taken a stand' to not comply. These are all the same standards, and again, the level to which you are rebelling or complying, with a few in the story coming up with new standards to look empowered.

This is all inhibiting you from showing up as You, showing up as Your Essential Nature. Your Michelin Man suit has just expanded and expanded, although for some buying into ego/mind empowerment, they love the look of their suit. More layers, the 'fluffing up of their peacock feathers'.

So, let us look at what true empowerment is:

True empowerment has nothing to do with the ego/mind. True empowerment is when you show up as You and as Your Essential Nature, when You Be Your Spirit. You can only truly be empowered when you are Being You, reflecting Your Essential Nature.

Empowerment does not have characteristics in the story and is not personal. It is a vibration and shows up as a Presence. It has no content. There is no single standard for how it shows up, actually a standard is an expectation, an identification, while functioning from the ego/mind.

True empowerment shows up differently for every single Being that exists. The Unique Presentation of You is how You show up empowered. Being You is Being empowered and every Infinite number of Presentations of Oneness is what shows up as We All show up empowered. It is the characteristics of each and every Unique Facet of the Infinite Diamond of Oneness. Competition is irrelevant as there is no one like You – ever!!

Being empowered means choosing and stepping into the potency You Be while in this world or any world You choose to frequent. Being empowered provides access to all that You know and choosing from this place has freedom from ego/mind bindings or confinements. It shows up as true freedom of Spirit. This is sometimes referenced as a target in the story, although here I am referring to an Infinite class.

No energy is consumed or required to maintain You showing up, unlike with the ego/mind version of the empowered you. Our societies have little concept of this as empowerment because it has no framework or form to establish predictability, measurement and control. The closest identification, as mentioned above, is being 'free spirited' for the rebellious ones in the story, those considered not to comply or conform.

When you meet someone who shows up as true empowerment, there are no buffers or layers or airs about them. They show up simply as Them Selves; not showy, not demanding, vulnerable, authentic, not needing anyone to notice them, and certainly not seeking followers. They are comfortable in their own skin with no self-consciousness. If they enter a room, you will pick it up immediately. Their energy emanates Presence, exuberance, vulnerability, authenticity, intimacy, irresistibility and no attachment.

Interestingly, when those functioning from the ego/mind receive someone Being Who They Are, they receive them in the narrow context of their ego/mind. A common presentation, for example, is misidentifying true intimacy as sexuality. The ego/mind has no reference to true intimacy, 'Into Me See'. The person Being Present does not have a point of view about it, only the person receiving the energy of the true empowerment does.

How You Being empowered looks in the world is a direct reflection of Who You Are; a direct reflection of Your Uniqueness. You Are That, an aspect of God that No one else is, a Breath of God.

As we have already discussed, it is difficult using words to capture such Unique Presentations of Essential Natures without creating a limited perspective of it, however, for the purpose of providing you with examples, I have used words. Notice the bundle of energy the words create rather than any fixed point of view of what the words access from your ego/mind. Here are some examples:

☐ Caring and gentle nature, grace, affinity with the elements and elementals, attuned to other Beings with no point of view, Master Creator for the planet;

☐ Leader, front-liner (pioneering and out in public), strongly expressive, innovative, inspiring, listener, compassionate and devoted to God;

☐ All seeing, wise, facilitator of healing, potent, allowing and Infinitely and Divinely Loving;

As gentle as a deer and all-knowing, softly spoken, expressive in silence, and beauty in stillness;

☐ Leader, expressively joyful, teacher and facilitator in wonder, no attachments, perceives beauty in the All;

☐ Zen, stillness and quiet, giver to all, simplicity in interaction, perceives acutely at all vibrations.

Even though we may repeat words to describe how each of Our empowerment can show up, it can never truly match the potency and nuances of Being Who We Are. For example, using words like 'leader', 'mother' or 'teacher' could never reflect the Infinite number of Presentations of this. Notice this as we continue in this exercise and beyond, as you experience Being You. Keep checking in on the energy the words create rather than the words themselves. That will give You the information.

It is only when you Be the fullness of Your Essential Nature that You are truly empowered and can access Your Infinite Potency.

Common characteristics that show up with true empowerment for All of Us are:

☐ True Joy,

☐ True Caring,

☐ Gratitude,

☐ Humility,

☐ Irresistibility,

☐ Authenticity,

☐ Intimacy,

☐ Vulnerability,

☐ Exuberance,

☐ Honouring,

☐ Beauty,

- ☐ Generosity,
- ☐ Non-attachment,
- ☐ Total allowance of what Is,
- ☐ A Divine Love for Allness and
- ☐ Devotion to God.

Sometimes, others cannot receive the fullness of You, may find You too powerful and can be intimidated by Your Presence. In this case, they are not functioning from their Being, rather are functioning from their ego/minds, and have judged You and measured You against the content they have stored there. They may not even be conscious of what it is about You that they are reacting to. They may misidentify it as ego/mind content. Being is not an experience they allow themselves to receive. You are not affected, as it is only the ego/mind that buys it as significant.

Now for the exercise:

In your journal, record in any way you choose how you show up empowered in the story, that is, when you are functioning from the ego/mind. Include:

- ☐ How much effort it takes to put on the masks and filters required to establish and maintain that empowerment;
- ☐ How did you determine which masks to put on to show up as empowered? Did you use anybody as a reference point?
- ☐ What are the environments in which you feel more empowered?
- ☐ Is it easier to feel empowered because of some expertise, experience or other familiarity or even how you look?
- ☐ Do you judge others in relation to your empowered state? Do you compare?
- ☐ Do you judge you in relation to your empowered state?

☐ Do others and the world judge you in relation to your empowered state? and

☐ Anything else you find interesting about when you show up empowered while functioning from the ego/mind.

Remember, these exercises are for you alone. It is to strengthen your muscle of observation, not to perpetuate any judgement of you. I am interested in you observing the level at which judgement is projected rather than dwelling on and making significant the content of that judgement.

Now, in your journal, write how You do or would show up empowered as Your Essential Nature. How does or would Your Spirit show up? What is Being truly empowered look like as You? Include:

☐ How it is different from the information you received in Part 2 of this exercise. For example, does relating to Your Essential Nature as empowerment expand your allowance and receiving of You?

☐ Do You have a point of view about how You show up?

☐ How much effort is required to Be You?

☐ Have you any judgement of how You show up?

☐ Are you aware of other's judgement of You?

☐ Are You aware of other's judgement of You? and

☐ Anything else that You perceive that could be a contribution to how you are noticing You. Notice if the information is from the ego/mind or from You.

Enjoy the process. Continue to return to this, as it is not about getting a comprehensive list of anything. Rather, it is about you beginning to recognise the distinction of 'you' and 'You' without placing significance on the information you receive. The more you choose to receive the information, the more information You receive. Remember, if You are open to receive it, You will perceive and access all the information You are seeking. This is different to 'you' looking for it, as 'you' will always have a position or significance around what you are looking for and thus filter and colour what you receive. Don't take my word for it, find it Your Self.

CONCEPTION AND INCARNATION

Let us now look at Our Souls with regard to conception and incarnation and how this shows up for me.

While working with clients I am so grateful for the innumerable Presentations of conceptions and incarnations that have shown up before me, and the wealth of information received around those conceptions and incarnations.

When applying your attention to something, it is interesting to observe the information rather than having a fixed view of 'needing' to look for something in particular. If you have a fixed view of what you are looking for or 'need' to look for it, what you find is limited and filtered to that scope and that content.

In observing, I also was not particularly interested in finding answers, I was noticing what showed up when facilitating others to Be more of Them-Selves. It was because of the identifications clients had with conception and incarnation that I even began noticing conception and incarnation beyond my own experience. It was more buffering between Who They Were and how they showed up in the world, often literally as the identification with the body and coming into the body.

Again, I am discussing this from the apparent individuation of Oneness into form, and consequently time/space and apparent linearity. In reality, there is Oneness even though we show up in this reality as form that seems separate and seems to be experienced as events unfolding in time/space, in a linear way.

So, what did I notice?

What became clear was that conception and incarnation are not events that occur simultaneously, in the same moment. Conception occurs and, at a later 'time', which is most certainly variable, incarnation occurs.

I did not experience any instance of conception and incarnation occurring simultaneously, that is, were one event. What I perceive at a vibrational level is that the two are at varying vibrational frequency ranges. The physical conception into form shows up at certain vibrations and the Being coming into form, incarnation, at other vibrational resonances.

I also continued to perceive in each Presentation I was privileged to observe, that there was a new form. Conception continually held an energy of a new form, not just a transformation from a coming together of a father's sperm and mother's ovum. My limited left-brain knowledge only knew this, whereas my awareness continued to consistently perceive something else.

The word label of 'conception' for me also reflected what I was noticing. The creating into form, coming together (sperm and ovum) while also an idea collapsing into form, funnelling down from the energy of the idea (concept), into form (conceptualisation), no different from 'Aum' vibration coming into form as Consciousness, then forming energy with an 'idea' and appearing condensed to form matter An idea taking form as it projects from Light and comes into apparent form showing up at the micro level of the sperm and ovum 'taking together' to initiate the process of the point of manifestation of another human form.

I continued to notice that a new form, a new idea was Be Coming. I noticed something more going on than just a 'coming together' and a carrying on or transformation of a form from that coming together. The content of that form included the information of the mum and dad not only in the biology but also energetically as a bundle of vibrational signatures and resonances, referenced in a similar way to the vibrational signature of karma as it is referenced lifetime after lifetime. Actually, it wasn't separate from that either. All the information of the vibrational signatures certainly informed the choosing of this mother and father and DNA presentation and the 'stage' of the lifetime being chosen. Even though it still felt like a contradiction in terms of Oneness and the non-separation of Allness, I continued to get this information from the level of apparent form.

A new question comes in now: Does the Being incarnating orchestrate the coming into form of a new form, or do they choose from possibilities already presenting from the coming into form of other Beings' choices? Where did the 'thought' to create a new form come from? These questions are really questions of a linear mind and are at the vibration of the linear mind. In the perception of Oneness, these questions do not show up as a separation. With no separation, the questions reveal the beautiful play of Divinity and Oneness of which We Are All an aspect. This includes the play of choice as we all choose incarnations or no incarnations and the stages of those incarnations and no incarnations, all to know Self. Our Souls choose from this expansive context of existence. This is where Oneness and non-separation is truly evident. We are not cognitive of it but the Divinity and Infiniteness of Who We Are plays out Magnificently in both conception and incarnation as We Be together in that Oneness. The reason for it all: To Be Come cognitive of Who We Really Are and know that Oneness is all that Is.

Seeing a totally new form and a point of manifestation of a new form was seeing a new projection of Light from Oneness, not an evolution from an existing physical form. While I did not need to understand it, only perceive it, I did hunt for some left-brain information to match my awareness and I found discussions on the creation of the zygote, a new cell formed from the pronuclei of the sperm and ovum (Moore, 1988).

The zygote is a new cell and considered 'the beginning of a human being'. This matched the energy I was perceiving even though I didn't fully understand the biology. This fit what I perceived: the point of manifestation of the body/mind complex, the projection of a new form by the Light from Consciousness.

As I continued reflecting on this, I happened to attend a course called *Matrix Energetics* (Dr. Richard Bartlett D.C., 1992)which I had previously booked to undertake. Already absorbed with my reflections, my attention leaped at the discussion on the heart torsion field (Jonsson). I heard that the heart torsion field accessed Our Infinite Nature and is the very first thing that forms, even before the physical heart. I perceived a deep relevance of this awareness to my internal reflections on conception. The energy was a match. The information on conception was continuing to unfold before my perceptual eyes.

As I allowed the information to project and merge with my awareness, I noticed that the coming into form of a new form simultaneously included projected matter and energy. It was not separate. The Infiniteness of the heart torsion field was Present while physically we had one cell, a hologram of Infinite Oneness. The projection of the new form by Light showed up equally in a form receivable by the five senses (zygote) and also energetically as a heart torsion field, both Presentations proclaiming the Magnificence of that new form, not separate from Oneness.

As I continued to observe this simultaneity, I experienced a Wave of Indescribable Joy, like a hundred million fireworks exploding in celebration of this new form, of all new forms Coming to Be. Then I noticed something else. Imbued in this Joy was a throbbing, a rhythm, and then I realised It: I was noticing the manifestation of the 'Aum' vibration in form. I was perceiving 'Aum' in the fabric of the form more tangibly than I had previously perceived. I was overwhelmed by an Immeasurable Magnificence reflecting our conception into form. Imbued in matter is the rhythm of God, 'Aum' pulsating. Not only did 'Aum' condense to form Consciousness, it maintained a 'Hum', a pulsating that echoed its rhythm in all form. Our heartbeat, our Breath, our lifeforce and our movement more obviously and eternally reflect this rhythm, yet it Is in All form. All form is a road back Home

Whichever direction I observed I was met with an Inconceivable Explosion of Magnificence.

As I remained absorbed in this awareness, my attention then went to incarnation. The Oneness and Divinity I perceived with conception I knew as the stage and its Joy and Beauty is Limitless, so what was there to Behold when looking at the Soul Itself, and more specifically, where exactly did Our Souls reside?

I did not have to wait long for the reply. I was blessed one morning to receive information on incarnation.

As I lay in bed, I began receiving a motion picture-like projection. What I beheld totally astounded and humbled me beyond measure. I was being shown a Soul coming into form and It came to the heart torsion field. The Soul, which looked like Light, merged, appeared to fuse, with the heart torsion field. It looked as though it became part of it rather than inhabiting it.

In what felt like an Eternal Moment, I watched as this Light, upon Be Coming One with the heart torsion field, began ricocheting through the heart torsion field. Sparks of Light were bouncing throughout the torsion field. It felt like no time in the sense of time reflecting Light, it felt Infinite. I was watching a Spectacular Light Show. Somehow, I knew that the Light couldn't occupy the whole torsion field and that was why I was watching this Light ricocheting throughout the torsion field. It felt like there was inertia in the centre of the torsion field and that the torsion field couldn't be totally occupied, rather, the Light continued to bounce around. It felt that without the inertia, there would Be a Glow. I was observing a Flame made up of all the ricocheting Sparks of Light.

Then the realisation came to me. OMG (literally). The descriptions of the Soul as a Spark of God and Flame of God were not metaphoric, they were literal!! We Are literally Sparks of Light and a Flame of God when we incarnate. The Infinite and Eternal Life of Who We Are is literally the Manifested God in His Own Likeness. That is what we 'look like' as an individuation of Oneness, of God. My perceptions of Us as the projection of Light from Consciousness, as the Facet of the Infinite Diamond of Oneness, the Manifested God, literally is Who We Are and shows up in our incarnation when we Be Come One with the heart torsion field. We Are and project an Inexpressible Light Show. I was in awe and felt honoured to have watched and perceived this information. We are all Sparks of God. We Are all Magnificent beyond comprehension.

Our incarnation is a literal Spectacular reflection of the Light of God and together with our conception and the development of the body/mind complex, God and Our Divinity is reflected wherever you look.

A few months after receiving this information, I researched more on the heart torsion field. I didn't really know a lot about it other than experience its Phenomenal and Infinite reflections of God and Who We Are.

I found the work of Russian astrophysicist Dr. Nikolai A. Kozyrev (Wilcock, 2006), who first identified these spiralling energies in all of nature. He found that they were what created our Universe and also our notion of time and yet of themselves travel at the speed of light and are beyond gravity and electromagnetism; they did not function in time/space. He found that these torsions create and change matter and are influenced by changes in Consciousness. He and others also found access to tremendous amounts of energy via these spiralling torsions when they are dynamic, particularly in the centre of the torsion field, zero-point energy. They were also very surprised to prove that there is no place energy is not, there is no empty space. They called this aether, which is what holds Our Universe in place, it is what holds matter in place.

'Zero Point Energy in our universe becomes a mind-boggling thought, for a cube of 1/3 an inch square is contained more energy than expended by ALL of the stars in OUR GALAXY in a million years!' (Setterfield, 2017)

In 1889 Nikola Tesla, stated that '..it is a mere question of time when men will succeed in attaching their machinery to the very wheel work of Nature. Many generations may pass, but in time our machinery will be driven by a power obtainable at any point in the Universe' (Tesla, 2017). Telsa dedicated himself to finding how to harness this Infinite energy for the benefit of humankind and the planet Earth.

This all matched what I perceived. I already knew we were Our Divinity Coming to Be in form. I know we have access to Infinite resources. I know we are All One. Kozyrev proved that the fabric of matter was beyond time/space and accessed Infinite energy and that there was no empty space, something was holding it all together. He called it aether, I call it Consciousness.

We have forgotten because of our ego/minds, yet Inspiration, which we will speak of soon, informs our knowing in the story and yet again are the roads that lead us back Home, to know Who We Are. In truth, everything is our own Divinity reflected back to Us.

The Unfathomable Beauty of our conception and development as a body/mind complex appears Miraculous and is imbued literally in the fabric of God. But wait, there is always more. Even at a more 'physical' level of apparent form we have access to God via the third eye, the spine, the chakras, medulla oblongata and life force or chi and our Breath, and let us not forget through every single cell and where the cell is not.

From the very first manifestation of our physical form we are reflecting Home and have a way Home, and have access to Infinity, Our Infinity. God has provided a roadmap back Home whatever route you choose to take.

We are Divinity in motion. We have just forgotten and bought as real what is stored in our ego/minds. If the ego/mind did not buffer us from Who We Are, we could function from the Infinite energy and Infinite Divinity We truly Be. The ego/mind buys as real that you get energy from food, water, and other things from outside you. Once we begin to buy out of the content and context of the ego/mind, we begin to receive and perceive Who We Are and can function as the Infinite Beings we truly Be.

We have the capability to function from this Infiniteness. I know Consciousness is expanding on the planet and we will Be This, No-Thing is separate. Until We all Shine as Who We Really Are we will not rest to expand Consciousness. What we are really 'doing' is facilitating each other to know Who We Are and to shed what cloaks us from Shining. When the cloak of the ego/mind is dismantled we do literally Shine. Even in the story, it is shared that Holy Ones who are Enlightened Shine and Glow. The eyes are the window to the Soul. Look how the eyes of Enlightened Ones' Sparkle. Similarly, when I perceive those that have released the ego/mind, I 'see' Light around their heads also. Again, halos are literal. They do exist and can be perceived at higher vibrations when the ego/mind has been shed. All of these characteristics display the Soul reflecting outwards when nothing hinders or cloaks its Presence. You are seeing God reflected to You. It is to enable you to see Your own reflection, You are the Light of God.

But wait, there is even more.

Earlier I spoke of the Soul having some content, the content of Your Essential Nature. This content is expressed within and as The Breath of God. It is Our Spirit, Respiro. It is God in Movement.

While, from my left-brain perspective, a new form does not breathe in utero, from my awareness I 'see' Breathing. The 'Hum' of 'Aum'. The Movement of God animating the new form has begun, not separate from the Movement of the Spectacular Light Show of Our Light ricocheting throughout the heart torsion field and integral with the Movement, the rhythm of 'Aum' within form, within the conception and development of a new body/mind complex, including more literally the heartbeat. The Breath transforms again at the moment of incarnation and communes with the rhythm of all cells and no cells and the heart torsion field and the heart itself, even before it develops physically. What began in conception merges as One in the Presentation of the Soul in incarnation, Breathing Life into this lifetime from the Source of Life. The Breath, the Spirit, seems to then Re-Present more physically the 'Aum' in form, the Access point of Infinity and all the access points to Infinity within the body/mind complex, including the physical heartbeat. At this vibration of no time/space all is Known and is an Isness. There is a rhythm, and a recognising of a rhythm, and this creates a linchpin for the current conception/incarnation Presentation.

Souls can bring their attention back to pre-incarnation and Be Present 'elsewhere', an example of what is called in the story 'an out of body experience'. At incarnation, commonly and repeatedly, the Soul leaves the body and then returns. While we are not cognitive of it at this early stage of development, this can continue until later in the development of the body/mind complex and sometimes even after birth. This linchpin is the anchoring, or more literally, the broadcast of information to the Soul to 'zero in' where it has chosen to incarnate. This information is also not separate from all the vibrational information Present.

As we develop and are born into this reality, the Breath keeps us moving in our body/mind complex and perpetually provides a road back Home in any moment. It continues to ripple the rhythm and vibration of 'Aum' throughout existence. This is 'The' Butterfly Effect.

When the ego/mind content is not present, or even if we adopt the Right Actions of breathing practices taught by yogis and others who have awakened within their bodies, we open to the Infinite capacities We Be, including healing the body/mind complex.

At the point of 'death' of the body/mind complex, when the Soul 'detaches' from the heart torsion field, I still 'see' Breathing, a rhythm. Its form as a Breath animating a physical form changes and transforms to Be Present while not in the physical. It still exists as the rhythm it Is. It remains inseparable to the Soul and Our Infinite and Eternal Nature. It is Our Spirit.

Another way I perceive the Breath is as Respiro, as the In-Spiration of God into our actions. Your Soul incarnating, the Breath, Your Spirit enlivens the body/mind complex and expresses as Inspiration, new ideas and creation when we choose to utilise the information we receive and perceive from Our Souls, Our awareness (the language of the Soul).

Without the story being cognitive of it, the same Inspiration that Breathes into a new form, is the same Inspiration that has formed all knowing in the story. The same Inspiration of new ideas/new forms that enable the technologies to measure scientifically that Consciousness holds our cells in apparent form.

Do you really think that new ideas come from a preprogrammed ego/mind, referenced by what already is known and concluded? No. The ego/mind is a library of what has already existed in the story. Inspiration is God in Movement. It is what informs advances or rather, expansion of Consciousness, in science, the arts, sport, our cultures, our humanity. It is not personal, it is God guiding us to Know Our Selves from which we are never separate. It is all part of the Divinity in and As Oneness.

Let us now reflect on the practicalities of incarnation.

Let me begin with some context. In the story there is much debate about the moment that a life has begun. I do not think the story differentiates conception and incarnation when we discuss a 'life'. In the story 'life' is generally bundled together as the body and the Being as 'a life', one life. A discussion on the Being is mostly not even in the equation. There is an energy of 'what you see is what you get': there is a baby and that is a new life. What I perceive as a Being, a Soul, incarnating into a new form from a conception is generally not differentiated.

I can only speak from my awareness, and I most definitely experience and know that conception and incarnation do not occur simultaneously. I am not saying that the honouring of a new form should not occur because of the distinction of conception and incarnation. For me it is all an Expression of Divinity. Where I do differ is the fixed viewpoints on how something should be, rather than perceiving the Isness of each Unique Presentation.

Incarnation of the Soul in any instance is not at a set time, it is variable. The incarnation of the Soul does not occur at the point of conception. It occurs some time later and varies for each incarnation.

I came across instances when the Soul incarnated soon after the point of conception. In most cases I observed, it occurred after the first few weeks. Also, the Soul comes and goes, that is, bringing attention to outside the body/mind complex. What I referred to earlier as 'an outer body experience' occurs often as a body/mind complex develops. There is no position on this, it occurs naturally and is quite 'normal'. This can occur even after birth, even a few weeks after birth.

In our lives we experience this sensation when we experience something traumatic or overwhelming. Rather than experience the full intensity of the event, the Soul chooses to 'pop-out' and diffuse the intensity. We experience this as an out of body experience. Anecdotal evidence from those that experience near death experiences also speak of being out of body (Various, 2018) although these out of body experiences can be to a greater degree as the body/mind complex can present as close to 'death' or technically at 'death'.

During the development of the body/mind complex, the Soul continues this out-of-body process as It adjusts to the incarnation, the confinement within a body/mind complex. While We are not limited to the body/mind complex, there is a sense of confinement experienced, particularly when we factor in that the body/mind complex has the vibrational content of karma, which of itself is what does not allow the fullest Expression of Self to Be Present.

I have also observed multiple Souls vying for a new body/mind complex, which is resolved quite naturally with no position or significance.

The Essential Nature of the Soul can also be perceived before incarnation. This includes a sense of male or female as part of Their Nature, even though this does not by necessity correlate with the gender of the new body/mind complex.

I also regularly perceive Souls waiting to incarnate. They 'hang around' for a while even before conception. At this level of Isness and Being informed by Allness, a Being chooses when and where they will incarnate and while there is no time/space beyond this reality, a Being will 'hang around' prospective parents/parent/family before a choice is made.

In a similar way, Souls that are related to clients through miscarriage or abortion also 'hang around' (similar to other family members who have passed over). I have found very frequent cases of the same Souls returning after a miscarriage or abortion, it was more common than not. That is, if a mother miscarried or aborted a child and they went on to have another child, the previous Soul, in a great many cases I observed, returns. There is no judgement on the part of the Soul. It is the story that has the judgement. At the level of Our Souls, where there is no time/space, All is Known, even if We will experience a miscarriage or abortion. Additionally, I always receive the information that any Soul that has chosen to incarnate is considered by Oneness to Be a child of that mother and father, whether the child survives until birth or not, and no matter how old the unborn child is in utero. It is considered part of the stage, the story and known to contribute to dismantling the veil of the ego/mind.

During our lifetime, the Soul generally remains with the heart torsion field until the 'death' of the body/mind complex, however, this is not always the case. Though it is not common, a Soul can leave a body/mind complex before the death of the body/mind complex and another Soul enters, merging with the heart torsion field. This can occur, for example, whilst under general anaesthetic during surgery or while the body/mind complex is under the influence of numbing agents. Know that for this to occur both Souls would be choosing it, and, again, it is not common.

How the body/mind complex shows up in life is definitely a reflection of the content of the ego/mind, the karma still buffering the Soul from showing up fully. It can bring the body/mind complex to the point of death, yet it isn't the body/mind complex that chooses 'death', it is the Soul.

At the level of Infinity and Who We Really Are anything is possible, even the healing of the body/mind complex in any moment. There is no separation in the Oneness. It is not the body/mind complex that causes a 'death', it is the Soul choosing and changing the form of the Breath that shows up as the Breath stopping in the body/mind complex. The Soul completes the process by then 'detaching' from the heart torsion field.

When I reflect on my own father's passing, and others that I have been privileged to bear witness to, the energy changes dramatically at that moment when the Breath changes from a physical Breathing and 'stops'. What is Spirit in the physical form now is Spirit beyond incarnation. We are now beyond this reality and what happens next is the release of the body/mind complex by the Soul. I literally saw my father's Soul leave his body. The body/mind complex is no longer Animated and Who We Really Are is now beyond this reality. The transition is occurring.

SOUL MATES

I cannot end this chapter on Our Souls without discussing the concept of Soul mates.

In the story there is much expectation on 'finding your Soul mate'. With this expectation comes a limitation that to truly find love in this world you need to find your Soul mate. With this also comes the polar opposite, that if you do not find your Soul mate, you have somehow compromised or been diminished in some way.

I wish to share my perceptions on this and hopefully clarify misidentifications that I see occurring within the story not only with individuals but generally at the macro level in the world.

Everything is vibration and Our Souls are no different. Each of Our Souls has a vibrational signature, a coding of information similar to DNA. This vibrational signature is how information relating to us is stored and projected (It is all not dissimilar to our computer databases, particularly when we get to the basics of how they are stored: ones and zeros, Light and Shadow, projections).

We have a resonance of how we show up in the world, that is, with all the content of our ego/minds, our karma; and this is stored as it is in any moment. We have a resonance of Who We Are, Our Soul and this Is as It Is while We exist. This vibration does not change while We exist as Our Selves. It is perfect and no other Soul will ever exist the same. It is a Unique Expression of God as That Soul.

When we incarnate, we reflect and project both the vibrational signature of how we show up (karma) and the vibrational signature of Who We Are, even though we do not pick it up with our five senses.

Even those whom I have referred to as 'Lost Souls' would be resonating both, as the limitation for them is that they cannot pick up any of the awareness of their Souls, however, It is always Present.

As we travel during an incarnation we reverberate, like a beacon, the vibration of Our Souls and the vibration of how we show up. Even with the layers of identifications that we are wearing and our own lack of cognitive awareness, we are transmitting these vibrations wherever we go. It is really how we look without the form and structure of our bodies, and is how we look when we transition from our bodies. All the information remains an Isness.

This vibration of how we show up is the net effect of all the content of the ego/mind, including all the content we have bought as real with regard to Soul mates. This content may be subconscious or cognitive including content from magazines, books and other media on the 'ideal partner' or what constitutes a Soul mate.

When we are functioning from the ego/mind and measuring a person, mostly an intimate partner, based on the criteria of what a Soul mate is within our ego/minds (and for 'Lost Souls' that is all there is in that moment), I do not consider that to have any relevance to what I perceive a Soul mate is. As such, I perceive this to be a total misidentification.

A Soul mate has no direct relevance to an intimate partner and reflects a vibration, not a percentage of ticks on some checklist.

It is not dissimilar to our discussion on empowerment. Empowerment in the story, is the level to which there is compliance or not to criteria within your society on what empowerment shows up like. Finding a Soul mate can be one of the criteria for ego/mind empowerment. True empowerment is a vibration, a Presence, Who You Are, Being You in the world. A Soul mate is similar.

While there will never Be a Soul the same as You, there are things and people in the world (incarnate or not) which have a similar resonance to Your Soul. This includes nature, our planet, people, actually anything that exists. We will look at this further in the next chapter as while we are functioning within the story, from our ego/minds, it is these things that more truly 'fill our cup' and facilitate transmuting our identifications. For now let us focus on people.

There will be people in the world that are familiar to You, despite being strangers. You do not even have to meet them. You can receive them over the TV screen or the internet, I know I have. There are people who feel like 'your tribe' or you immediately 'hit it off' upon meeting them. There are people who 'feel' like you have met them or known them before, whereas you may or may not have in this or any other lifetime or when not incarnate.

There is a distinction to be made here. There are two reasons for the familiarity. Firstly, some Souls will feel familiar to You because of past and/or future lifetime experiences. You share karmic story with these Souls and You may experience a Soul connection with these Souls in this incarnation. This does not reflect that, by default, they are Soul mates. The familiarity here is the same as the foundations maintained when functioning from the ego/mind. Secondly, the familiarity is due to a high degree of resonance with Your Soul's resonance. These are Soul mates.

Soul mates are not from karmic connections, if any. They have a high degree of common resonance with Your Soul's resonance, not dissimilar to having common DNA characteristics. These Souls are indeed familiar (like family) as they are familiar to the resonance of Who You Are. Notice that there is no content checklist, only a receiving of an energy: what it 'feels' like.

It is not as common as you think or perhaps desire. It is much more common to encounter Souls You have had karmic connections with. Additionally, it is not directly related to being male or female or have anything to do with being an intimate partner. Our Souls do not have a position on this. There is no significance around this. It Is as it Is.

The reason we receive these people as familiar is because the resonance of Our Souls is a vibration of Home, of Oneness, and when we meet someone that resonates like Our Souls we recognise it as a home-like 'feeling'. Unfortunately, this is when misidentification occurs. We implant this information (what we are 'feeling'/receiving about a Soul) into our ego/minds and we think that our yearning is dissipated because we 'have found the one'. It is not real, only a temporary 'fix' from this reality. It is not a returning Home which is the true yearning of Our Souls. The 'one' is not Oneness. It is another Soul that 'feels' like You. You could also further disempower yourself by misidentifying that someone outside of you 'completes you', misidentifying the feeling as a need for intimacy with that person.

If you were to meet someone who shares a high percentage of Your Soul's vibrational resonance and you are not in your awareness, you may find that person irresistible and recognise that person as somebody you are yearning for, but in actual fact you are yearning to reconnect with God. It is like you have been given a taste of Home but you think the person is it, no, they are not It. Consequently, you misidentify this feeling as love in the story rather than what it is, a glimpse of what Familiar and Home feels like when You return to Oneness.

People who are Enlightened can provide this feeling of Home also. This is why we are drawn to certain teachers; you are drawn to their Soul resonance when there is a similarity to You. They return to guide us back Home. They can provide a true experience of and pathway to Home, however, only You can 'go There'.

There is no real need for a Soul Mate to show up in any lifetime. There is so much that exists in our world that resonates like You and that facilitates you awakening to You and returning to Oneness.

If one or more Soul mates do show up in a lifetime, they may not show up in the form you think or desire. Your Soul mate may be a best friend, a teacher, a child, a work colleague; someone you would not choose as an intimate partner. In these cases, you will most likely have the love experience but not misidentify it as romantic love in the story. Also, Souls which resonate like You may not be incarnate during your present incarnation or may not reside in your 'neck of the woods', the stage where you have incarnated.

In my 20 years working with clients, I have met five people who have met a Soul mate in the form of an intimate partner, and only one maintained a long-term relationship within the story. Another was separated by the death of their partner. The others could not sustain a relationship in the story. While misidentifying their partner as 'the one' they experienced anguish when it just did not work out because of how they each showed up in the relationship and in the world.

We forget that while a Soul mate may show up, we are still functioning from our ego/minds and thus function from the content of the ego/mind. A Soul mate may resonate like You but if You or Your Soul mate are not functioning from Being, you will have your Michelin Man suits show up in the relationship.

In the story, the notion that a Soul mate brings with them the 'happy ever after' is a lie and a fantasy; we can leave that in the movies.

Intimate relationships with a Soul mate not only have the usual relationship issues but they also can present an internal confusion. When you 'feel' a connection to a Soul mate, and particularly if you buy the lie that this person is 'the one', you experience disbelief, loss and confusion when they do not live up to the title because of their behaviour or other content showing up from their or your ego/mind. There is no rightness or wrongness, it is what it is.

The decision to stay with someone based solely on the notion they are your Soul mate is equally buying the lie that someone is 'the one'. This is when truly the misidentification of Soul mate is very evident.

If you do feel you have a Soul mate in your life, knowing what is going on may help. It can be useful to have a Soul mate around you as it enables you to experience aspects of Your Self in the story and fills your cup rather than draining it. But while functioning in the dualistic reality, it can very easily flip to the polar opposite if a dependency or exaggerated expectation is imposed on or by either person.

When we function as Who We Are we are not deluded by the familiarity of something outside of Who We Are. The need to 'find a Soul mate' is known as irrelevant and a distraction. You know You are One with All, in the kaleidoscope of vibrations of All that exists. Soul mates and actually anyone or anything that exists and resonates like You, can be perceived as useful to facilitate returning Home. That Is It.

What if we embraced inclusion of all vibrations and resonances that exist, and enjoyed our lives as we awaken to Who We Are? Everything is available. Let us stop seeking outside ourselves and enjoy the contribution of All that Is on this beautiful planet of ours and even when we transition from our bodies. There is no away. In the New World that is instituting, we will receive the contribution of each of us to each other and the planet, to an honouring and receiving of that contribution which is chosen or not. The rigidity of needing to get it right will dismantle and it will become possible to drop judgement, receive and embrace all our diversity and Be together in Oneness.

Four

LIVING AS YOUR SELF

LIVING AS YOUR SELF is buying out of all the content of the ego/mind. The charge on that content has 'flat-lined' to illicit no reactive response. Life is lived through your perception, using the mind as a tool to facilitate choosing and creating how You Be in the world and in existence. You are in allowance of All that Is, even the stage of the world. You have an acute and potent capacity to Be in the dualistic reality while not buying it as real. You are Being You, and enjoying the ease and joy of Being. Everything is about the expansion of Consciousness and all Being in Oneness, even if this word labelling is not utilised.

Life is known to Be a reflection of Divinity in All things. There is nothing to achieve, choices are made in daily life in every moment. These choices are made as a contribution to showing up in the world as Being You. All yearning dissipates as You realise You are not separate from anything and there is no away.

There is No-Thing You are not, and while you may not be cognitive of it All in any moment, You have access to perceive It. There is no line to the finish, there is no line, no linearity. There is Allness and Isness and It includes You.

Those who are not yet cognitive of this, are also not separate. This is why we reincarnate, as it is known that All will return Home, no exceptions, no exclusions.

Being cannot be forced. It arises when enough ego/mind content has been shed, dismantled, bought out of or transmuted. As this occurs we remove the charge on that content until there is no charge, the true 'flat-lining' and death, the death of the ego/mind, You Being You as an Isness.

For the majority of us, we continue to transition from living as ourselves, as determined by the content of our ego/minds, to living as Our Selves, with no content, no position, no point of view. Let us now explore how we are functioning in the world, living our lives and transitioning to Our Selves.

Most of us do not allow ourselves to know this is what we are transitioning to. We remain in the confines of the ego/mind. We think living is within the context of the societies we have chosen to incarnate in or have cognitively chosen to belong to. We buy as real all the identifications we define ourselves as. While, the language of Being, the awareness of the Soul, may be perceived, this is coloured by all the content of the ego/mind.

For most, input received via the five senses and perceived from awareness is referenced against the library of content within the ego/mind and the ego/mind then interprets it, deciding what it thinks it is. What you think you receive and perceive is what your ego/mind wants you to receive based on all the content within that ego/mind.

I have referred to this as your perspective. Now let us notice that nothing can really be received and perceived as what it Is while the filters of the ego/mind are in place interpreting and changing the information.

Would you know what honey is if you didn't know what honey is?

Life is the position we take based on all the expectations, correlations, conclusions, judgements and decisions held within the ego/mind. It is like a pinball reacting after being triggered, joining the dots every time we receive and perceive information. This is our reality in any moment, and for many, nothing else is considered possible. As we remove the charge on our ego/mind content, our reality does change. Our perspective changes, our positions change, until eventually we hold no position on anything. While functioning from the ego/mind, we think this target isn't even a target. The thought of not having a position or point of view is deemed ridiculous and impossible. What is actually possible is no attachment or charge to anything 'needing' to be a certain way and the total freedom to choose whatever we choose.

We create our positions based on our ego/mind content in any moment. Positioning is always on the spectrum of totally agreeing to totally disagreeing, this is the dualistic reality. The few who come up with further measures are again on the spectrum between totally agreeing and creating additional content for others to comply with; or totally disagreeing and creating additional content for others to comply with. These are often people in the story that others mimic when they judge themselves as less than. Each stage has its own spectrum of benchmarks.

Our sense of self often relates directly to our perspective of our position, both overall in our families, societies and the world, and/or in certain areas of our lives, specialisations where our position may be deemed by the ego/mind to be superior to other aspects of our lives. This can also be labelled as ego/mind empowerment, and is where you position yourself in relation to empowerment.

This is all referenced from the ego/mind content which shows up as identifications. These create a foundation for us in the world. Whether these identifications show up as agreeing or disagreeing with the environment you have chosen to incarnate in, it all provides the 'solid ground' from which to function in the world. Often, we pick a particular identification and create a sense of self from that. This can occur both cognitively and unconsciously. We then mimic how the identification presents in the world and then feel a sense of self, of belonging and proceed to identify 'self' as that.

I have noticed that when we are functioning from the ego/mind this 'solid ground' is critical to the level to which functioning is deemed successful. We need this 'solid ground' from which to jump off into the world, no matter what that world looks like for us. If the sense of self in compliance with the ego/mind is maintained, a foundation is created and there arises a potentiality to function in the world.

I have noticed that there is a progression through which we can function in the world. Visually I see it as concentric circles expanding out as our sense of self stabilises. In the centre is ourselves. At this point there is a functioning with self only. Do not misidentify this as Self. This is self as the ego/mind and as such we are speaking of all the form and structure required to function from the ego/mind.

Until you deem yourself stable and have 'solid ground' as 'your self' you cannot function beyond this. In the story, any efforts to integrate these people into the broader scope of society would be futile and also too overwhelming for the persons involved. Any responsibilities that they have beyond self, for example, children, work, health, cannot be fulfilled as there is literally an inability to respond. Even responsibilities to the self are most often neglected.

To change this, their sense of self needs to be strengthened before they can function beyond themselves to the next level of functionality, their immediate family. Depending on the content held within the ego/mind, examples of remedies that such individuals can choose both cognitively and unconsciously while functioning with no foundation of self can range from:

- ☐ Joining a gang and living with or as that gang;
- ☐ Joining those taking drugs and being friends in that community (common unity);
- ☐ Cultural attachment to the exclusion of all others;
- ☐ Religious attachment to the exclusion of all others;
- ☐ Joining those that are homeless and feeling like nobody else understands them or they can't be anywhere else;
- ☐ Joining any particular group that advocates and requires secrecy and/or ostracising and excluding all others.

To:

- Behaving like and/or mimicking someone or something else;
- Joining a group with a clear identity, differentiated from others while not ostracising others (differs from above in degree of exclusion and scope), including groups identifying in culture, race, sex, social status (including being unemployed), sport, health, religion.

This is a level of functioning which maintains 'fight or flight'. It is not about judging good or bad, wrong or right. At this level, if identification and a foundation is not established, functioning is hard work, overwhelming and often no relief is experienced, which of itself, can appear to 'force them' to partake in numbing behaviours. If a foundation is established, functioning can remain within a very narrow scope of living in the world.

The next level of functioning is within immediate family. I generally see this presenting as those that live with you in your home and are related to you, for example, your partner, your children, and for some their parents (when culturally defined as immediate family or when you are still living with them) and for some, their pets. Often, at this level of functioning, the identifications are those of the immediate family and may range from adopting those identifications to rebelling against them.

If the immediate family environment is not providing a solid foundation from which to function in the world, living can be limited to this scope. Other identifications can also be adopted to replace the lack of foundation found in the immediate family, including the examples given above. I have also seen examples where another family or group has been adopted as the 'immediate family' foundation because the foundation of their actual immediate family was fractured or unstable for whatever reason, for example, separation, financial instability, abuse or conflict of any kind.

Another way we attempt to establish a 'solid ground' in immediate family, which I see often with clients, is by trying to fix those around you, wanting them to be different. This can be like hitting your head against a brick wall, as unless anyone is willing to make changes, you trying to make them change creates nothing but conflict. Not only may they not be choosing it, they may not see what you see, and don't 'believe' they have anything to change. In this case, they see you as the instigator of conflict and unrest within the immediate family environment. If this is showing up, notice the information that you are willing to make changes. I recommend bringing the focus back to you, to self and strengthening that foundation again. I have found that in attempting to change others around us, we may question ourselves and judge ourselves, fracturing the foundation of self. The ego/mind has judgement, position and significance to handle a situation. Someone is right, someone is wrong. Leave it! Practice observing those around you rather than reacting. Come back to self and revisit what is required to maintain a solid foundation with immediate family. For example, it may be practicing allowance of how they are, moving out, not judging yourself or creating your reality within your bedroom and 'chunking up' your interaction with immediate family to social pleasantries. It is not your job unless awareness (not the ego/mind) informs otherwise, leave that to God in the bigger picture of everyone awakening to Who They Are.

If we have a solid foundation at this level, we can function beyond to extended family. This can sometimes merge with the next level of community, particularly for those that have no extended family available or increasingly, connection to extended family is weakened or lost.

As our sense of self solidifies further and we are more assured in our environments from the ego/mind perspective, we progressively expand out and become available within our society, country and the world. At these levels of functioning, the foundation can be rocked by events like war, political unrest, famine, natural disasters and terror attacks that occur away from us geographically. While those immediately affected are most likely functioning at 'self' or 'immediate family' levels, even if temporarily, such events can also have a domino effect for those functioning at community, society, national and global levels, potentially collapsing them right back to needing to re-establish functioning as self if the events trigger a reaction where lack of safety or security are felt.

At any moment, if we feel we can obtain a more solid sense of self from another identification, we can find ourselves jumping into the foundation that the other identification provides. This can show up, for example, as a total change in behaviour, presentation in looks, clothing, and for some even sexual, cultural or religious orientation. For many the change resonates more with how they feel based on the content of the ego/mind in that moment, this includes how they feel in their bodies.

The above levels of functioning reflect where we are living in the world whilst functioning from the ego/mind. The content of our ego/minds is what is informing the conclusions of belonging or not belonging, of feeling solid in our foundations. This includes whatever content the ego/mind interprets from any awareness received and perceived from Our Souls. This adds another dimension to our discussion. Depending on the level to which the awareness from Our Souls is received clearly or coloured and distorted, will impact our foundation and how we function and live in the world.

When we live as Our Selves, no solid ground is necessary. Our 'foundation' is the formless knowing and Isness of Consciousness. Content is irrelevant. How we show up is informed by our awareness and knowing. This is the target for all of us whether we are cognitive of it or not.

Let us now spend some time looking at this further dimension of the level to which we are perceiving and receiving the awareness of Our Souls and what our ego/minds are doing with that content. I will refer back to the scope of functioning in the world as we transition to living more as Our Selves.

Let us begin with those that I have labelled as 'Lost Souls'. These are people who function solely from what is stored in their ego/minds. This content has so much charge that it overwhelms and narrows their perspective to just what they think they know. It is not that there is so much content that it overwhelms. No, I do not think we have any capacity issue with our ego/minds (that is another reflection all together). It is the relentless and massive charge on the content that creates the blockage to receiving any awareness from their Souls.

Should they choose to receive and add more content into their ego/minds, it would most likely be in strict alignment with the existing content, or at the same vibrational resonance as that content.

This can show up at both ends of the empowerment spectrum. It can be dogged and forthright, with no level of flexibility in thinking. When they observe others around them and in the world having different points of view and even flexibility in thinking (I am not even talking about awareness here, only the content of ego/minds), they defend their 'right position'. They do not justify their position, as their position is the only correct one. These people take no prisoners and do not see another point of view as worth considering. They can show up as empowered in the story, often with much force, and can function at the world level due to their solid sense of self. They definitely would not label themselves as 'Lost Souls', they may label themselves as leaders.

At the other end of the spectrum, 'Lost Souls' can also show up as totally withdrawn from the world, most likely creating a detached personal reality that imprisons them in a way of thinking that they feel they cannot escape and they never get relief from. Thoughts and the charge are insistent and persistent. Even one thought can prove inescapable. Interactions with those outside of them will most likely be extremely dysfunctional (based on story benchmarks). These 'Lost Souls' show up totally disempowered and cannot generally function beyond themselves. They may function beyond themselves only in a fantasy or altered reality, in an attempt to live in the world. Often, they may turn to numbing agents to survive the intensity of their experience. Mental illness may also show up in response to this intensity.

Showing up as a 'Lost Soul' can also occur for some people from time to time. A clear example is when overwhelm with the content of the ego/mind is experienced and to manage it, the body/mind complex shuts down and disconnects the mind function. This can be temporary but has the potential to become permanent. Usually, overwhelm triggers the body/mind complex to show up as an out-of-body experience only. For a 'Lost Soul' experience, shut down, disconnect and out-of-body experience can all show up. Functioning in the world can quickly revert to the level of 'self' only.

There are also those who, while not 'Lost Souls', define themselves purely from the content of their ego/minds. While they can receive other information and awareness, it is heavily coloured and altered by the ego/mind and is generally rejected. They do not alter the structure and form of identifications worn and this is perpetuated generation after generation as a goal, and a huge matrix of belonging is entrenched. This can be based on any identification, more obviously, race, culture, and religion, and more commonly presenting as functioning from the levels of 'immediate family', 'extended family' and 'community'.

Even reflecting on changes in our humanness over history, functioning from this place would have created our diverse cultures, languages and traditions. Geographic isolation contributed to the isolated thinking. We are no longer geographically isolated, yet for some, that same thinking is in place, to live life purely from what they know as the content of their ego/minds, living solely from those identifications.

Any content that is added to the ego/mind would be congruent with existing content. This firms the foundation of who they are, different to everyone else. Often this shows up as excluding all others as wrong; other times this shows up as maintaining isolation as a superior group or out of deemed necessity to maintain status quo to avoid tainting how they show up.

Sense of self is assured when 'self' shows up as a replication of everyone else within the group (for example, family, culture, religion, race and even sexual orientation). Functioning can be to the level of the world when there is a solid sense of self within those identifications and it is deemed that these fixed identifications can fit in and belong in the world. Equally, this may not be considered possible, and the scope of functioning is limited to the level at which the identifications are deemed as fitting into or belonging to structures such as family and community.

Safety and security (the maintaining of the foundation) is when everything shows up in alignment with the content of their ego/minds. When someone or something does not conform, for example, losing a job, abuse in any form, a family or community member going 'off the rails', being in a relationship with someone not the same as 'them', including all judgements around culture, sex, age, race, the polarity of this reality shows up. There is the intervention to get them back in the fold. The feeling that something is not right or the rejection and/or ostracising of anyone not conforming is necessary to maintain stability and status quo of what is deemed right and what is deemed as necessary to maintain order.

There is a desperate attempt to maintain a fixed matrix of content and identifications, anything else is chaos, wrong and judged as inferior, intolerable, inappropriate, scandalous, unacceptable; the list goes on.

This showed up for the majority of the population in the past. Consciousness on the planet has expanded, awareness is being increasingly reflected, and this containment within fixed identifications is, for the majority, lessening. The above is now beginning to show up as the minority, even though it can feel like a significant influence on how the story shows up both at the micro level and the macro level.

The expansion of Consciousness is even reflected in a tool that has connected us all, the internet. There is no coincidence here. As Consciousness expands our Inspiration is increasingly evident in the world. It is all unfolding whether we are aware of it in any given moment or not.

Interestingly, we can observe in the internet the same presentations of ego/mind functioning that I speak of here. There is no away in Oneness, it is all reflected, after all, it is all of us that input content into the internet. It is like the collective ego/mind. Now that's an interesting thought!

For some, despite a general 'acceptance' that change is occurring around them, their ego/minds determine that change is not possible for them and they maintain how they function in the world. This can be justified with statements like:

- ☐ 'I am too old to change'.
- ☐ 'I have done this the same way forever, why would I change now?'
- ☐ 'This is how we were taught'.
- ☐ 'Why fix something that isn't broken?'
- ☐ 'The world is going mad, we need to hold on to how things should be done'.
- ☐ 'This generation doesn't know what work is'.
- ☐ 'The old ways are the best ways'.
- ☐ 'We need to learn from the past'.

For others, the ego/mind has dropped the charge on having a set of fixed identifications and is open to receive change that can be adopted as new identifications. We are even creating new identifications reflecting the changing level of Consciousness on the planet. We are beginning to use terminology that mimics the awareness of the Soul, while for many it is only recognised as coming from heart. We recommend: 'do what you love', 'follow your heart', 'follow your dreams', 'find yourself'. We are using these terms to advertise products. These are all buying out of the existing and fixed identifications we have incarnated with, and the asking of 'what else can I choose?'

This, however, does not delete the need to maintain a foundation from which to function in the world. We continue to seek to maintain solidity, an expectation of how things should be. While functioning from the ego/mind, maintaining the foundation of our sense of self remains critical, relative to the charge held within the ego/mind. For many, the broadening of scope of identification to a global scale can generate an even greater reaction within the body/mind complex when they cannot maintain foundations at that global level. I have noticed this particularly with young people. Technologically, they are born into a global environment, that is part of their stage. While they continue to function from the ego/mind, the progressive foundations I speak of are still required to maintain a capacity to function in the world. If they are unstable at the level of self, this can show up as increased incidents of mental illness due to the inability to cope with a vastness they know of, but cannot function in. It can equally show up in other illnesses and allergies to life and to the world. It does not surprise me that the senses need to be actively managed, for example, using earplugs/headphones plugged into technology (a stage of their world), illustrating a need to receive all the information while also needing to maintain stability by blocking out other stages. It is like any other numbing strategy. Interestingly, this generation has an increased capacity to receive information non-linearly and in vast quantities, yet without foundation, it is too intense to live in that world. Even targets they may have can jump directly to a global level but without the stability of foundations, their capacity to fulfil them will mostly be obscured by a lack of capacity to function in the world.

For all of us, if something unexpected does occur, for example, an accident, illness or the death of someone close, the degree to which it rocks our foundation requires the same degree of rebalancing in an attempt to maintain stability. Our whole lives come into question, and while this can be the very thing that begins to awaken us to Who We Are, the ego/mind will desperately seek to return to normality, to fit into the identifications that have been adopted as who you are. No matter if there is an acceptance by the ego/mind of different identifications, it will always try to get you back to the 'you' the ego/mind determines you to be.

This may take time, treatment, recovery, acceptance, forgiveness or other action, all in an endeavour to return to stability. This may not be attainable. For some it is not attained and a void is experienced. This lack of foundation can itself prove fatal or can result in the need to numb with alcohol, food, TV, drugs, withdrawal from the world, check out from the mind via insanity. It may open you to question 'what else or who else are you'. For others, there is a period of readjustment until a new foundation with new identifications shows up, commonly including what happened to you as an identification. Examples are victims of crime and cancer survivors. I am not judging this as a wrongness. It is what may show up in order to function again in the story.

If something occurs unexpectedly in our community, country or the world, our foundation is also rocked relative to the connection to us, that is, relative to the level to which we are functioning in the world. For example, if a traumatic event occurred in the world and the event is very geographically distant from us, we may feel no rocking of our foundation. If we are functioning at the world level we are more likely to be unsettled or drawn to do something to rebalance the situation. This will show up increasingly as generations live their lives connected via the internet. Often, stability returns as time passes, or we get used to the outcome of the events and/or when the media coverage ceases. 'Out of sight, out of mind' works well in maintaining foundations.

For many, events and conditions that rock the foundations of others just become part of the content of the ego/mind, like the props on the stage of our lives. They do not rock our foundations. The ego/mind processes these as 'givens', not requiring any action. Examples are:

- ☐ famine and drought in Africa
- ☐ war in the Middle East
- ☐ marine life dying
- ☐ global warming
- ☐ animals becoming extinct
- ☐ poverty on the outskirts of our cities
- ☐ farmers affected by drought

This is where separation is truly evident. As we continue to dismantle the charge and content of our ego/minds, this separation will diminish. We are beginning to see it already.

For those that have already begun dismantling the ego/mind, these events and experiences of others can be received with an opening of their hearts. Their foundations are not threatened and awareness received by the ego/mind no longer creates a reaction of instability. It can invite an opening to assist others. This may initially be adopted as a new identification. They have put the significance of themselves aside and they bear witness to another. Action may be taken or not. Merely redirecting attention to something or someone other than themselves transmutes further the charge within their ego/mind, while simultaneously contributing to others and transmuting content for them also.

Another way of looking at the need to maintain a foundation is by looking at validation and acknowledgement. In a nutshell, if we each received acknowledgement in the story no matter how we showed up, we would not need to prove any sense of self, as we would have an assuredness of ourselves. We would not be measured against anything to determine whether validation and acknowledgement of us is justified. An ease would arise in us being who we are even when cloaked in the identifications of the ego/mind. We would not be grasping at and for identifications to belong to or fit within. This is definitely something outside of us confirming that we are more than OK. While functioning from the ego/mind, this is a useful crutch, however, it is not likely to occur in the reality of the ego/mind as the very structure of the ego/mind is comparison of right and wrong, good and bad. For someone to be the best, someone else must be less than. This will certainly change in the New World and is changing already. Acknowledgement is the new gratitude.

Only those who have begun to allow awareness to inform their choices can receive the possibility of acknowledgement for all, no matter how they show up. When we Be Our Selves, there is no need for anything, and everything Is, and the 'need' for acknowledgement would not Present, yet we may choose to acknowledge, particularly when awareness informs the contribution it will be to those functioning from ego/mind. Our Magnificence is known. Do we 'need' to validate the Magnificent Presentation of all the Unique Presentations of nature? We Are no different. Until we can all perceive this, acknowledgement by those that are open to gift it, is how true caring can show up in the story and allow someone to be seen and heard.

For many who are invalidated, the dismantling of the ego/mind begins by firstly building up the ego/mind so that there is a sense of self and then a capacity to function in the world. Their sense of self even from the ego/mind perspective is virtually non-existent, showing up as an invisibility in the world, as negligible, showing up as a 'doormat' and being 'trodden on', as gullible and as putting themselves last. Building up an ego/mind sense of self is the first stage of functioning in the world. Once that is established (notice the energy of structure here) and lived in the story, the same questioning arises as to whether the ego/mind has all the answers. The dismantling begins as the sense of self is progressively no longer required. This may not occur in the same lifetime. If the world took up just this one Right Action of acknowledgement, this would make a huge contribution towards the expansion of Consciousness on the planet. Imagine if we all received acknowledgement of who we are, even in the story, no matter how we show up. Imagine growing up and being acknowledged and received all the time, for all that you Be and do, all without judgement. What choices would we make? What would we create? The world would be a very different place.

However a foundation is created, we continue to function with this need to maintain a foundation until the need begins to loosen. It begins to change as we dismantle and transmute the charge on the ego/mind. We begin to cognitively recognise that the ego/mind does not have all the answers and that our awareness provides a contribution to our understanding of life.

This is still in the language of the ego/mind. We are still trying to work things out to maintain stability. We are trying to understand.

Awareness is received as our gut feeling or even intuition rather than the language of the Soul.

Whether change arises from a rocking of our foundations or from other means of transmuting and dismantling the ego/mind, (and which we will examine later in this chapter), as soon as the hold of the ego/mind as all knowing and as 'captain of the ship' weakens, we create space between thoughts and may question 'Is this all there is?'

In this space, which is Consciousness, we have opened to the possibility of perceiving awareness with little or no translation by the ego/mind. This shows up as no difference between the perception of the Soul and what is received within the mind. All of Our Souls and All That Is, of which we are not separate, is guiding us out of separation.

I have observed that those incarnated with very bright minds struggle more with the dismantling of the ego/mind than those that have incarnated with simpler minds. The scope of their minds is so vast, they think they can solve every problem in the world with what they know. This is not so much an ego/mind judgement of superiority (although this may show up for some) as an experience of what it feels like to be able to solve problems in their day to day lives, at work and on a global scale.

As they do begin to function from awareness, using the mind as a tool, the resulting Inspiration is the very thing that contributes to expanding Consciousness within the story. For example, advances in technology and our expansion of knowledge of how things are as they are in existence. As we all get close to God, our capacity to articulate Magnificence expands. This is the gift of the brilliant mind. Science and spirituality: there is no conflict when we perceive from the bigger picture beyond ego/mind.

When we first begin to realise that our ego/minds do not have all the answers, some resistance can appear. Initially, as only the personal position of the ego/mind is experienced, there is a personal defence in not knowing everything and thinking that perceiving awareness is a weakness. The awareness of the Soul is yet to be experienced as You and thus it is held separate, almost as though someone else is imposing information because you don't know it. This is the competition of the ego/mind, the positioning, the win/lose of the dualistic reality. Beyond this duality is the possibility to perceive information that Uniquely expresses through You, via Your Essential Nature, Your Spirit. No one will ever show up like You and Being open to perceive awareness and express it as You, is the gift of You and You Being Your Self in the world. How can there Be competition?

We can each take a single piece of awareness and it can Shine as You.

Others may show up as more open to perceive awareness, however, get confused between what is coming from their ego/minds and what is awareness. This is common as we transition to Be Our Selves and is part of the strengthening of our observation muscle. I will give you a clue: awareness has no point of view, no charge, it is information. Also, when You observe perceiving awareness, it is instantaneous, in no time/space. Often in the story we talk about our initial gut feeling. This is it, the first glimpse of information before thought. If your awareness has a charge or you have a point of view or any position or superiority around the awareness, you have input the awareness into your ego/mind and it is no longer clear. This is what many people do at this stage. They are receiving and perceiving awareness and then inputting it into the ego/mind. The clarity is now gone and the ego/mind will change, hypothesise, question, contort, reject; it will do its thing. Notice if this occurs. Practice noticing the moment you switch to function from the ego/mind. Processing begins; the joining of the dots begins. Don't judge it, just observe.

I want to mention here also, that a great many people, particularly in the spirituality arena, know the language of the Soul and awareness and they think that they are perceiving awareness when it is all their ego/mind. What you think is awareness isn't. It is the ego/mind masking itself as awareness as the ego/mind knows you are looking for awareness. What a trickster!

Until they are willing to perceive even this ego/mind content as information, they will remain functioning from the ego/mind. Again, the clue is having superior position, particularly of themselves and 'their' awareness, 'their' teachings, needing followers, having a point of view, including rigidity of thinking. If they have the answer and you need to go to them for the answer or to heal you, that is their ego/minds playing out.

They may perceive the awareness and then input it into their ego/minds and declare to the world the awareness as theirs. They create superiority and further identification. Their ego/minds may even convince them that they are here to heal the planet and what they know is crucial. In truth, it just doesn't show up that way. This is an arrogance of the ego/mind still wanting to maintain control and importance of 'you' rather than 'You'. What shows up is a limiting of capacity as soon as the awareness is input into the ego/mind. You have locked yourself out of Infinite capacity. Infinite capacity will only show up when you don't have a point of view, when You are One with All That Is rather than you being the one.

There may also be an attempt by the ego/mind to imitate the potency of Being. Structures and control are utilised to establish authority and 'knowing' in the story. They think they are Being because they feel potent, whereas, they are adopting ego/mind empowerment and control. They are not open to change or receiving and perceiving awareness. They think they have the expertise, the experience, 'they got this'. They may not even be able to hear these words and think they are Being. Another lie of the ego/mind. Being always has space (Consciousness without content) for other possibilities.

Another interesting presentation while transitioning to Who We Are is that we are open to perceive awareness relating to others but cannot perceive awareness directly related to us or those immediately around us. As we transmute judgement and expectation, often we drop the judgement and expectations relating to others before we drop it for ourselves. We transmute any charge on having a point of view of others, we are in allowance of them no matter how they show up, but remain in position and point of view for ourselves. This is also why practitioners can Be Present with clients while not Being fully awakened to Who They Are.

This self-judgement maintains filters that do not allow information from awareness to be clearly perceived about ourselves and those close to us. We may turn to others to perceive that awareness. Having strong foundations 'seems' to strengthen our capacity to perceive information but this is a filter. Should that stability be rocked, all clarity will go in an instant. A stable foundation is a crutch and not true empowerment.

Notice what you notice for yourself and practice being in allowance of you too. A crutch I often recommend is treating yourself as you would a child of yours. Judge yourself as you would want your child to judge themselves. For most, they would not want their child to judge themselves at all, we can see past any ego/mind filters to how amazing they are, even if we limit ourselves to how they show up in the story. If You could only know the Magnificence You Be and no matter how you or You show up in the story, it is perfect for the unfoldment of Consciousness on the planet and in existence.

Practice being kind to yourself. Be in allowance of self-judgement. This allows an observing of that judgement without buying that judgement as real and feeling the effect of the judgement. Once you can observe it as what it is in this moment, you have freed yourself. Then practice Being You and all needs dissipate in true caring for and as You.

For many who are toggling between Being and functioning from the ego/mind, self-judgement is often also perpetuated in relation to the degree we think we are not 'there yet'. We seem to maintain an endless checking in that we can clear more, do more, change more about ourselves. We continue to see more 'wrong' than 'right'. It is such an unkindness to ourselves, and our bodies will continue to reflect this. Often, this includes actively facilitating those around us without receiving and perceiving awareness to Be and do so. We receive the information and 'take it upon ourselves' (even literally in our bodies) to help. At this stage, it is not so much an ego/mind superiority but a lack of clarity relating to ourselves, even if we limit the observation to the level of self-care.

There is a lack of acknowledgement of You Being You in the world. You are a tremendous gift to All. Recognise and acknowledge that. Acknowledge your commitment to the expansion of Consciousness. This is innate in Being, and without any need to do anything, You are a huge contribution.

The lack of acknowledgement is a function of the ego/mind and strengthens the hold of the ego/mind. It shows up as needing to do more but there are no such needs in Being, only choice. When Being, no framework exists and an ease and joy in Being Is. There is no getting 'there' in Isness. It is known that God has our backs.

A most fundamental obstacle for most when functioning from the ego/mind is perceiving awareness relating to the mortality of ourselves and those close to us. The illusion of fear created by the ego/mind establishes a total resistance to information which may reveal the imminent death of the body/mind complex or something that will contribute to that death. The scope of our life is deemed by the ego/mind to be this one body/mind complex and it maintains a high alert to avoid any information that may rock the foundation it has established for us in the world, whatever the scope of that world is. This is particularly the case during the expansive phase of a 'lifetime'/ incarnation.

I have dedicated a whole chapter to the concept of death and I encourage you to read it if this conversation has elicited a charge for you. We do surpass this also, usually after the realisation that We Are an aspect of Divinity that cannot die. We surrender and let go.

Let us now discuss Right Actions. While we will discuss this further in the next chapter on karma, I will discuss it here also as we reference transitioning to living as Our Selves.

I define Right Actions as recommended behaviour within a family, society, group, culture, religion, anything really, that mimics behaviour which occurs naturally when we Be Our Selves. I do not think that this is remembered in the story, rather, each of the above groups would advocate their recommended behaviours as right behaviour. A clear example is right behaviour that is identified within that group as what a 'good' person would do. This adds further filters within the ego/mind rather than removing content. While functioning from the ego/mind and the dualistic reality, those recommended behaviours could also very possibly be in conflict. Thus, for me, it is futile judging which recommended behaviour is right or wrong, and yes, we will go to war for it.

We are looking in the wrong place to overcome this; we are looking via ego/minds even at the macro level. Once we begin to observe from a vibration higher than the density that creates the point of view (come over it), we see the origin of recommended behaviour. The origin is awareness, Unique awareness, either perceived for one individual or perceived as a crutch for others to facilitate them while still functioning from the ego/mind and not able in that moment to perceive the information for themselves. What happened is, that awareness, and, I am sure, many pieces of awareness perceived over the time and space of history, was perceived, and once entered into the ego/mind was converted to be recommended behaviour for all. Unfortunately, each ego/mind and each collective ego/mind within a family, society, religion, group, will take that information and it will be changed to match the content and charge and vibration of that ego/mind at both the micro and macro level. It is futile judging it; it is a function of the ego/mind.

In the next chapter I will discuss how recommended behaviour and Right Action can be useful. The point to look at in this moment is that recommended behaviour is a product of ego/mind and Right Action, while definition and structure within an ego/mind reality, can be a crutch which mimics how we show up when we Be Our Selves.

When we Be ourselves it is known that everything is about coming to Oneness for all of us. All Being and doing naturally contributes to this.

We don't know this when we are functioning from the ego/mind. Without cognitively knowing it, initially recommended behaviour, and progressively Right Action, is adopted as behaviour in the story. We do it to be a good person or to do the right thing, yet it remains an imposed behaviour. I say 'progressively Right Action' as Our Souls are guiding us back to Our Selves and as we get closer to Being Our Selves as an Isness, we do begin to behave like Our Selves even within the dualistic reality of the ego/mind. We increasingly maintain a level of Presence, even while toggling between Being and functioning from the ego/mind.

If we can be cognitive of this process as it unfolds, we can remove any self-judgement on needing to behave a certain way. Self-judgement is a sticking point for Being You as you think you need to show up a particular way. That is a lie of the ego/mind, even at the macro level.

When the ego/mind has dismantled sufficiently, there is no need to impose any Right Action because Our Nature fulfils any intention of Right Action within the story. Coming from Our Essential Nature, behaviour is informed from awareness and shows up as the Unique contribution of You.

What changes is that the generic Right Actions that are recommended and are static within an ego/mind dualistic reality no longer apply, and we can follow our own awareness as to what Being and doing we are drawn to in the story, all for the expansion of Consciousness.

I will give an example. Your spiritual teacher or leader recommends being of service by staying home and taking care of the children. The recommended behaviour is static and advocated as a generic requirement. Within this recommended behaviour can show up the Right Action of humility, caring, generosity and love for those to be cared for. These show up naturally when we Be Our Selves. Here the Right Action is also static in how it shows up content-wise, that is, staying home and taking care of children.

For those buying the identifications of the ego/mind, there is little resistance to the recommended behaviour. They do not question the behaviour as it is congruent with who they think they are and who the world thinks they are. Their sense of self is secure. Their foundation is solid. Not doing the behaviour is more likely to illicit a rocking of their foundation.

For some, when the ego/mind is still 'captain of the ship', undertaking such recommended behaviour may build resentment and judgement of self and those involved. There is no or little accessing of awareness, only the identifications of right and wrong, and what they 'should' be doing. Even though the ego/mind content wants to show up differently, there is a battle between 'want' and 'should'. There is a perpetual loading of more content and charge while judgement continues.

For others there is a cognitive choosing of the recommended behaviour and the identifications which result from choosing it. There is a consequential satisfaction with the action and themselves; a positive judgement of self, maybe even an empowerment with this identification. They, and probably those recommending the behaviour, think that having complied is closer to Being Them Selves or closer to God, but it is not the compliance to a set of recommended behaviours that achieves that. If when Being Them Selves they show up in the same way as the recommended behaviour, that is, the recommended behaviour is a Right Action for them, then that will bring them closer to Being, to Oneness. It is possible that if there is a match to Being, they may toggle out of the dualistic reality, slip into Being and Be Them Selves in the action. However, if, having complied, they judge themselves in any way, they are adding more filters, the Michelin Man suit has expanded.

Others may be cognitive of having shed much of the significance of self within the ego/mind and have chosen a willingness to be of service within the story. They are not yet cognitive of the Unique Presentation of Being and, as such, think that all recommended behaviour, particularly requested from a teacher or leader they look up to, is ideal. They misidentify it as a 'must do'. They may also misidentify the outcome of complying with the behaviour as satisfying the yearning to commune in Oneness. Having shed the significance of self, they may recognise the Right Action within the recommended behaviour. However, if there is a mismatch to Their Essential Nature, they will not feel fulfilled in the behaviour. They may not be able to identify why they are feeling unfulfilled as often they will be devoted to the task. The reason for the unfulfilled feeling: they are not in congruence with Them Selves, how they would show up Being Them Selves. The resonance is not a match. The humility, caring, generosity and love that are Right Actions may show up in a different form when Being Them Selves. It may show up equally in the workplace, being humble, caring, generous and loving in the work environment. It may show up without any doing, from Being. If there is a match with Their Essential Nature, they will recognise a sense of bliss and joy in the behaviour that is Infinite in Nature. This is beyond the ego/mind dualistic reality and is living as Your Self.

What begins to show up when the ego/mind dismantles further is knowing that static recommendations of behaviour are not 'must dos'. We can receive the recommendations as information with no charge, the same as we receive and perceive awareness as information. If we choose to do anything, we choose action which resonates like Our Being. There is no right or wrong, no need to justify any behaviour, and no need to do anything. As everything is about the expansion of Consciousness and there is no away in Oneness, anything we Be and do is a contribution to this. The Right Action showing up as staying home to care for the children may not present at all. The story may judge you for that but Consciousness does not. The story cannot make sense of not needing to do anything. The dualistic reality does not know a reality where all Being and doing is a contribution to the expansion of Consciousness and the return to Oneness. This is unfolding. It doesn't matter that the story does not acknowledge it, it is occurring regardless. Often, hearing that you can follow your awareness rather than adopting a rigid and generic recommended behaviour can be a relief. It will certainly create a sense of ease. Additionally, not being attached to the outcome of any action buys out of further identifications within the ego/mind including those relating to recommended behaviour or Right Actions, and thus, you have further transmuted what hinders you from Being You.

What shows up as we choose that which resonates like Who We Are is the Infinite Nature of Us and this is living as Our Selves. These are Our Unique aspects of God, Our Essential Natures, plus how we all show up, with humility, love, caring, generosity, vulnerability, authenticity, intimacy, gratitude, beauty: Presence.

Here is another example.

We are taught in spiritual and religious teachings to be humble, to practice humility. This recommended behaviour is a Right Action but often not how we think while functioning from the ego/mind. Practicing humility while functioning from the ego/mind generally shows up as an imposed diminishment of you to present a non-elevated personal position. You 'make' yourself smaller, less visible, softly spoken to mimic what you think being humble is. This is another filter. This is not what humility is and it certainly is not the humility which arises naturally when functioning from a non-dualistic reality, when Being. It is only Our Essential Natures that may show up for some with those characteristics and rather than being weak they arise as Infinitely potent.

When we Be Who We Are, humility is knowing that our awareness is not personal. We know We Are an aspect of Divinity reflecting Our Unique Expression of that Divinity while also not owning or taking credit for that awareness or knowing. You don't have to fake 'no personal position', no personal position arises when we Be. There is no diminishment of Who We Are. This is true humility. You are not the one, You are reflecting Oneness. There is a joy in awakening Home. Being reflects this in the world and in existence with no point of view, showing up as Your Essential Nature, Your Spirit.

Many of us are toggling in and out of Being. Choosing something that resonates like Who We Are has the capacity to switch us out of the ego/mind dualistic reality to Being. As we experience this toggling, we build trust in the information we perceive. We build trust in our observation of what stems from our awareness and what is content of the ego/mind. We make choices creating our lives and cognitively choose whether to follow awareness or ego/mind options. Judgement begins to fall away and we experience life as an Isness. At this stage there is a continuing Presence of Self. You 'keep your lamps burning' (Luke 12:35 NIV) even when functioning from the ego/mind ('asleep in the dream').

Simultaneously, as we continue to toggle between Being Who We Are and functioning from the ego/mind, the ego/mind charge continues to transmute. The fretting feeling of the ego/mind needing to know it all relaxes. I remember saying to my ego/mind 'There, there, it's going to be OK. Let me just give this a go and let's see what happens', and I would choose to act from my awareness. I was conscious of the separation, and chose to follow the energy to ease my ego/mind, which only existed because of separation.

I am still toggling between Being and functioning from the ego/mind but one thing that has changed is that the ego/mind no longer perpetually resists awareness when I perceive it. Often my mind comes into play as a tool to facilitate the awareness showing up in the world. The ego/mind receives awareness in the mix.

When you trust You can perceive awareness, trust is no longer required. Trust is a crutch until You know. It is the same with belief. Belief is an imposed point of view until You know. Knowing is your awareness expressed as You, not separate to You and All that Is. Do you believe in Wi-Fi? No, it is a given. The only thing you put trust in is the service provider. No need to doubt The Service Provider. Awareness is Infinitely and freely given, no charge!!

In your everyday, You continue to dismantle the thoughts that the ego/mind is the mastermind of what is unfolding. You notice synchronicity and clues that seem to flow with ease. This is not separate from choices You make. You are part of All That Is and at this vibration everything is known, even which choices will be made.

Whatever you or You choose will be metaphysically matched by the Universe. It is a response to Itself asking as You or you are not separate. It may unfold over time/space as it comes to Be, it will be created to reflect and project the vibration of your choices.

The analogy I often use is that of a puppy dog. The Universe is like a beautiful, unconditionally giving puppy dog that is sitting up, paws in the air, smiling and wagging at how Magnificent you and You are, and waiting to be asked what to create. It doesn't have a point of view, It will create whatever You or you are choosing.

The way the Universe works is from vibration. Whatever you are choosing will be perceived at its net vibration and this will be reflected to you in what is created. You are never separate from this process, however, in describing it here, it may appear so.

If You are Being You and You choose to create something, there is no gap between what You are choosing and what is Being perceived by the Universe. The vibrations match. You will create what You have cognitively chosen.

If you are not Being You, and still have content of the ego/mind filtering You from showing up, this will impact any choosing. If you choose to create something, you will be cognitive of content relating to that creation. You will not be cognitive of the unconscious content of the ego/mind relating to that choosing, even though you may perceive an energy of what that is. The net effect of all the content relating to that choosing will be perceived and that is what will be created.

I will give you an example. 'I choose to get a new job'.

If You are Being You, the question may not show up that way. It may be more of an energy of question reflecting what is being chosen. So, if Being You, You may show up perceiving the energy of the job You currently have, choosing to change that, then beginning to create an energy of what You are wanting the job to Be like, whilst also having an energy of question, of what is possible, of letting go. There is no attachment to whether the current job changes to match that energy or if there is another job that will turn up. It is known that Allness works out the how, the unfoldment. You perceive the net energy that You have created around your job situation and You choose that. You then receive and perceive any Being and/or doing in any moment that is a contribution to creating that choice.

Any amount of ego/mind filters, whether thought, emotion, decision, judgement, expectation, conclusion, doubt, belief, that you hold in relation to a job, and getting a new job, will turn up as a net energy, a net vibration, and that is what will be matched. Oneness has no point of view. It is waiting to create for you what you are choosing. It knows You are not separate, though you don't know that yet. Everything stored in the ego/mind which relates to your choice is what is perceived as what you are choosing.

If you are not receiving what you have chosen, either what you think you chose does not match the net vibration of your content relating to your choice or you haven't actually chosen.

Very commonly we think we have chosen something but we haven't, we only observe the choice. Using the example above, some people simply think about the idea of getting a new job. They contemplate the idea of the choice and may determine it is not possible or is too risky considering, for example, that their foundation is solid in their current job and they need to remain stable to meet existing responsibilities. These thoughts may never be verbalised. If they are there vibrationally, they are present. The form is not required for the Universe to pick it up. Even if the 'thoughts' are not yours, if you adopt them as your own, they are in the mix. You may think that you have chosen, but thoughts in your head contradict your choice, you to and fro with the idea and, in a nutshell, don't choose. The net vibration of what is even cognitive doesn't match the choosing. The Universe will keep reflecting even the ambiguity because that is what you are choosing in that moment: ambiguity and uncertainty!

Others choose in a particular moment and then no longer pay attention, they think the job is done and the Universe will sort it all out. They 'go with the flow'. Firstly, the moment attention is taken away from the energy of the choice, the vibration has changed and it is no longer the same choice. Secondly, this reinforces the separation of you from Oneness, which adds more filters, and again the net vibration has changed. I often say 'choosing is not a passive exercise'. If you choose, stay alert to perceived awareness as you are not separate from the Universe that will unfold your choosing. If awareness says 'turn right', turn right!

It really is simple: the net vibration of your choosing is what is created, no matter what reality you are functioning from.

We have forgotten about Being a part of the Universe. It shows up as something separate to us and a higher power away from us. We pray 'to' it. This creates a disempowerment, a diminishment of us. This is not God's intention, the knowing has been lost. We have forgotten that we are One with this Magnificence. This is what is meant by Being made in God's likeness, we are not separate. At the end of our prayers we say 'Amen'. Do you know what that is? We are asking, directing, that whatever we are asking be returned to before form, to the 'Aum' vibration, and returned to us in the form of our choosing. This is an empowering statement to and as Oneness. This has been forgotten and having been input into the ego/mind, it has created a static disempowerment, asking a separated and higher power, for something. We become invisible in this, often a pathetic and begging energy, and this is not Who We Are. We are now coming back to Our Empowered state as Being Who We Are and we are becoming cognitive of what we have forgotten. Wherever you find yourself on the stage of the world, You can Be You no matter of the matter.

Observe, notice, ask and choose. Also, the more you choose to transmute what filters You from showing up, the more ease you will have in creating living as Your Self. Let us now look at more of what I have noticed when it comes to transmuting what filters us from Being Our Selves.

Let's go:

All the identifications you listed in the exercise in Chapter Two, and all the identifications you are not yet cognitive of, are what is buffering you from living as Your Self.

If we can transmute those identifications and remove the charge they have, You would show up in the world and have access to Your knowing that returning to Oneness is all that Is.

There is no implanting of this information. It arises as knowing, similar to You showing up as the Essential Nature You Be, as the Spark of God that You Be.

When we speak of removing a charge, we are referring to removing the significance and importance placed on the identifications. This is the pride, the control, the insistence, the inflexibility, the point of view. This is what is stopping us from Oneness which includes All, and what is stopping us from living as Our Selves.

If we did not have a charge, we would receive everything as information. We would choose and not exclude. As David Hawkins said 'In choosing chocolate, you don't have to hate vanilla.' (Hawkins, 2003).

So, let us keep this really simple from a practical perspective also. Everything is about transmuting the charge until we have our only true death, the death of the ego/mind; the death of what is buffering You from showing up not only in the world but in existence.

This is your Michelin Man suit; the gap between Who You Are and how you show up in the world. Whether you are incarnate or not, it is there until it is not.

While working with clients and in observing my own experiences and awareness with regard to my own Michelin Man suit, I have observed that there are two approaches to bridging this gap:

☐ From the outside in; and

☐ From the inside out

From the 'outside in', we transmute all identifications, both cognitive and unconscious from a 'doingness'. We 'chip away' at all the content of the Michelin Man suit. We dismantle the hold it has on us, we reduce and eventually remove the charge, with the target being conscious choice of what we choose to wear without any charge or point of view.

From the 'inside out', Being instantly buys out of all identifications. It is certainly the speedy way to remove the effect of identifications and content. While the ego/mind is in place, this is difficult to sustain and certainly cannot be forced. Consequently, practicing both approaches can facilitate 'you' showing up as 'You', and each approach facilitates the other.

When you bridge this gap everything that you yearned for, felt as missing and unfulfilled, will dissipate. The misidentifications in the story which exist to feel like you belong, to want more, to fit in, be successful, all dissolve in a relief, a freedom, a coming Home.

While you are dropping the charge on identifications, the story will continue to hold identifications as significant and necessary, certainly before we all transition to Oneness.

As you choose to get clearer, those around you may not be choosing to do so. Choose for yourself but do not impose this on others, as then you are creating another identification on the significance of dropping identifications, often showing up as 'fixing', and the ego/mind plays with you again.

Be in the world, not of the world. This is really what we are referring to here. Not that long ago, the choice to Be Who You Are in the world necessitated You to leave the distractions of family and society and live in seclusion or with a teacher. Thanks to all facilitating more Consciousness on the planet and in existence, we can now stay where we find ourselves and Be Who We Are, even in suburbia. Now we can function from this place of Being in the world and not buying the world as Who We Are.

We will continue to Be in the world of story and may go to work, meet friends, we may feed ourselves, take care of our families, do what we do, but we would not choose as real all the identifications of that world that judges, has expectations, has hierarchy, etc. It shows up as creating another reality that is non-dualistic in nature. That doesn't mean that we have just given ourselves permission to 'run amok' and be irresponsible. It just doesn't present that way when we Be Our Selves. It would only show up that way if you think you have bought out of all the identifications but you are actually fooling yourself and adopting a rebellious version of the same identifications: the polar opposite, products of the dualistic reality. Being Our Selves invites our individual contextual potentialities from Infinite possibilities to Be in the world rather than conforming or rebelling against a fixed point of view.

What we do perceive very quickly is that the dualistic reality cannot fully receive Who We Are. This can vary in degree from some stages not receiving Us at all to stages that embrace diversity and remain open to receive You on the condition You met 'acceptability' benchmarks for that stage.

When we Be we know this as an Isness. We do not take it personally, seeing it as reflections of Michelin Man suits.

To participate in the dualistic reality (Be in the world) we perceive moment by moment what is required to interface that dualistic reality. If we are not received we may not interact or we may choose to listen, we would certainly not inform those not receiving Us that they are mistaken and narrow minded. That would be a superior ego/mind, not Being. We would receive all the information and choose what we are choosing. Actually, rather than superiority, a childlike wonder arises with no point of view or reaction to whoever is before Us. There is no need to prove any position. What arises is an allowance of the ego/mind perspective showing up before Us, knowing that this has nothing to do with Who They Are.

If you find yourself at work and You have received and perceived awareness for a task at hand, awareness also informs how to communicate it to those around you. Awareness will inform the words that will work in any situation. Functioning from ego/mind provides only fixed points of view and position; awareness does not.

When I facilitate clients, I do no preparation other than logistically preparing the room. I know awareness will arise unique to that interaction of Consciousness to inform what is required in any moment. I have no idea what will come out of my mouth. I hear the awareness when the client hears it. I marvel at information that my ego/mind could never have thought of.

Noticing that an interface exists, that we meet the dualistic reality rather than diminish ourselves to belong or fit into it, will assist in acknowledging what Is in any moment, including an acknowledgement of Who You Are and You Being You in the world and in existence.

Let us now look at each approach in detail.

FROM THE INSIDE OUT

This is the direct route to Your Self. This is the most powerful and quickest approach. It is Being in the Now, in the moment. Your Life would be an Isness, as to Be is beyond time/space.

When You Be You something really interesting happens. All the charge of the identifications you carry within the ego/mind is no longer Present. It is bought out of as a reality, it is known that it does not constitute You. There is no gap between Who You Are and how you show up in the world. When you bridge this gap everything that felt missing and unfulfilled no longer arises, all yearning is satisfied. This is where true happiness and joy is.

This is not an imposed thought. It arises when You Be You.

All identifications are accessible as information and are known not to define You, they are known as the stage You Are in whilst Being in the world. If Being is sustained, this can be labelled Enlightened. Enlightenment at this point is not significant either; it is a label for Being You 'all the time'. The Nature changes from an apparent linearity of time/space to an Isness. It is only when you are still functioning from ego/mind that the 'goal' of Enlightenment has significance attached to it. Enlightenment literally means 'to remove the dimness and blindness, to shed light upon' (Etymonline.com), that is, you shed light on what cloaks you from knowing Who You Are, that You are Light, You are a Spark of God, not separate from All That Is, Oneness.

Most of us do not sustain Being as an Isness, rather we are experiencing moments of Being. These moments are of the same Nature as sustained Being. It is because we come out of Being and function again from our ego/minds that our lives, including our bodies, reflect that content and charge rather than our contextual potentialities from Infinite possibilities.

When we follow the energy of Being, there is a return to the centre, the core of You. This seems to Be an innate knowing. Even in the story this shows up as following the heart and gut feelings. We innately return to our physical centres when thought is taken out of the equation. While we are Infinite and can never be limited to our physical Presentation, the knowing that we have access to our Infiniteness via our physical bodies including the heart, and more potently, the centre of the heart torsion field, arises when the ego/mind is bypassed.

We can obtain glimpses of this also when there is a disruption in our foundation or when bearing witness to another's story. These are examples in the story that bypass the ego/mind.

While working with clients, and bringing my attention to Who They Are and what was buffering them from Being Who They Are in the world, I noticed another piece of information which consistently Presented. This information related directly to returning to the core of Who We Are.

What I noticed was a core energetic bandwidth from above the crown right through to below the feet, similar to a spine. This core bandwidth is energetic in Nature and its Presence relates directly to a client's capacity to sustain Being.

This Presented not only as a reflection of the capacity to Be but also functioned to transmute what ego/mind content and charge still remained when not Being.

When clients were Being Them Selves, this core strengthened and when the core was strengthened, their capacity to maintain Being became exponential. When Being, these clients were strong, potent and unwavering in a core centreing, and the energetic bandwidth was quite wide down the centre of the body.

For clients who were not Being in their lives, not living as their empowered and potent state, I could not perceive the presence of this core bandwidth at all. This often correlated with clients who were not Present in their bodies, experiencing life as an out-of-body experience most of the time, and often these clients were also those whose foundations, even in the story, were equally unstable, volatile or unreliable. There are innumerable content experiences that can allow this to show up including trauma, abuse, rejection of the body not belonging in the story. This can correlate for some whom I describe as 'Lost Souls'. When I brought my attention to a core bandwidth Being Present for them, it often began to show up. It cannot be forced, however, it seemed that bringing attention to it was sufficient to switch it on. There was little strength in the energetic core but it was Present.

For others, I would perceive a feeble and loose thread of core. The strength was negligible, however, they had some access to Being, the core was Present.

I noticed that as clients were more Present as Them Selves, and as they were in allowance of Self, their core bandwidth became stronger and more tangible. Even if they were not Being in any moment, this core bandwidth remained in place and choosing to Be was a quick and immediate stepping into their centre, when chosen, almost with no effort required, reflecting again the no time/space Nature of Being.

This energetic bandwidth became a quick check-in for me when facilitating clients, providing a wealth of information instantly. It also provided further confirmation of the awareness that Consciousness replaces the need to maintain a solid foundation within the story.

We try so hard in the story to be seen, to be accepted and validated, and to establish who we are in the world. We then further misidentify it with position, competition, superiority. This density of building a foundation from which to function in the world requires much effort and force to sustain. A stable foundation is required before we 'jump off into the unknown'. It is like we need a foundation to hold us before we question anything, seek something else or choose to change.

The thought of dismantling this foundation can be a frightening prospect for those still relying heavily on it. What shows up is that Consciousness Be Comes the foundation, a formless foundation. The Universe has got your back rather than the finite nature of a family or society which, within the dualistic reality, can turn to the polar opposite in a second.

This energetic core bandwidth Presents tangibly and literally: the Universe has your back and It Is You. Its strength correlates directly with the extent to which You are functioning from Oneness, from Consciousness. Consciousness is unlike the foundation of the story, with its separate parts. Functioning from Consciousness is Being and the Isness of This is the formless foundation We Be. There is no separation. Consciousness Is not separate from You, it Is You. The energetic core is a reflection of this Consciousness 'foundation', or more literally 'found action' as You Being You in the world.

Thus, a useful target for all of us may be to strengthen this energetic core bandwidth, as the stronger it gets, the less you need the foundation of the story. It is a direct correlation. It is not the same 'getting' of the story. It is what shows up when You Be, and, bring Your attention to it, and the energetic core bandwidth will Be. It is like the 'chicken and the egg', Being contributes to the energetic core strengthening, and bringing your attention to it, strengthens it and can even create it, allowing Being to arise with more ease.

Let us now play with Being.

Exercise Five

Get comfortable where you are sitting as you read this. If it works for you, record the instructions and lie down, close your eyes, listen and follow the instructions.

Give yourself the space to Be Present. If you don't know what that is or feels like, Be in allowance of Being Present. If you need to schedule a quiet time for yourself, call on others to help. Otherwise, give yourself space by going to bed 30 minutes or so before going to sleep. You may find you sleep well after this exercise. Don't judge yourself if you sleep during it, fall asleep in its embrace.

If you choose, Be open to just the words I speak. If a thought comes by or you judge something I say because it has a charge for you, notice it and let it go by. Reassure your ego/mind 'There, there, let's give this a go. Let's see what happens'.

Take a deep breath and let it go. Let the breath simply fall out.

In this space you have gifted yourself, there is nothing you need to do. Everything Is as It Is.

Take another deep breath and let it go.

Wriggle around and get comfortable whether you are sitting or lying. If you can, uncross your arms and legs and be as relaxed as you can. If you need to prop up any part of your beautiful body, honour it by doing so.

Take another deep breath and let it go as it ripples through your body.

Bring your attention to your feet. Notice your feet and all the travels they have taken you on. Notice that no matter what happened to your feet, they never judged you. They always aim for balance. Take a deep breath from your feet and let it go. When you take your next breaths, gather up any content that is stored in your feet. Notice the energy of this content rather than what the content is. Continue to gather the content until you feel done. In your next out breath, release all that content and anything else that does not allow your feet to Be. 'Thank your feet' and visualise yourself kissing your feet, first one, then the other.

Now bring your attention to your legs below the knees. Notice your ankles, your calves, your shins, notice your body there. Notice if you have not noticed this part of you. Notice that this part of you strives always to Be Present for you whether you are moving or not. Take a deep breath from this part of you and let it go. When you take your next breaths, gather up any content that is stored here, not only from this lifetime but from Always. Gather up any content that may be hindering this part of you from working as it would like to. Continue to gather the content until you feel done. In your next out breath, release all that content and anything else that does not allow this part of your body to Be. Thank this part of you, and visualise yourself kissing your ankles, your calves, your shins, all around this part of your body. Lots of kisses everywhere, maybe on parts you have never consciously touched.

Take another deep breath and bring your attention up to your knees and let it go. 'Hello knees. Thank you knees'. Notice how much your knees Be and do for you. Take a deep breath into your knees and notice all the content that is stored there. Notice any content that has manifested in tears, or soreness and pain. Look behind your knees, is there more content hidden there? Notice how your knees strive to move forward, to maintain flexibility, to be fluid in Being. Take another deep breath and gather up all the content that does not allow your knees to Be. Continue breathing and gathering the content until you feel done. In your next out breath, release all of that content and anything else that does not allow your knees to Be. 'Thank you my awesome knees,' and visualise yourself kissing your knees, first one, then the other, then kiss behind your knees, first one, then the other.

Now take a deep breath from your thighs, the thighs that hold you up and never want you to fall, and then let the breath go. Notice the strength held here from Always. Even without you noticing, your thighs have maintained awareness and Presence to stand strong in the River of Life. Take a deep breath from your majestic thighs and let it go. As you take your next breaths, notice any content that does not allow your thighs to Be as they choose. Gather up this content, and when you feel done, release that content with your next out breath. 'Is that better, thighs? I am grateful, thighs, thank you for being there for me'. Visualise yourself giving your thighs a massive, squeezy hug and kiss them both, first one, then the other.

Now visualise your hips, your pelvis, your reproductive organs and systems. Take a deep breath into these parts of you and let it go. If you need to make a noise as you release your breath, do so. Take an even deeper breath into these areas and let it go. Scan these parts of your body as you take your next breaths and gather any content stored there that does not allow these parts of you to flourish and flower as they would like to. On your next out breath, release it with the chanting of 'Aum', returning that content to before form. Repeat this until you feel done. Acknowledge this part of you as a vehicle of new life in whatever form you choose. Now visualise a flower bud within this part of your body, whichever flower you choose. Watch this flower bud. As you continue breathing, observe this flower bud unfurling, and allow this blossom to Be within your now blossoming body.

Now bring your attention to your buttocks. Notice any tension you are holding there. Notice if you have not noticed the Presence of your buttocks. Take a deep breath from your buttocks and as you let that breath go, sink deeper into where you are sitting or lying. As you take your next breaths, notice any content that does not allow your buttocks to Be. Continue to gather the content until you feel done. In your next exhalation, release all that content and anything else that does not allow your buttocks to Be as magnificent as it is. Acknowledge your buttocks. 'Thank you buttocks for being there for me' and visualise yourself kissing your buttocks, first one side, then the other.

Bring your attention back to the front of your body. Notice your belly and all the organs and systems within this part of your body. Allow this part of your body to nurture you from the inside out. Take a deep breath from your belly and all the organs and systems around your belly, and if you can, fill up your belly with breath, then let it go. As you take your next breaths into your belly, notice any content that does not allow this part of your body to Be. Continue to gather the content until you feel done. In your next out breath, release all that content and anything else that does not allow your belly and all the organs and systems within this part of your body to Be. If you choose, receive awareness from this part of your body. 'Thank you', and visualise yourself giving lots of kisses to your belly and to all your internal organs and system, even those you don't know much about and which allow you to be incarnate.

Now bring your attention to your diaphragm. It is the silent achiever. Continue to notice your diaphragm as you take your next few breaths. Gather any content that does not allow your diaphragm to Be, including anything that does not allow your diaphragm to expand fully. In your next out breath, release all that content. Thank your diaphragm for allowing the Expression of Your Spirit, Your Inspiration, to Be Present in the world. Perceive the creation of You and God's 'De Light' in You, and God's 'De Light' in You Breathing Life into this body. Visualise yourself hugging your diaphragm in rhythm with its rhythm, a rhythm of Consciousness, of God.

Now take a deep breath into the base of your spine and let it go. Stay here as you breathe and notice anything that does not allow ease in this part of your spine. Notice if you are relying on anything outside of you to 'have your back', to be your foundation. On the next out breath and with the chanting of 'Aum', release all that does not allow the base of your spine to Be. Continue releasing until you feel done. As you take your next breaths, slowly bring your attention to your entire spine, from the base slowly up to your head. Notice on the journey along the spine, the Eternal Nature of your spine. The River of Life that is your spine, within which flows the glistening nectar of Infinity, both with form and without form. As you continue breathing, notice any content that does not allow your spine to Be. Continue to gather this content until you feel done. On your next out breath, with some awareness also on your diaphragm reflecting Your Inspiration, release anything that does not allow your spine to Be the full Magnificence it Is.

Now bring your attention to your hands. Visualise yourself looking at your hands. Notice that in your hands is stored everything that has ever happened to you, not only during this lifetime but in every lifetime. 'Thank you hands for Being there for me'. Take a deep breath from your hands and let it go. Give your hands permission to release everything that they are holding on to for you and for anyone or anything else. As you continue breathing, gather up anything else that does not allow your hands to be free and to be joyful. On the next out breath, release all that content, and celebrate your hands. 'Thank you hands'. If you choose, allow All of You to Be with your hands from this moment on. Visualise yourself giving your hands a kiss, first one, then the other.

Take another deep breath and bring your attention to your arms and let your breath go. As you continue breathing, notice your wrists, forearms, elbows, your upper arms and your underarms. Notice how much work they do that you may not have noticed. Notice how beautifully their mechanics play out in their Being. As you take your next breaths into every part of both your arms, notice any content that does not allow them to Be. Continue to gather the content until you feel done. In your next out breath, release all of that content and anything else that does not allow your arms to move smoothly and weightlessly, with total ease. Thank your arms and give them a big hug. Notice how easily they give, and now is a moment for them to receive. 'I love you, arms'.

Take a deep breath and bring your attention to your shoulders, and let it go. Also notice your shoulder blades and all the systems that allow your shoulders to Be. As you take your next breaths, notice any content that does not allow your shoulders to Be, including everything you are shouldering and have shouldered in any lifetime. Continue to gather the content until you feel done. In your next out breath, release all that content and anything else that does not allow your shoulders to Be free of any weight. Now take another deep breath and wriggle your shoulders free of any remaining content that may have become stuck there for a long time. Continue until you feel done and your shoulders are resting with more ease. 'Thank your shoulders for bearing the weight of anything you have not previously been able to respond to, to take responsibility for'.

Now bring your attention to your neck and your head. Take a deep breath from your whole neck and head and let it go. Visualise standing in front of yourself and notice the front of your neck. Notice how it moves as you breathe; notice that it does not have a point of view. Look at the back of your neck, how it cradles your head as well as being the doorway to the spine and the brain, where access to Consciousness is readily available. Observe the sides of your neck and the subtle holding that often goes unnoticed. Take a deep breath from your neck and let go anything that does not allow it to Be. Now look at your head, glimpse the Unfathomable that plays out within your head that provides in any moment a reflection of Infinite Magnificence. Look at what adorns your head: your face, the jewellery of Being. The glistening eyes from which Your Soul can Shine, the forehead, the nose, the cheeks, the ears, the mouth, lips, teeth and tongue from which to receive information and facilitate You Being incarnate. As you take your next breaths, notice any content that does not allow your neck and head to Be. Continue to gather the content until you feel done. In your next out breath, release all that content and anything else that does not allow your neck and head to Be. 'Thank you neck, thank you head'. If you choose, allow yourself to be Present with your neck and your head as you receive and perceive from the five senses and beyond, from awareness.

Pause for a moment now and watch yourself sitting or lying down. Take a couple of breaths in and out as you see your whole self and Your Whole Self.

Bring your attention to your chest. Notice it framed by your diaphragm, your lungs, your spine, your ribs and adorned with your nurturing breasts. Take a deep breath within your whole chest, including the back of your chest, and let it go. If you need to sigh your breath out, do so. As you take your next breaths, notice any content that does not allow your whole chest to Be. Continue to gather the content until you feel done. In your next out breath, with the chanting of 'Aum' returning that content to before form, release all that content and anything else that does not allow your whole chest to Be.

Continue to notice the Exquisiteness of this part of your body, and how it functions in harmony with all things. Now notice what abides within this Exquisiteness: your heart and Soul. Notice the Infinite Nature of your heart and Soul. Take a deep breath from your heart and Soul, and let it go. Keep your attention with your heart and Soul and now ask to be shown the literal Spark of God that You Are. Can you see Your Soul within your beautiful body? Can you see Your Soul animating your entire body and beyond? Can you notice there is no beginning and no end? Can you notice how Your Soul is Who You Are, Radiating Light in and as All That Is? What can you see as you reflect on this journey you have taken Being with your body, noticing how no part was ever intended to be alone?

As you continue to notice the Radiance of Your Soul, bring your attention to all of you, and now notice the space within you. Notice that in this moment even the parts of your body that appear solid can now be experienced as space, as Consciousness. Notice that when you bring your attention to space, there is no beginning and no end. Be there. That is what Consciousness feels like. It has no content, no judgement, no point of view. It is Divinity made from the 'Aum' vibration. Be in the no time/space of Consciousness, of Being. Notice that this is the fabric of your whole body, there is no separation, there are no separate parts. Know that this formlessness is more truly Who You Are. This is the Oneness that is Our Home.

Take a deep breath into You and let it go. Notice all of you. As you take your next breaths into you, notice any further content that does not allow you to Be. Continue to gather that content until you feel done. In your next out breath, release all that content and anything else that does not allow you to Be. If you choose, notice from this moment on, anything that does not allow you to Be You.

Acknowledge yourself for All that You Are. Radiate Divine Love to You, from You and as You. Notice this higher vibration of You as you again bring your attention to your body sitting or lying. Stay with You for a moment. As you begin to wriggle your feet and hands, and awaken back into the stage and the story, notice the flow and harmony of your body. Remember Who You Are, an Exquisiteness of Divinity, not separate from Oneness, here to awaken All to know this. Move a little more now. Notice what you haven't noticed before. Have you noticed more of You? Can you feel space? Can you notice that space is You? As you move a little more, begin to open your eyes. Be caring to yourself as you observe any change in your reality. Continue to observe as you feel more grounded in your body, and you begin to notice again where you are sitting or lying. Does your body feel more solid now? Has thinking returned? Did you notice a transition back to a dualistic reality? Continuing to observe is a gift to you and all. When you are ready, get up slowly and continue Being and doing whatever you choose.

Repeat this journey with your body as often as you like. Allow your awareness to inform what you notice. As you get familiar with the exercise, bring your attention to different aspects such as your cells, your skin cloaking your body, other parts of your body you become aware of, maybe your energy bodies. After a while, play with noticing only the space that holds matter together, and, as your experience deepens even further, practice letting go to God, surrendering all the content to God.

When Being You, when centred in the core of Being, You have access to All There Is. In the Magnificent Presentation of Our physical bodies You have access to Infinity and Infinite resources. We all have systems and access points Divinely orchestrated to facilitate awareness, insight, perception, wisdom, knowledge, connection, communion, Our return Home, no matter the route we take. Within our Magnificent bodies are Present:

- ☐ The Chakra system;
- ☐ The Spine;
- ☐ The Medulla Oblongata;
- ☐ The Third Eye;
- ☐ The Heart Centre (Soul and Heart Torsion Field);
- ☐ The Breath;
- ☐ Chi / Life Force; and
- ☐ Every cell and where the cells are not, all projecting in Light as Consciousness in form.

Play with exploring this Divinity that Is You, maybe select a system and take a journey with It, and receive your awareness.

It is in practicing this observation at high vibrations that not only transmutes the charge on content within your ego/mind, it facilitates it for all, there is no away. Practicing is an invitation to Being, there lies the Eternal Moment. Even if you glimpse Being, that is success. Your body/mind complex will remember, and the more You Be, the greater ease in Being. Experience the ease and joy that is Present when We Be Our Selves and increasingly live our lives as Our Selves.

Notice also if there is a lessening of thought while practicing the exercise, even if you justify it with listening to instructions. Continue to observe it rather than judge it. Continue to check-in where you are functioning from in any moment.

This observing goes a long way toward facilitating more of You to show up. Know however, that Being You is Infinitely Potent and has the capacity to transmute identifications instantaneously.

I use the words 'transmute' and 'transform' because nothing is destroyed or dies, it changes form. So while we witness decay, 'death' and the dropping of unconsciousness, it is only changing form within Infinite existence of which You are an integral aspect.

The Nature of Being You is beyond the limitations of this reality and the more you show up as You the more the buffer and content of your ego/mind dissipates and transforms, it transmutes. I am not speaking of doing anything, only Being You. Being You buys out of the content and transmutes it. Double whammy! When you remove charge, you create space, or rather, with the charge no longer present, what holds everything remains and that is Consciousness, which we experience as space.

Be in allowance of receiving Being from All that Is and in every moment you will be transmuting what is not allowing You to show up. Let us again slip into a reality beyond the dualistic reality, let's 'do' another exercise.

Exercise Six

If you choose, begin to notice trees.

Trees are a beautiful metaphor, Divinely given, to remind us of Being. Notice that trees are not in a rush to go anywhere, they don't need to do anything. Trees facilitate our Being here on the planet, our ability to breathe. They allow our Inspiration to Be and expand Consciousness on the planet.

Trees hold the space in our fields, protecting and mothering crops, grasses, plants and all living things. They nurture the sapling until they can stand alone, and then transition and transform with no resistance. They hold the space on the sides of our freeways as we rush to where we are going. They maintain silent vigil while we awaken to Who We Are.

Trees create the energetic core of our forests, our planet. They Be above as below, for the seen and the unseen.

Trees bear witness to our history, they store our history. They let go of that content and transmute it as they transform, all the while knowing there is no away. They grow and contort to our changes, to our unconsciousness, while having no point of view. They respond to all conditions in an attempt to rebalance, to remove the charge.

Trees will receive our hugs, our cries, our silence, our exploration, our discovery, our celebrations and our unconsciousness.

Trees welcome those that live with, from and on them. Trees give freely and reflect the generosity, humility, care, love, vulnerability, authenticity and intimacy that All Essential Natures Are.

Trees await all of us knowing Who We Are. They do not judge any lack of Being. They know, and do not resist. Trees receive us no matter how we show up.

Trees are so beautiful in their Magnificence, in all their Presentations, so Unique, each a reflection of a Unique aspect of God, like All of Us. Trees know Who They Are and will continue to show us. We embrace and relish their diversity yet cannot receive each other in the Beautiful Diversity with which we all Present.

If you choose, begin to notice trees.

When you choose from Being and fully awaken to Who You Are, then real magic can happen as there are no limitations, expectations or rules in relation to matter and form. While the story may label these as miracles, more and more, particularly as the New World expands, this will be commonplace. When we Be there is a gratitude, humility and honouring that arises rather than a disbelief of 'Can this be possible?'. Additionally, without attachment, significance and point of view in relation to an outcome, even more is possible.

In this reality, it is limitation and a belief in limitation (both content of the ego/mind) that is buffering us from accessing our true potency and Self. The 'miraculous' is not exceptional, it is Who We Are.

Working from the 'inside out' in this way can be instantaneous and because the vibration is so much higher than the issues being carried, the changes are noticeable and material when we return to functioning from the ego/mind. The change in form means that you will never be the same again, form has been transformed.

The reality that shows up when we Be Our Selves is not something detrimental to the world. The world does not know it yet but it is the only hope for the survival of the planet.

FROM THE OUTSIDE IN

The 'outside in' approach is a slower process, it is a 'doing' process from outside of you. You have access to the finite resources of the body/mind complex at a physical and dense level, including what is stored in the ego/mind as knowledge.

While I have separated 'outside in' from 'inside out', I do so for illustration only, as in truth, the two approaches cannot be separated and occur simultaneously to varying degrees. For most of us, the awareness of the Soul is received and perceived by the ego/mind, even if the awareness is translated by that ego/mind. It is the net vibration that will determine the outcome.

When you are choosing to resolve the charge of identifications from the 'outside in' you are in the realm of content, both cognitive and unconscious; you are in the 'thick of it'. You have all the past reference points and future expectations at play. Predominantly, the focus is on what is cognitive to you, that is, what you have observed is something that you are no longer wishing to carry. For example, 'I have a pattern of being codependent; I am scared of heights; I wish I could have money; I want to lose weight; I am bored; I am not appreciated; I am not successful; I want to stay popular; I keep getting into abusive relationships.'

We know we want to change something about ourselves or our life and we choose to 'do something about it'. This could be some of the innumerable actions like diet, meditation, medication, affirmations, extra study, picking up a hobby, walking the dog, reading a book (fantasy, fact or fiction, or self-help), volunteering, prayer, 'me' time, changing something or excluding something or someone from your life.

The level to which we open up to even these choices outside ourselves is also dependent on our identifications. If our identifications deem that seeking help is weak or not appropriate, assistance would not be sought. The judgement will remain, and no action is taken to remove the charge on them. Despite this, events and conditions will continue to change within our lives to activate change. The Soul will always seek to guide us back to Self. While filtered by the ego/mind, this is where we are truly buffered down the river with the ego/mind as 'captain of the ship'.

We could also seek out a counsellor, a wholistic practitioner, psychiatrist, psychologist or other form of doctor, friends, pastor or other religious or community leader or anyone we think can help us deal with the issues we have noticed we have a problem with.

Everything always gets back to vibration, even when it comes to the 'outside in'. We may not be cognitive of this. We certainly don't discuss it in those terms in the story. Yet, it is the very thing that will determine whether an issue is resolved or not, transmuted or not.

How we show up with all the content of the ego/mind has a certain vibration, usually quite dense. This density varies for everyone as a whole and varies when we look at particular identifications and particular issues and situations.

For example, the judgement that you always attract abusive partners is much denser vibrationally than, say, your judgement that you have beautiful eyes. Notice the energy difference between those two judgements. Energy can be described by the vibration it has.

When we choose a particular action or remedy for our issues, the content of the action or remedy is not primary. If the net vibration of the action or remedy is greater than the vibration of the issue, a material and permanent change will occur. Metaphysically, you will never be the same again.

If the vibration of the technique, action, or person(s) (incarnate or not) that we seek for our issue is less than or equal to the issue wanting to be cleared, nothing materially will change. The form may change but a material change will not be experienced in the quality of life. The vibration is about the same level or less than the issue so the outcome will be relative at about the same vibration or less. Any change is often short-term. You may, however, get permanent changes in other identifications that do vibrate at a lower frequency than the technique, action or person(s) which you have sought help from. This also occurs on the macro level of governments and countries.

Apparent miracles occur when the vibration of the technique or person(s) is substantially higher than the issue being sought to be resolved, and the net vibration of the asking provided an outcome of high vibration and showed up as dismantling the issue.

This brings me to another interesting observation. When someone or something is functioning from a very high vibration (incarnate or not), that is, they are Being Them Selves, what can show up is a 'zeroing in' on the issue they are facilitating for someone even if they do not perceive the specifics of the situation. This is often not necessary. I observe it as a laser beam type action. The action is direct, potent, and focused. The high vibrations Present with such potency and attention that what they bring their attention to can change immediately. At these vibrations there is no time/space. It is functioning from Infinite awareness, accessing 'zero-point field', Infinity, where there is no charge. Their target is to facilitate the person before them to be more Them Selves, there isn't anything else. Applying this sort of power changes you.

If the technique or person(s) is at a low or dense vibration similar to the issue, the effect is like a diffused light rather than a laser beam. It has a muffled and broad-brushed effect. Some change may be experienced but not materially, and usually not long-lived. At these vibrations, often those facilitating are attached to needing to 'fix'. This only shows up when functioning from the ego/mind. Even those seeking the change often want to be 'fixed'.

'Fixing' does not show up at higher vibrations as there is no away in Oneness, and whatever is presenting for the person Is. Those functioning as Who They Are are facilitating Oneness, not 'fixing'. They allow the awareness to show up and follow the energy of what presents. At these higher levels of vibration, a material change does occur even if the issue appears to be the same. If the desired result is the outcome of the facilitation, it is known that that was the contribution to awakening the person to Be more Them Selves. For others, not resolving the issue is a contribution to awakening to Them Selves, even if it means the 'death' of the body/mind complex, the transition from this incarnation.

Let's summarise. Seeking assistance at higher vibrations than an issue is the only way to make a material and permanent change. Being facilitated by something or someone at these vibrations guarantees a change. It may not be the 'fixing' what you are seeking, yet metaphysically, you will never be the same. The laser beam effect potently transmutes content that awareness draws them to. This could resolve the specific issue or may not, it could resolve other issues. You will be different, even if you are not cognitive of it. There will be less content buffering you from Being You in the world and in existence.

You can have two different practitioners conducting the same practice and the results will be totally different as a direct reflection of their vibrations of Consciousness.

When utilising the 'outside in' approach it is all about the tools available to facilitate the transmuting of identifications. What has shown up for me and for my clients is the gathering together of a Kit Bag of tools and crutches that facilitate you specifically.

I use the word label 'crutch' to reflect the temporary nature of an adopted action or behaviour. It is something we do consciously even though we know that when we are Being Our Selves we will not need to do it. Consciously noticing and choosing a crutch allows us to more easily maintain Presence rather than unconsciously doing something.

Choosing to adopt a crutch does not disempower you. It is an allowance of what Is in this moment and an acknowledgement of you choosing to change something and consequently using a crutch to facilitate that change.

In any moment we can choose the content of our Kit Bag. I do notice the contradiction here, as up to this point I have been discussing removing our charge and transmuting content. The 'outside in' is an approach adopted while we still have ego/mind in place. Thus, a Kit Bag is a crutch itself until it is no longer required, which, if we were functioning as Who We Really Are, would be unnecessary.

Even when we have not chosen to make changes in our lives and we are functioning from our solid foundations we are also utilising a Kit Bag. These Kit Bags are at vibrations that match the content of the ego/mind and their target is to maintain status quo, to reaffirm our belonging and fitting in. The Kit Bag is used to perpetuate content and positions rather than transmuting it. Actually, we would not separate it as a Kit Bag, rather, it is what we do, it is who we are. I am labelling it as a Kit Bag to bring some level of conscious thought to the process.

I have included some specific examples below. Even though some of these may be crutches for those choosing to make changes in their lives, what I am speaking of here are actions we carry out in the context of perpetuating our identifications.

- ☐ Shopping and retail therapy so that you can keep up with deemed expectations;
- ☐ Consuming alcohol to match a social setting, for example, a glass of wine while cooking, beer at the pub, champagne at the races;
- ☐ Turning to food to feel safe;
- ☐ Going to church on Sundays;
- ☐ Gossiping to justify your position as right and someone else as wrong;
- ☐ Going to work to make money to pay the bills;
- ☐ Never showing emotions because you are 'the man of the house';
- ☐ Aggressive protesting to affirm the wrongness of others;

- ☐ Going to get your nails and hair done every week to make sure you are presentable and fitting expectations;
- ☐ Going to the football in your team colours.

Do not judge the content of your Kit Bag, only observe which crutches you currently utilise as what resonates as you in this moment, what 'feels' like you in this moment. The transitioning to an expansion of Consciousness, to Self, to You, cannot be forced. You cannot look at a flower bud and demand it to bloom. You can observe it, commune with it and delight in its unfurling. You are no different. Delight in your unfurling, not separate from the bloom.

The Kit Bag we utilise when cloaked in the story and in the content of our identifications will contain crutches consciously and unconsciously determined and/or behaviours we assume to be part of who we are. You are drawn to those things of this world that match you and your identifications or match the fantasy identifications you aspire to have or be in your life. The fact that we are having this discussion on Kit Bags and tools and crutches, opens up the possibility of noticing it even if it has been unconscious, as once you notice something it is unconscious no longer and you have just shifted some content. If the action is chosen when conscious, that maintains a Presence. That is success for me: more of You showing up in the world.

The target is to identify the things of this world that vibrate like You, not the contents of your ego/mind or what you desire to have as content.

The reason for this is threefold. Firstly, those things that vibrate like You are of a high vibration and thus will transmute the charge on the dense content within the ego/mind. Earlier, we discussed that anything or anyone that has a vibration higher than our issues or content can facilitate a material and permanent change. Now I am making a further distinction. I am narrowing down all actions, person(s) (incarnate or not), methodologies, etc. that vibrate higher than the issue(s) you wish to resolve or higher than the content of your ego/mind, to those that vibrate like You. This is for the second reason, that selecting those things which resonate like You, are the closest things that will match You Being You and they will strengthen your capacity to Be. You may still choose to have items in your Kit Bag of high vibration that do not resonate like You. How they feel to You will not be as 'familiar', like Home, as those that do vibrate like You.

For some, choosing what vibrates like You can facilitate the beginning of toggling between Being You and functioning from the ego/mind. These are the things of this world that bridge and transition 'you' to 'You'. What can show up is that whilst adopting a crutch from your Kit Bag, you slip into Being You, and the toggling between realities begins.

Thirdly, I have observed that while functioning from the ego/mind, the only things that truly recharge you, that 'fill your cup', are those things which resonate like You. When you are drained to your core with what happens in the story, it is only those things that resonate like You which will automatically give you energy. This is because they too access the Infinite energy that becomes accessible when we are Being Our Selves. It is like the Universe, from which You are not separate, perceives you choosing to Be You and Infinity is accessed.

In practice, when you do not have a Kit Bag which vibrates like You, and you are exhausted 'to the bone' by the story and the world, you may turn to numbing agents or rebelling or distracting activities in your dense Kit Bag of content. This will only give temporary relief. Such dense things will never recharge you, transmute content or provide relief from yearnings.

The crutches that perpetuate your positions will continue to keep you on the mouse wheel of your reality. They fuel the turning of that wheel that the ego/mind deems is your life. That which vibrates higher and as Who You Are will facilitate the jumping out of that mouse wheel into a reality of your own choosing.

Only those things that vibrate like You or are at a higher vibration than what you are carrying, will give you relief. That's it!! And this is a crutch until you Be You.

As you transition to You in the world, the contents of your Kit Bag will transition to those things that vibrate lighter and higher than your identifications and content. Most of us, in this moment, will have a Kit Bag of items that:

- ☐ do resonate like Who We Are;

- ☐ are of varying vibrational frequencies, with some items vibrating higher than our issue(s) and content and some vibrating lower;

- ☐ we think are high vibration but they are not. For example, when someone facilitating you is functioning from their ego/mind, while speaking the language of the Soul and you misidentify them as functioning from a high vibration.

- ☐ perpetuate identifications for us;

- ☐ we decide are good for us from a thinking point of view. These are those items which do still reflect the content of the ego/mind and are things the ego/mind is OK with us 'doing', for example, eating more healthily, going to the gym, 'me' time. These are new identifications we have or aspire to adopt.

As we transition to Being more Our Selves, items may be the same within our Kit Bag yet their vibration presents higher. For example, if you had 'being out in nature' as an item in your Kit Bag when you functioned from a denser reality of story, how you experience that as you transition to Be more You in the story, will be more vibrant and expansive in nature. You may even choose to Be with the space in nature.

When you begin to consciously choose a Kit Bag which resonates as Your Essential Nature, as Who You Are, you begin to take charge of and facilitate your way out of ego/mind content from the 'outside in'.

Your Kit Bag is a crutch until you don't need it any longer.

Only you can determine what the content of a Kit Bag that resonates like You will contain in any moment. Here are some examples to illustrate:

- Being with animals, Being with that feeling of giving and receiving;

- Being in nature: the earth, mountains, sky, cosmos, sea, waves, trees: always Present and Being there for us to know Who We Are;

- Reading a book of high vibration that feels like a match with You. Sometimes we are drawn to a book and know we are to read it;

- Being with others: watch the company you keep as this is a huge contribution to your vibration, others functioning at a dense vibration will impact you if you are not Present;

- Being alone: for some of us, me included, Being alone is expansive and an initial 'go to' in our Kit Bag;

- Creating geographical distance from the identifications and content. This is an interesting one. I have found that when we take ourselves away from an issue or trauma or anything that contributes to us not Being Ourselves, creating space by removing ourselves will provide the space for clarity, for awareness, the space that is Consciousness. Examples are:

  o Taking a long drive away from a situation;

  o If, at an event, taking a moment and going to the bathroom and sitting for a minute or two or three;

  o Going outside and being with the children or nature;

  o Going on holiday. This creates a space away from your identifications and then you are receiving a contribution from those things around you: nature, sights and sounds, being with yourself; being with others without the content.

☐ Experiences that you have established a matrix of energy around and when activated trigger an immediate shift in vibration. For example:

   o A favourite spot to sit or walk or meditate;

   o A favourite song or piece of music;

   o Cooking;

   o Painting;

   o Sitting in church or temple;

   o Seeing a sunset or sunrise;

   o Being with a teacher you are drawn to;

   o Hearing birds in the morning;

   o Hearing children laughing.

☐ Sounds and music that resonate like You. The content can be of such high vibration that we physically feel our hearts being contributed to and Our Souls touched. Notice too the space between the notes;

☐ Smells that resonate like You: flowers, essences, spices, smoke, fruits, rain, sea spray, a forest floor;

☐ Being with the space between everything;

☐ Any Being and/or doing that opens your heart unconditionally;

☐ Practicing mindfulness and Being in the moment;

☐ Reflecting and being with children who have not bought as real the story and identifications which many will buy into. In the New World the target is for all of us to not buy the identifications and Be childlike in our wonder and exploration of ourselves, others and the world we find ourselves in;

☐ Ritual and ceremony as an Expression of You. This can include smudging, prayer, rites of passage, honouring ceremony, anything that marks an occasion or is an acknowledgement.

The distinction I wish to make here is that it would be a reflection of Our Magnificence, not a diminishment of anyone. Being diminishes no one, only ego/mind does;

- Laughter, particularly when you 'lose yourself' and drop self-consciousness because you are laughing so much;

- Healing sessions with someone Being Them Selves;

- Meditation and contemplation with Your Self;

- Communion with God;

- Devotion to God;

- Movement in resonance with You. For example, yoga, dancing, running, walking, swimming, surfing, riding, skating, twirling, skipping;

- Being with things that shine and feel like the projection of Light that We Are. For example, the sun's rays, the moon's glow, the sun shimmering on water, the glow of crystals and diamonds, the sun reflecting through crystals and rain projecting the rainbow as we are projected, of dew on the leaves, and sun through the clouds. I remember as a child, while lost in the world, I would always seek out the sun radiating through the clouds because I saw it as heaven on earth and it was like Home to me;

- Deity and Enlightened Ones who show us Who We Are. Even icons and statues of them are useful in establishing an immediate recall of energy that can be a wonderful contribution to You Being You. It is not about diminishing You and praying up to them, it is about knowing You are not separate and for you to know and remember that beyond doubt;

- Being in, by and with water;

- Any 'Right Actions' you are drawn to that mimic Your Essential Nature.

A key characteristic of Kit Bag items that resonate like You is their unconditional Nature. They are an Isness with no point of view or position. They are void of content other than their apparent projection into form. It is the information of their Unique projection that provides the Unique resonance. Even deities are a projection into a form they are recognised as. We are drawn to the deity that vibrates as Who We Are. Some unconditional items project resonances that feel like Home for most. Examples are the sun's rays as described above, the cosmos and the stars.

Having a Kit Bag that resonates like You is the target, however, when You are Being You in the world, the Kit Bag is no longer necessary or relevant. As mentioned earlier, most of us will have a Kit Bag that has items that resonate like Who We Are and some items that continue to satisfy identifications still in place within the ego/mind. I know I do. Don't judge it, observe it. Let's spend some time looking at how a Kit Bag would show up for you in this moment. Know that as 'you' transition to 'You', as your perspective changes, the content of your Kit Bag will also change until You no longer need it. A gift of a Kit Bag is being conscious of using it.

Exercise Seven

Part A

Notice what items of this world and in existence you perceive as resonating like You. Utilise the clue that these items have no position or point of view, rather they are an Isness. Do not judge yourself with regard to 'where you are at'. Write in your journal what arises when you bring your attention to what resonates like You, what feels familiar and like Home to You. Use your imagination and see what you can come up with.

Part B

Now I want you to notice what you 'do' in a day. Notice if there are specific crutches you utilise in a day to function as 'you' in the story. For example, having brunch on a Sunday morning at a local cafe, after having walked the dog, creates an ease and maybe even joy in you. Reflect on which items of this world are in your Kit Bag as you function from the ego/mind. Do you need retail therapy when you are stressed? Do you have a ritual way of getting ready for the day? Do you need a drink? Do you start the day with a coffee? Do you need to eat? Do you need to care for others? Do you need to be needed? Do you call your mum every day? Do you watch TV in the evening? Do you need acknowledgement? Do not judge any of it, just notice. Be willing to be totally honest with yourself and 'eyeball' it all. Be accountable to no one. There is no need to justify what you choose. Maybe spend a few days noticing what your 'go tos' are, what tools and crutches you use to reflect 'you' in the world. We are transitioning to no judgement so please do not perpetuate judgement of yourself or others, just notice. These items are generally those things that provide a sense of belonging, of fitting in, of replicating a feeling that relieves stress for you, which provides information relating to your position or status in the world. Write, draw or document your ego/mind Kit Bag in your journal. When we begin to notice, we make them conscious. Consciously choosing, even if we continue to choose the same item, allows the Presence of You.

Part C

Are there any items you identified in Part B that are also in Part A? Are they at the same vibration? With this exercise, I ask that you begin to notice where your awareness may be informing your choices within the ego/mind. I ask that you begin to notice if there is a translating of that awareness or whether your ego/mind has dismantled in regards to particular actions to allow the clear perception of your awareness to be received without distortion.

Acknowledge yourself, even in considering this possibility, as you write, draw or record the information in your journal.

Choosing to live as Your Self is a choice, and like any choice, it is not a passive exercise. Choosing the content of your Kit Bag and transitioning its contents to reflect more and more like You is part of the active nature of transitioning to You. Do not force it. Do not push for a result you think is better. That is your ego/mind. Be kind to you.

Notice if you have made a choice to Be Your Self or if you are watching this discussion or watching the choice. Your Soul will be guiding you back to Your Self in the context of existence and lifetimes. If you choose to actively participate in the unfolding, you have dismantled much separation between 'you' and 'You'.

As we continue to transition to Who We Are, our awareness increasingly informs all the choices we make within our day. The separation of 'you' and 'You' begins to dismantle and there is an Isness to how we experience our lives. The ego/mind may still be in place, however, it too has dropped much of the charge on receiving the perceptions of the Soul, our awareness. It no longer illicits a threatened response to the information it deems as outside of what it knows.

Additionally, personal positions that were so critical in the past, no longer show up. There is an allowance of others and their positions and perspectives, with no need to conform to anything or anyone. This does not show up as superiority, or as noticing that they 'still have stuff and I don't'. When this shows up, the ego/mind is playing with you again, and still has a charge on position. No, it shows up as an observation of what Is.

When I work with clients I notice this. I perceive Who They Are and notice the content that doesn't allow them to Be in the world as Them Selves. I know they are not the cloak they wear. Judgement doesn't arise. What does arise is joy when any amount of buffer is transmuted and more of Who They Are Becomes Present.

Your awareness also knows what you know and have stored in your ego/mind. Life is lived from perceiving awareness and utilising all resources to facilitate Being and doing. The mind is used as a tool and everything you have ever known and all else is accessible to You. For example, if you are a surgeon, while functioning solely from the content of your ego/mind, you would be limited to what you have been taught, what you have learnt, and what you have gathered from past experiences. So, when you perform a particular surgical procedure, you know the steps, the anatomy, the correction, all based on your knowledge and experience from the past. If something unexpected occurs during the procedure, you only have available whatever references you have in your ego/mind. You may be able to come up with something, but it will always be based on what already exists.

If you have dismantled your ego/mind sufficiently to allow your awareness to be received by the ego/mind, and you find yourself in the above situation, you may perceive an Inspiration to address what is presenting in a way that you had no previous knowledge of or in a way that has never existed before. Your awareness together with the content of your mind commune to create an Inspired result. Additionally, as you have an allowance for receiving and perceiving awareness, the vibration is high, higher than the issue being sought to be resolved, thus even vibrationally, you have risen above the issue you are facilitating and the person before you will never be the same.

As Consciousness expands on the planet, we will be functioning with an allowance of awareness. The Infinite will be valued and no more doubted or deemed to require belief.

Acknowledging that this is occurring allows it to present more and more, and the more it turns up, the more the ego/mind is dismantled. We always have access to what we know in our minds. The bonus is accessing what we can know from existence and beyond. It is this knowing that expands Consciousness. It is this Infinite resource that will facilitate the transition of our world to a world in balance. Balance and no charge is always the target at all levels. This simplicity has been lost and is Being regained.

This way of living takes the pressure off and creates a sense of ease because you don't have to hold anything, only Be. You continue to follow your awareness and consciously choose any Being or doing. If

You require information, you access it in any moment, whether it is stored already or received and perceived from awareness. Everything Is as it Is.

The expansion of Consciousness on the planet is unfolding. If you choose, continue to observe and notice the unfolding and actively participate. If You Be, You will perceive the vastness of a reality, beyond the dualistic reality, that has one intention, to return you Home to Its embrace and for you to Be with the Immense Joy, Love and Familiarity that dissipates all yearning.

Five

KARMA

Karma is a word, like any other word. A great many societies, and religious and spiritual teachings within those societies, have used this word to label certain content. I am not here to begin a comparison or to invalidate any other discussion on what karma is. My attention will be on what my perceptions are when I notice the bundle of energy that I call karma.

When we get down to the basics of any discussion on karma, bringing our attention to its purpose is the most useful. That purpose is very simple. To bring to Light what does not allow You to Be You in the world and in existence, and thus return to Oneness, to God, to the All/No-thing We All Be. The word labelling may be different, the descriptions may be different, but the target is always the same.

What I am 'doing' in this chapter is discussing the information I am perceiving and relating it within the context of karma. Many talk about karma when referencing Enlightenment, so a discussion on Enlightenment feels incomplete without a discussion on karma.

Notice any level of resistance to even opening a discussion on karma. Notice what shows up, even if it is judgement. Throughout, my aim is for you to practice perceiving your own awareness rather than adopting anything I or anybody else says, as that creates more layers or filters rather than less. What follows is no different. Word labels alone can trigger so much charge and point of view. Notice this as we discuss karma.

So, what is karma for me?

Karma is all the content and charge that buffers Who You Are from showing up in the world and in existence. Everything that filters You from Being is your karma. Karma is not about how you got the buffering, but that the buffering exists. It is your Michelin Man suit.

The net effect or net vibration of that content, of your karma, is what presents in any moment. How you show up in the world and in existence is the net effect of your karma in that moment. The Universe does not look at the content and analyse or judge it in terms of good or bad. Consciousness does not have a point of view about it, it knows that everything is about you returning Home to Oneness. It is what it is in this moment. It is only the dualistic reality that judges karma.

Karma is generated whenever 'you' have not followed the awareness of 'You'. What results is a charge on the chosen behaviours and activities, like a prostituting of Self. It is irrelevant how the story judges the behaviours and actions. Every instance where awareness is not chosen directly relates to the level of karma generated from those actions or behaviours. The degree to which karma is generated relates directly to the variance between the vibration of 'You' and the vibrational frequency of the thought, feeling, emotion, action or intention.

When choices are made from awareness, there is no charge, only choice and if the measure of karma is the deviation from awareness then no karma arises or is measurable.

If You Be You in the world, even all the existing content is bought out of and You show up as Your Self. No need to transmute karma, You are functioning in the non-dualistic reality of Being. Enlightenment is when this shows up as an Isness, rather than experiences of Being You.

The only reason you do not have access to your awareness is because you have bought into a reality that tells you who you are, the dualistic reality. You bought into all the identifications you are wearing and this filters 'you' from 'You'.

When you make choices from the dualistic reality of the ego/mind, karma is still generated based on whether or not you are following your awareness, which you may not be cognitive of. That's right, you heard me. You are generating karma when you are not following your awareness, an awareness you may not have access to.

What is also interesting to note is that when you function from the dualistic reality, you may no longer perceive the awareness of karma that I speak of. You concern yourself with karma if the society, religion or group you have bought into, has adopted karma as a benchmark within the story. The awareness of what karma is changes from being non-dualistic to dualistic in the form of benchmarks, that is, expectations and judgements.

So, for those that consider it relevant, what they 'do' is try and work out what actions and behaviours they 'think' would not generate karma. We look for reference points within our reality for how we 'should' behave. We are replacing Our Unique awareness with judgement within the dualistic reality of what is good and what is bad. These often conflicting judgements, depending on the society, religion or group, are static and generic in nature and may not vibrate like You. Your awareness will always, as an Isness, vibrate like You.

For those functioning in stories that do not refer to karma, they also use reference points of what is good and what is bad, this is the nature of the dualistic reality. They are still in the effect of their karma, despite it not being a measure or label within their story, they use other measures and other labels.

We are replacing our awareness with recommended behaviours outside of ourselves that may or may not generate karma. The story may even list the recommended behaviours that do not generate karma and/or transmute karma ('good karma') and those that generate karma ('bad karma'). If the recommended behaviour is a Right Action for you or vibrates like You, it will not generate karma. Anything else will, even if the story thinks it is an appropriate, acceptable and even desirable behaviour. Models such as churches and other religious institutions were developed around these recommendations.

Recommended behaviours can be useful when we do not have access to Self and when those recommended behaviours have some level of awareness remaining. All recommended behaviours would have been processed through the ego/mind. Depending on whether awareness remains, that is, its vibration remains high, will determine the level to which karma is generated. For example, recommended behaviours that mimic the Right Actions of caring, humility, love, gratitude that are innate in all Our Essential Natures would not generate karma if actioned at vibrations like Who We Are. Recommended behaviours that we judge as 'good' will generate a degree of karma if they are not in resonance with You or your awareness. Some recommended behaviours may have been so contorted that complying with them would be a total prostituting of Self, yet you think you are behaving as you should.

Notice that my focus is on the vibration of the action. Everything comes back to this whether we are discussing Who You Are, creating in any reality and generating karma or not. However, in the story, the measure is generally the completion of the action and a consequential judgement of 'good' if completed and 'bad' if not completed. A recommended behaviour may be actioned by one person at very high vibrations, maybe with an opening of their heart, or even vibrating like Who They Are (which could also slip them into Being) or it can be actioned at low and dense vibrations, with someone merely going through the motions of the recommended behaviour.

While the story may judge these the same, Consciousness perceives them totally differently, with no point of view. It is what it is. For one, no karma, for the other, karma, a buffer to Who They Are.

At the level of vibration, we are not limited to only recommended behaviours. Any 'doing' that vibrates like You will not generate karma and will transmute karma, even mindfully watching a seed floating through air.

This is where, as discussed in the previous chapter, a Kit Bag that vibrates like You is most useful when you do not have access to your awareness as an Isness. Right Actions are a great tool as they mimic how You would show up Being You. Your Kit Bag that vibrates like You is full of Right Actions Uniquely for you.

Later in this chapter we will discuss the transmuting of karma, more particularly from the context of recommended behaviours and Right Actions. Everything we have already discussed about transmuting the charge on the content of our ego/minds, our identifications, is the same as transmuting your karma. What we are referencing is another perspective within the story.

For now, let's make a distinction between karma and the systems of management and control within a particular society or group.

How a society deals with what it judges as good or bad behaviour is part of the systems utilised by that particular society to maintain order and stability. This is all part of the stage.

For example, if someone commits a murder, some societies may do nothing, others may respond by reciprocating the action, others may 'throw them in jail', and others may collect the evidence and seek to determine what a reasonable person within that society would judge the behaviour as. Whatever action, if any, is taken in response to the murder, is determined by the identifications and content of that particular society or group.

Those societies that have karma within their benchmarks, may judge the action of murder somewhere on the spectrum of 'good karma' to 'bad karma'. Karma is judged by the action rather than the vibration of the action and outcome. It is certainly not determined by reference to the awareness of the murderer. Being cloaked in content, both society and the individual perpetrating the action may not have access to any awareness. The static and generic responses come into play. Any course of action to correct the situation would also be judged on the spectrum of 'good karma' and 'bad karma'. A society, for example, may determine that a balance is achieved with punishing a murderer and putting them in prison for a certain period of time. The society may see the particular circumstances of the prison sentence as a transmuting of karma, as correcting a wrong.

147

This includes content like duration and conditions of the sentence (for example, level of comfort during the sentence).

Irrespective of what is determined by any society or group, karma is only generated if the Soul of the murderer perceives their action as charged or imbalanced, as a prostituting of Self. Awareness does not concern itself with content or story, that belongs to the dualistic reality. The context of the murder will, however, influence the perception of the Soul and there may be situations where the Soul does not perceive murder as generating karma.

For those reading this and thinking that this can be used to justify your actions, that is a trick of the ego/mind. Your society will have its judgement on your behaviour, and you can play the game of justification. Awareness cannot be tricked, no matter your thinking. You will not escape karma with justification.

When we look at the corrective action of a society in the above example, a prison sentence alone, as an action, does not guarantee the transmutation of karma.

You may have two inmates in prison, both convicted of murder. One may continue to build the identifications they are carrying around, while the other is experiencing a shifting in their Consciousness and as a result is transmuting their karma. The society that sentenced them believes that they are in the same situation, being punished for their unacceptable behaviour. Consciousness would perceive it quite differently. Similarly, if another murderer is not caught by that society, they may have escaped jail, but if their Soul perceived their action as imbalanced, they do not escape their karma.

In the story, we also have identifications on what karma should look like. We judge people's behaviour and expect them to reflect that in the world based on the karma we think they have generated. For example, you have judged someone as doing something wrong or bad. You determine that to be 'bad karma', and you expect that 'bad karma' to be reflected in the way their life shows up in the world. You get frustrated and don't understand when they go on to create great success and others love and follow them. You want them to be caught out and for everyone to know they are not a good person.

What you are seeing is your own perspective. You are judging based on your identifications including expectations, correlations and judgement, including what success is to you, and what being caught out means for you. Karma is not based on your content, and neither is the transmutation of someone else's karma. It is determined by their awareness. It has nothing to do with 'you', the product of your ego/mind content.

You are within the confines of content, of the ego/mind. You are looking for the transmutation of what you determine as 'bad karma' in the actions of the story and in the stage of the story, as determined by you. It is always the net vibration of an action that determines what is created. While filtered by your perspective, this information may not be received. You see the actions and judge them. You are not perceiving the vibration of any 'doing' either in relation to the generating of karma or the transmuting of karma. When functioning from the ego/mind you do not 'see' the big picture.

While we are All One and we can perceive the awareness of others, when we do perceive awareness, the information relating to others shows up with no point of view. It may present differently to how information relating to You shows up, yet this is known as the Unique Expression of Our Essential Natures. Awareness does not have charge on content or expectations, correlations and judgement.

Here is a crutch. While we still function from the ego/mind, someone else's karma is not your concern. It is not your responsibility to make sure that they 'pay for their sins'. There is a clear distinction between how the story deals with the action and what is someone's karma. Leave that to God. Karma is a person's relationship with God, as truly it is what separates them from Oneness, from God.

How we show up in this moment is the net effect of our karma in this moment. Someone's perspective on this can never capture all the information. It will be clouded by content. Using the above example to illustrate, having judged success and being loved and followed as 'not bad karma' is like looking at the outside of a box and judging what is inside based on what you see. The ego/mind provides a conclusion based on your personal content. It works out what is in the box. This has no relevance to karma. When we perceive the vibration from our awareness, the form and structure of the box collapses, and the clarity of the information is received. No hiding in boxes, awareness perceives All. There is no 'getting away' from or with anything, and it Is what it Is with no point of view.

Let us now begin to look at the transmutation of karma. Throughout this book we have been looking at the transmutation of the charge on all the identifications we are wearing, our Michelin Man suit.

Your Michelin Man suit is your karma. It is what separates you from Oneness, from God.

Everything we have spoken of is relevant here, as transmuting identifications is transmuting karma. My focus here will be on the content within the story 'specifically designed' to address this separation, more particularly religion.

THE TRANSMUTATION OF KARMA

Every action or behaviour (including thought, feeling, emotions) you have chosen since you have existed, either generates karma or not, transmutes karma or not.

Whenever 'you' have not followed the awareness of 'You', you have generated karma, the net effect of which shows up in this moment, as an Isness, whether in a body or not.

When the net vibration of an action or behaviour vibrates like You or when you have followed your awareness (which also vibrates like You), no karma is generated, and you transmute some of the karma that you have previously generated. This is another way of describing the transmutation of content when we rise above an issue. We don't know what content is transmuted, yet you will never be the same.

If the action or behaviour does not vibrate like You, you will generate karma in varying vibrational frequencies relative to how it vibrations like You. Similar to creating more identification and content. More buffering 'you' from 'You'. Even the identifications of name and address add to karma when charge, attachment and significance remain. 'You' do not have a point of view about it, yet 'you' may have all manner of charge on them.

I spoke of a Kit Bag of things of this world and in existence that vibrates like You. This is Wonderfully useful in transmuting content. The attention is on the vibration, and where the vibration of the tool is greater than the issue, or the karma, a material and permanent change will occur.

I included Right Actions in this Kit Bag, being any action or behaviour that mimics how You would show up when You Be You. When You Be You, karma is irrelevant. There is no gap or separation from Oneness.

If you were to choose to transmute your karma, using the tools within your Kit Bag that vibrates like You, will be very effective. Remember that these are crutches, as mimicking You is not Being You. Whilst within the confines of the ego/mind, mimicking You is a high enough vibration to transmute all karma, however, this cannot be sustained, as Being is not an Isness and your vibration will drop. Tools that do not vibrate like You, yet do vibrate higher than your karma, will transmute karma that vibrates lower. Ultimately, remaining karma would all be transmuted at the vibration of You.

For those of us toggling between Being and functioning within the dualistic reality, when we Be, we more potently transmute our karma as we have accessed the Infinite capacities of Consciousness. It is because we buy into the dualistic reality again, that karma buffers Who We Are again.

Even if you do not consciously choose to transmute your karma, Your Soul will be guiding you to Oneness, to Who You Are. Whenever a 'doing' is at a high vibration, and most certainly, at a vibration like You, your karma will be transmuted, even if you are not seeking to transmute it. Everything gets back to vibration, whether you are cognitive of it or not.

Experiences like trauma and illness, that rock our foundations, may not vibrate high when we look at the trauma and illness in isolation, as an experience, however, they often facilitate the dismantling of ego/mind content, the identifications that define who we think we are, and the net vibration is high. Karma is transmuted.

This is the only reason we are here: to know Our Selves. Transmuting karma removes the separation of 'you' from 'You', and You know Your Self. We continue to choose incarnation to transmute karma and to awaken others to know themselves, that is, to facilitate the transmuting of karma for all. This facilitation is informed from awareness, not the ego/mind, as it is known that until we all awaken to Who We Are, Oneness is incomplete.

Many who have already awakened to this have returned to show us the way Home. These are the prophets and sages throughout history. It is the awareness of these Souls from which religion and churches have been founded.

There are also a great many who are not recognised in the story. They have appeared throughout history. There are many peppering the planet now. I perceive them as the Sparks of Light they Are, with no filter to them Shining as Who They Are. Their Presence alone is transmuting karma for us all. Even others amongst us who have awaken sufficiently to know, are facilitating others to Be Them Selves.

All these individuals may not use the words I use or that anyone else uses. They may live a quiet life in their 'neck of the woods', yet their vibration is so high as to contribute to the transmuting of karma for all. Equally, there may be some that live a public and, what some would label, a wealthy life and without being attached to or identified by this, they vibrate so high as to contribute to the transmuting of unconsciousness for all.

This is the contribution of Being. When we have transmuted the karma cloaking us, we facilitate the transmuting for all.

I will give you one beautiful example. I often notice that children who incarnate and do not remain incarnate, often through illness, are like Pure Souls that come to transmute the karma of all. They have such a pure and innocent Nature, willing at a Soul level to give their life for the benefit of all so Consciousness on the planet can raise. Their Selflessness is such a gift to us all.

When we all release our bodies, there is an opportunity to transmute karma. What unfolds both before releasing the body and when releasing the body transmutes karma for the majority. The process is known to contribute greatly to transmuting karma.

How karma is stored is via a vibrational signature. This is an Isness, irrespective of whether we are in a body or not. When we transition from a body, we continue to carry the cloak of content. We are not automatically Enlightened when we leave a body. Any transmutation of karma is reflected in that vibrational signature in any 'moment'.

When those who have capacities to perceive in other realms, perceive information about our loved ones, it is both this vibrational signature around their Souls and their actual Souls that they are gathering information from. They are perceiving how we show up in existence. Our loved ones are very much alive, minus the body. It is all One Life. The more content that gets dismantled and transmuted, the less the form with which we show up. The vibrational frequencies we frequent are more and more formless until we are Being as the no content of Consciousness.

Those whom are fully Enlightened frequent these formless realms, many remerge in the All/Nothing beyond manifestation, the Unfathomable. When we call on those in these formless realms and beyond, they re-project their Selves into form, to show up for us.

Being is the no charge of Consciousness. Being incarnate or not is irrelevant.

Wherever we frequent, if we have karma cloaking us, we can continue to transmute it, and Our Souls will be guiding us to Who We Are.

If you choose to reincarnate, the content and its charge, your karma, that remains filtering 'you' from 'You' will continue to be present in the new incarnation. For most, the process of incarnation does remove access to information readily available when not incarnate. Even though both are dualistic realities for most, incarnating is much denser and we forget again and begin a 'new life' needing to remember Who We Are. While some of the content may change, such as our physical appearance, due to the parents we have chosen to facilitate our incarnation, the net vibrational signature of karma will remain as it is.

For most, what we choose as the stage for our incarnation also reflects a choice by the Soul of what can facilitate further transmutation of karma. There isn't anything else. Look around you, it is all for you to 'know Thyself'.

As an aside, as we continue to choose incarnations, the significance of content from past incarnations reduces and is pushed into the background, filed away so to speak. This is why, when perceived, we show up predominantly like our most recent incarnation, not previous incarnations. Information on these can bubble up to the surface (cognitive mind) when we 'work' to transmute our content.

It is often said in the story that if you don't overcome a lesson one lifetime you will return to repeat it until you 'get it'. This is not an absolute. You may draw similar content lifetime after lifetime, if karma/content has not been transmuted. This is because the vibration of the same behaviours match and we attract 'like' to 'like'. If you continue to generate karma by what you choose to 'do', it may perpetuate a pattern or make it even denser and lower in vibration. If some karma has been transmuted, this will lighten the vibrational signature and how you show up in the world and in existence, eventually matching Who You Are. This can occur while not incarnated. Any change in the vibrational signature will change how you show up. Content is also not pigeon-holed into categories from which we choose specifically what we transmute or generate.

Additionally, it is only the story that places significance on the 'problem' of repeating patterns. Consciousness does not judge the content, It perceives it the same as all other content: more buffering you from Being You. The reason I mention this is, if we lessen the focus on the 'problem', we instantly remove some of the charge plus we create space to choose what will be a contribution to more of You showing up rather than 'solving a problem'. This is another example of practicing to rise above an issue.

Every 'doing' is perceived, and karma changes dynamically, generating more, transmuting, whether incarnate or not. The net vibration changes constantly even with a thought, and it is what it is.

When we get back to the simplicity of this all, and don't get distracted with the content, we can notice that every action is about transmuting what does not allow You to show up.

Wherever we look within the dualistic reality there are examples of content that are attempting to reflect this awareness. I see it in the recommended behaviours within our societies, our religions, and more recently, in the calls globally of how we are all in this together and recommending embracing all as one.

Yes, the dualistic reality is functioning from ego/mind, and the awareness has been translated and contorted by the dualistic reality. While we continue to function 'here', this reality is a road to God, to Oneness, to You. There is no away.

It is about strengthening your muscle to notice the vibration of those recommended behaviours, and how they resonate relative to You. It is about consciously choosing our 'doing', asking if this 'doing' would be a contribution to more of Who I Am showing up. It is about being active rather than passive in our choices.

It is also knowing that functioning at the level of ego/mind is not Being. By being selective in your actions, you can get closer to God, to Who We Are. While within the confines of the dualistic reality, you cannot know God.

The dualistic reality of the ego/mind can only get you to the brick wall of this reality, it is like the brick wall in The Truman Show (Weir, 2006). It hits a 'dead end' of form and structure, the product of the dualistic reality. Who You Are is not the construct of a reality that someone else decided is you, that everyone looks at and judges; Who You Are is beyond this reality. Like in the movie, our willingness to go beyond into the unknown is what is required. It is only unknown to the ego/mind. Your ego/mind will tell you that you will die if you do not listen to it. Choosing to go beyond, or more literally, to rise above it all, appears most difficult only because the ego/mind tries to convince you to choose otherwise. Once chosen, an ease arises as Consciousness has your back, You are strengthened by Your Self.

What creates a doorway in the brick wall of the ego/mind are Right Actions and anything that vibrates like You. Opening your heart is an example of this. It is like the doorway magically appears, it is not magic, it was always 'there'. You rose to a higher vibration where the doorway could be perceived. It was always waiting for you. Being at the doorway is not walking through. Mimicking You is not Being You. When You Be You, the doorway itself, and in fact all form and structure, 'dissolve' into the formless Nature of Consciousness. You have risen in vibration beyond form, the doorway is not and You Behold God. You 'look' around and All is Oneness in a formless Exquisite Beauty.

In the story we have Right Actions, originating from this awareness, that are useful when we face the doorway to God. This is the opening of our hearts, prostrating, the kneeling in church, and the bowing of our heads, even to others. It is the humility and love that arises within Our Essential Nature, yet while we choose to mimic Who We Are by adopting Right Actions, we 'do' actions that may seem imposed. Don't buy into any personal disempowerment that the ego/mind may declare. What you are 'doing' is mimicking the buying out of all identifications, the letting go and surrendering of all content, and showing up 'naked' before God. With this, with the opening of our hearts to God and to Who We Are, one can slip into Being, and the doorway dissolves in a Divine Love, and You realise It was always 'there' for You. Consciousness Itself Delights in Your return Home.

This is what is meant in the Bible when Jesus said:

'Again I say to you, it is easier for a camel to go through the eye of a needle, then for a rich man to enter the kingdom of God' (Matthew 19:24AKJV)

The rich man is representative of all the identifications of the ego/mind, and the judgement that success is achieving those identifications, creating a strong sense of self from the perspective of the ego/mind. You will never find God there. You are cloaked from that Oneness by the very things you measured as success. Only when you let go the identifications, will you find God, find You, the Spark of God that You Be.

The Kingdom of God, Heaven, is Oneness. The story will tell you that heaven is on the other side of the brick wall and that you go there when you die, when you drop your body. You will find a beauty there and greater ease of Being, yet, this heaven is a fraction of what is truly Heaven. Heaven is You Being You and communing in Oneness, whether you are in a body or not.

While recommended behaviours are instituted within the dualistic reality, a gap between 'you' and 'You' will exist whether you are incarnate or not. If those recommended behaviours resonate like You, you can slip into Being, and the brick wall of the dualistic reality is no more.

This is where the benefits of recommended behaviours and particularly Right Actions are crucial while we function in the dualistic reality. Those that vibrate at a high level would still be reflecting the originating awareness that knows it is all about Being You.

Our religions that advocate such recommended behaviours and Right Actions should be encouraged within the perspective of guiding us to the doorway of Oneness.

Do not dismiss religion because of the many instances where the ego/mind has totally corrupted the original awareness. Strengthen your muscle of noticing the vibration, and you will receive the information about the vibration of the recommended behaviour. You choose. Never adopt what anyone says as mandatory. Get the information yourself. Remember, karma is determined by the level to which your actions are congruent to You, not your family members, teachers, community members, religious leaders or any other leader.

For example, let us consider the one recommended behaviour of confession. It is advocated as a necessity to 'cleanse your sins'. The action itself can be useful. Asking someone else to 'cleanse your sins' is not dissimilar to seeking facilitation from a practitioner to rebalance any charge. It is no different to any Being and/or doing that transmutes karma. The vibration will determine the net effect of the action. Where we lose the potency is in depending on the point of view of an imposed authority figure to 'cleanse our sins' and not choosing the action in potent choice to transmute our karma, our charge on content.

If you come to God and surrender all the content, that action alone raises above the issue and it changes. This potency has also been lost to an impotence of diminishment with the story labelling you a 'sinner'. The priest facilitates and invites the communion with God, with Who You Are. Putting significance on the face value of 'laying bare' before a priest is not the awareness, it is the product of ego/mind contortion of awareness.

If the priest is received as a facilitator and their vibration is high, that will change the content both as a function of their Presence and the invitation created to Be Present to Oneness. The vibration of Consciousness with the one facilitating you will create space to 'lay bare' before God and You and the facilitator not separate from God. If the priest's vibration is not functioning high, that is, they remain cloaked in content and charge, it will not facilitate much change in content nor facilitate a communion with God. It will facilitate a communion with the priest's ego/mind environment. This is the same with any practitioner/facilitator. The vibration provides the net effect of the change.

Sin is not what is labelled as sin by any benchmark outside of you; not any system of justice or recommended behaviour. It is always the gap between 'you' Being 'You'. That is it. The awareness of unique presentation has been replaced with static generic applications of recommended behaviour or not recommended behaviour and a predetermined charge relative to the behaviour perpetrated. Even the Ten Commandments are a crutch until we know. When we know, a Divine Love and caring for ourselves and others and all things arises naturally as Who We Are.

The more you shed the content that buffers 'you' from 'You', the clearer you will get the information until perspective becomes perception, and no gap exists, and no karma is generated.

Religion, at its core, is a road to God. That is its only purpose. If you are drawn to a crutch of any religion, feel free to choose it, no matter how the story judges you. Often, we incarnate into a family whose content includes identification with a particular religion. This may feel familiar to you. Do not adopt it blindly. Continue to notice the vibration in all practices and in all that it advocates including recommended behaviours. Some may have lost their way in the dualistic reality. Others may have retained the originating awareness. What is very relevant is who is delivering the content of those religions, again, notice the vibration from which they are functioning from. If a religion declares others as 'wrong', they have lost the original awareness that all roads lead to Oneness. Why did the Enlightened Ones come into this reality in so many different forms, if not to provide a diverse array of roads to God?

Any attachment to the religion itself, any form of belonging, righteousness and discrimination will delay reconnection to God. The road then becomes the roadblock and all you can see is the content rather than the way back to Self. The content of religion is what the road is made of, it is not the destination.

The vibration will give you the information. Choose it or not. It is a crutch like many others, like walking in nature, another road to God. All roads lead to Oneness, even if you are not cognitive of that. Know also, the roads lead you to the door, only Being You 'dissolves' the form and You realise the Oneness of All.

There is one particular practice that I have noticed has lost its way from the original awareness, while on the face of it, has been adopted like an awareness, and that is belief.

Belief may seem a Right Action, a mimicking of Who You Are, yet it is not. Belief is a disempowerment. The practice of believing in something, in someone, in God, is an imposed thought, an imposed point of view, not founded on any of your own knowing. It is another identification of the ego/mind. It is a separation. It can only take you to the brick wall of this reality. It does not even 'show' you the doorway to God, unless it awakens in you your own knowing.

The original intention of belief was 'Let me share my awareness, and know this for yourself: 'know Thyself''.

If belief was acknowledged in the story as a crutch until you did know, then I wouldn't be highlighting it here. I have noticed that belief seems to be the destination. We are being told we need to believe in God, believe in ourselves, and believe in other people. Sometimes we are instructed to believe in a God only according to our particular religion's perspective of 'Who God is'. Fundamentally, we are being told that we cannot know for ourselves so we have to be told what to believe. Believing in God is only a hope to know God.

You can never find Oneness when you continue to impose another's point of view as your own. All the points of view of the ego/mind are imposed points of view. This is content outside of you. A gap always remains.

I want you to know God. Even a glimpse of the Divine Love that Is God can Be an Eternal Moment and then You know. I want you to know Who You Are, a literal Spark of God, reflecting that Magnificence in the world and in existence. I want you to know that this is Who We All Are, no exclusions, no exceptions. Even those cloaked from perceiving this are no different. Do not believe in what someone or something outside of you told you to adopt as a behaviour, seek what You know.

If you don't know, you can choose to know. That is where to begin. Use a road, any road. If you are choosing the structure of a crutch, choose it. Oneness is incomplete until you find your way to You. That cannot Be until You know what You know.

Let us finish this chapter on karma with a discussion on another practice, a Right Action that is often misidentified in the story, particularly in religion. It will also be a prelude to our next chapter on healing. I am speaking of prayer.

When You know, one of the things You know is that Being an aspect of Divinity, of God, any asking will Be. You are not attached to any outcome of the asking. You perceive this asking as part of Divinity unfolding in existence, and You are in allowance of what unfolds. You are not separate, You are facilitating creation.

Prayer is a request for a changing of matter from one form to another. That is why we finish a prayer with 'Amen' or an equivalent to 'Amen'. This awareness has not been lost, however, the potency of it has. It has become a blank reciting of a word at the end of a prayer or at certain points in a ritual. 'Amen' is declaring that we go back to the 'Aum' vibration where the matter took form and reform matter according to the asking, the prayer.

We define 'Amen' as 'So Be It'. From its Hebrew origins it means both 'he confirmed, supported, or upheld' together with 'the idea of certainty or dependability' (CatholicAnswers, 2011). This is a word labelling pointing to the potency I speak of. It mirrors the vibration, derived in its origins from the knowing of 'Aum'. Ask and it Is with no doubt and absolute dependency. 'So Be It' works too if we access the original vibration. Know the Infinite potency of 'Amen'.

When choosing and asking is actioned from the no charge of Being You, the Universe, Consciousness, reflects back by unfolding Your asking. The vibration of what You are choosing matches what is perceived by Consciousness and Your prayer is created.

This is the resonance of Being. Everything is choice with no charge or point of view. Any asking, which is prayer, which is choice, is known will unfold, again, with no charge or point of view.

In the story, and particularly in religions, we have lost the knowing of this empowered capacity. This goes hand in hand with the disempowered practice of belief. We hope to believe in a God and to pray up to this God for what we are lacking. Check the vibration of this.

Prayer is asking for a change in form. It is not an asking that is then judged whether it will be granted or not. There is no separate authority checking if you deserve to be granted your asking. Consciousness will match the vibration of our choosing. That is it.

When we pray while functioning from the ego/mind, the Universe will continue to match the net vibration, including all the content relating to our prayer. However, with content buffering you, what you think you are asking may not match the net vibration of the prayer perceived by Consciousness.

Consciousness does not look at the content of our prayer and determine what you meant to say. Consciousness is vibration. It will reflect back a matching vibration. That is how creation comes to Be.

Within the story, awareness is still present to help us bypass the ego/mind. For example, the Right Actions of putting our hands together, centring in the heart, to remember to bypass the ego/mind and when bowing, honouring others as Who They Are, or wearing a bindi on the 3rd eye as an adornment to a doorway to God, or kneeling to reflect the removing of the significance of ourselves. These examples of Right Actions become ineffective when they are actioned at low vibrations, that is, when we go through the motions rather than adopting them as crutches that mimics Who We Are until we Be Our Selves. Strengthening our capacity to notice vibration will allow us to receive awareness that continues to inform us as we awaken to Who We Are.

If you strengthen your capacity to notice the vibration of everything, you will begin to notice the vibration of what you are asking and perceive Who You Are in the facilitation of creation. The net vibration of your prayer, of your asking, will be created. Take charge of your life, do not be buffered down the river based on imposed points of view. Do not go passively. Create what You are choosing. Be Your Self and even karma becomes irrelevant.

Chapter

Six

HEALING

BEFORE YOU BEGIN READING this chapter, pause.

I wish to acknowledge you. The You that is Infinite and the you that is cloaking that Infiniteness from fully showing up in the world.

Thank you for Being here on this planet. Thank you for everything you have contributed to expanding Consciousness on this planet, whether you are cognitive of it or not. Thank you for Being a part of the All that is showing up in this moment on this planet.

I absolutely know that we are all the lesser without you Being You.

I wish for you to truly know this.

We are all Magnificence personified. We are all part of the Infinite jigsaw puzzle of Oneness. One part is no more significant than another, yet crucial for the full picture. Oneness is incomplete without All.

Oneness is Manifested Consciousness. It is creation, and everything in Oneness is created from this fabric Consciousness, of which We are not separate.

When we experience our lives, particularly in the dualistic reality, we forget that all creation is made from Consciousness and thus has access to knowing in any moment. It is innate in its fabric. This knowing will always lead us to Being Oneness, to Who We Are. There isn't anything else.

Healing isn't about 'fixing', it is about removing the charge and rebalancing to 'know Thyself'. Rebalancing, coming back to balance, is more accurately the definition of healing. Healing is returning to no charge guided by awareness. It is no different to the removing of charge on content we have already spoken of at length as, in truth, it is this charge on content that shows up in our bodies as dis-ease, and for which we seek healing.

Embedded into every creation is the capacity to return to balance. Both at macro and micro levels this is a knowing. We see it with the planet, in nature, and our bodies are no different.

The cycle of creation and destruction enact a dance, each contributing to the other as everything changes form. A flower emerging from a seed and then the soil, growing stem and foliage, flowering, possibly providing food to others, then in perfection, the flower closing and the leaves and stem returning to the ground to contribute to whatever becomes. A new plant may emerge or not. There is no position, there is no fretting or yearning, there is no separation. The sun and rain make their contribution with no position, no yearning. The flower does not say that it is the most significant part. The shrivelled leaves don't think they are ugly.

When we see a lion kill an antelope, neither judges the other or has an attachment to this lifetime. There is only this moment. The lion is seeking food which nature has provided. The antelope runs as its knowing triggers a fight or flight response, but it is what it is, the response will work or not. If not, the antelope's body will change form to not only become food for the lion, and perhaps other animals, but also to feed the soil and continue to be a contribution. There is no personal 'I'.

Everything is in balance and an aspect of Oneness. No charge, no position, simplicity, Being.

We as human beings are the same. Our bodies, guided by a knowing not separate from any aspect of Us, will continually seek to achieve balance in that moment. You cut your finger and your body repairs it; you get too hot, your body cools you down; you are in danger, your body produces chemicals to enable a fight or flight response; you eat something that your body isn't choosing, your body will discharge it; you become emotional, your body will release it. Your body removes the charge!!

Without the identifications we have bought as real and which show up as our Michelin man suit, we would be able to access our awareness, our knowing, in any moment.

We would know the dance of form, of transformation, in our bodies from incarnation to transitioning beyond incarnation. We would not have a point of view about it, delighting in Its Magnificence and Glory.

We would choose in any moment, informed by our awareness, and accessing this knowing from Our Selves, whether in the form of a body, not body, other form, other not form. There is no separation. 'Our Selves' is part of Oneness.

The content of our identifications, however, has created a separation and our ego/minds have created charge and taken charge and projected another reality.

Healing then is within the context of the dualistic reality of the ego/mind. At this vibration, we cannot see the full picture I speak of. Rather, we break it down into categories and fix parts.

While our knowing is in the fabric of all form, it is being buffered by the content of our ego/minds that does not receive it. Rather than accessing Infinite knowing, we rely on the finite resources of our ego/minds. Our personal position is now separation and balance is no longer the target, fixing our personal situation is. As soon as we decided something was wrong, we increased the charge and lost further access to knowing.

Even at the macro level, we have created separation. Modern dilemmas such as overpopulation, sustainability, global warming, deforestation, salinity, extinctions and food production are simply the result of losing access to knowing that is ever Present, whose target is always balance.

The planet does not have a point of view. It will continue to access Its awareness. It is not clouded from that awareness with charged content and personal positions. It remains in allowance of all contributions. It will perpetually seek to rebalance. At all levels that rebalance may include 'death'.

In our day to day, actually moment to moment, as an Isness, our bodies, made from the fabric Consciousness, will, like the planet, seek to maintain balance. Our body/mind complex, not separate from Oneness, has access to knowing in varying degrees relative to our Michelin Man suit.

As we make choices, if those choices arise from knowing, the outcome of those choices contribute to returning to balance (no charge, no karma). If choices are not made from knowing, made from the ego/mind, balance may not be maintained. When this occurs, this is the prostituting of Self that generates karma and now we are calling that 'imbalance in the body/mind complex'. It is all an Isness, the different word labels are another way of articulating the same knowing.

The choices we make include the environments we live and work in. The speed and unkindness of our modern world, together with the great amount of content at the macro level resulting from not following awareness, can quickly overwhelm and stress us, requiring the body/mind complex to go into overdrive to rebalance. Other examples of choices not congruent with our awareness are:

☐ Upsets, taking what someone thinks of us personally;

☐ Wearing responsibility rather than choosing to act in an ability to respond;

☐ Taking on the facilitation of others and 'plugging' them into our body, commonly unconsciously chosen;

☐ Trying to change someone else, wanting them to be different;

☐ Wanting you to be different; and

☐ Bottling up emotions, not expressing them in a caring manner.

We do have capacities to shift content in any given moment. For example, we may cry, we may release a guttural sob in our grief, we may verbalise a release, shake it off, release through our bowel, or it may be expressed through any emotion. Ideally, the body/mind complex will release the charge as it is created. It will discharge and shed, it may create short-term illness to facilitate that shedding. If the charge is too overwhelming or if the body/mind complex is already overloaded with content needing to be balanced, the charge will be stored away, similar to cataloguing content in a library. Often common content is stored in the same body part or organ. I wish to acknowledge John Veltheim, founder of The BodyTalk System (Veltheim, 2013), for his awareness on the body/mind complex including the storing of content within the body including anger being generally stored in the liver, worry in the spleen, joy/sadness in the heart, grief in the lungs. This can also be when we have out-of-body experiences as we are not choosing to feel the full intensity of the experiences. The charge may be released at another time if the body/mind complex knows it can release it without intense overwhelm.

The body/mind complex is always juggling the load to produce the best outcome. When it can't keep up, it may need to prioritise its resources. This can mean the tipping point for certain parts of the body particularly if that body part or organ is 'full up'. This may present as the body/mind complex reducing capacity or shutting down function.

Dr Bruce Lipton speaks of this tipping point in relation to predispositions within our genetics. It is not a given that if you have a genetic predisposition that you will get the illness. Bruce identified that it is environment that contributes to the predisposition 'turning on' (Bruce H. Lipton, 2005). This is like the tipping point I am speaking of. The body is innately working to keep you below the tipping point. When the environment we are choosing is not chosen from awareness, and the body/mind complex cannot keep up with the rebalancing, it will do what is required to achieve optimal balance in the circumstances, including creating what we call illness.

Note that a genetic predisposition or any physical presentation chosen as the stage for a particular incarnation may be chosen from awareness, from a choice to transmute karma, and thus would not, on the face of it, be generating further charge, rather transmuting it.

If the pattern of not making choices from awareness continues, the target remains the same, and the 'death' of the body/mind complex may be the ultimate response to maintain balance. The point of view only exists within the ego/mind, which creates the separation from awareness.

We can equally have this discussion using the word labels of vibration. If you make choices that do not vibrate like You, you will create a charge, karma, that the body/mind complex will attempt to rebalance. That is, the body/mind complex will innately attempt to transmute your karma. If the body/mind complex cannot keep up, it will store the content within the body. This is also why illness may seem dense yet it is a response to create balance and the net effect may be transmuting karma. It is because we are functioning from the ego/mind that the Infinite resources available when we Be are not in play. We only have available the finite resources within the dualistic reality, even though access to Infinite resources is always Present.

If we were to get back to Being Ourselves and receiving awareness and knowing for our bodies, all information informs the maintenance of balance, no charge. If illness did present in the body, there would be an allowance. Knowing would inform choices of action/no action. Knowing automatically accesses Infinite resources. While it is known that rebalancing is possible, there is also awareness of whether the issue in this incarnation will be rebalanced or not, again, with no point of view. The illness could show up due to the unfolding of past karma or may even be a conscious choice to transmute the karma of others as it is known we are all One, and until we all return Home, Oneness is incomplete.

For those who are experiencing moments of Being and toggling between Being and the dualistic reality, awareness perceived while Being can inform any action or no action in relation to discharging charge. Access to Infinity shows up. The brick wall of the ego/mind is no more in that moment. Awareness in this moment is of a much higher vibration than any content retrieved from the ego/mind when no longer Being. Being also transmutes charge, without any doing. Strengthening your muscle to notice where you are functioning from and noticing the vibration of any form/no form will be a great contribution when making choices.

While not Being, and functioning from the dualistic reality, seeking out tools, techniques, practitioners, etc. that vibrate higher than the issue will be what can effect a material and permanent change. As we have discussed in other chapters, while this may not change how the issue is presenting, it will make a material and permanent change.

The dualistic reality does have practices and choices targeted to address the imbalance in our bodies. Again, notice the vibration of the remedy, rather than adopting the recommended behaviour from a disempowered position. Examples are 'good' diet, yoga, meditation, exercise, medication, medical intervention, therapy sessions, crystals and other contributions from nature. Some may be Right Actions, notice if they are for you. Others reflect ego/mind content.

If we continue to function solely from the dualistic reality we will not perceive the full picture of how balanced or imbalanced we are showing up. The ego/mind will continue to create separation and categories: 'I have heart disease', 'I need to lose weight', 'I am diabetic', 'I have cancer', 'I have mental illness'. This is the symptom of the imbalance, not the imbalance. It is how the karma or the transmuting of karma is showing up.

Choices within the dualistic reality have come to be standard, for example, a specific pill for a certain condition, a specific treatment for a specific body ailment. In truth, every single presentation needs to be observed as a unique presentation, accessing what uniquely will facilitate balance in that instance. Treating symptoms is like treating the tip of the iceberg rather than the whole iceberg.

I am not saying ignore the treatments within that dualistic reality. Much of our medical and scientific 'progress' (and any advancements actually) is informed from awareness. Most of us have some degree of Our Soul's awareness and knowing being received within the ego/mind. While it may be contorted and translated, it is received, and it is this that has been progressively applied to develop the treatments and therapies throughout history. What needs to be checked is the level to which the original awareness informing the advancement is still present or whether is has been significantly contorted by ego/mind content.

Equally, we pigeonhole Consciousness and awareness-based practices and modalities as alternative, wholistic, spiritual or religious. They too need to be checked for ego/mind contortion. Additionally, they are also 'doing' exclusion. There is no alternative in Oneness, you can't have wholistic without everything, including western medicine, and certainly the segregation of religion and categorising of spirituality is separation.

This is why I keep saying to practice strengthening your muscle of observing information and its vibration and exclude nothing in your consideration of what you are choosing. Get all the information and choose for your unique presentation.

I want to acknowledge Gary Douglas, founder of Access Consciousness (Douglas, 1991), for his awareness on choice and 'Being question'. Being in allowance of his awareness expanded my own awareness and has also contributed to giving me a language to reflect my knowing.

If you are choosing to transmute some of the charge showing up for you, firstly notice where you are functioning from. Observe it. This of itself is success, as many who are asleep in the dream of the dualistic reality do not allow themselves to 'see' anything else.

If you are buying only the dualistic reality as real, even if you have awareness being input into your ego/mind, you will buy the options provided in that reality, and more specifically, the society you are 'living in', as your choices to heal. You may also depend solely on the opinions of someone outside of you as to what your problem is and whether it is something that is 'fixable'. Your attention will more likely be on what is not working. You will treat the symptoms, the condition, mostly in isolation. You may diminish yourself in the process.

Even prayer and asking at this level of functioning will be from a disempowered vibration. Most likely an energy of pleading for a change because you have already been told that change is not possible and you have bought that as absolute. This is the finite reality of the ego/mind.

More is possible. Even acknowledging that there could be more than what the ego/mind wants you to 'see' will allow knowing to begin to flow.

Knowing is Who You Are. There is no test to qualify to perceive it. It is You. As soon as you open to questioning beyond the ego/mind, allowance opens space (the experience of Consciousness with no content) for knowing to be perceived.

Observe what you are choosing, even whether you are choosing to transmute any charge, any imbalance. Receive all the information.

This is where the potency of prayer and asking can be utilised. From an empowered choice to make a change, ask that the form be changed. While we remain functioning to some degree within the dualistic reality, there may be an agenda to the asking. That is, there is an attachment to the outcome. Notice it. Notice also whether this is reflecting an unconscious belief that change is not possible. Remember that the net vibration of your asking will be reflected.

When any Being is Present, Infinite resources are accessible. Anything is possible when we Are in the formless Enlightened states, where matter and form are fluid transformations with an instant thought. We will discuss these states of Enlightenment in the next chapter. For most, even though the former could Be in an Eternal Moment, asking shows up as karmic and contextual potentialities from Infinite possibilities.

While cloaked in content that is both cognitive and unconscious (karma), asking is affected by that karma. This content also includes all the judgement and expectations about whether any asking will be created as well as context, that is, where we confine our reality by contextualising potentiality. This is the framework we adopt as real, what we deem as 'realistic'. The outcome of asking reflects back the net vibration of all the content. When we remain functioning from ego/mind creating will be within karmic and contextual potentiality from Infinite possibilities. The Universe does not have a point of view. It reflects back the asking based on the vibration, it is not personal. The more you drop the charge, the greater the potentiality and the more expansive the context, with the target being the transmutation of any form and structure, no limit to potentiality, that is, Infinite possibility and no context, that is, no relationship to anything. This is the Infinite Nature of Who You Are.

When we Be we buy out of karmic influences. This is short-lived if we toggle out of the experience of Being back to functioning from the ego/mind. Instantaneously, the vibration changes from Infinite to finite, back within the confines of an ego/mind reality. Any asking will change vibrationally to again reflect karmic content. It is what it is. There is no proving or justifying or measure of deservedness, the vibration in any moment informs what is and that will reflect back to you.

As we continue toggling between Being and functioning from the ego/mind, we increasingly maintain Presence. The vibration of functioning is higher and the scope of potentiality is vaster in direct correlation with how much charge remains.

When Being is an Isness, while karma is no longer relevant, knowing is Present and it is known whether any karma is continuing to play out. Choices may also be made to transmute the karma of others.

Being Who We Are also initially remains influenced by context. While there is any individuation/ reflection of form, there is context, thus, Being is still referenced by context, and what we are asking for is limited to contextual potentialities from Infinite possibilities to the level to which we have not dismantled context in our reality. This is Magnificently Vast relative to the ego/mind reality, yet there is so much more, it is Immeasurable. For example, a seed that has the potential to be a sunflower cannot be a dog or a table if you ask that it be so. The caterpillar wraps itself in a cocoon, and the imaginal cells develop into a butterfly, it would not create a rhinoceros if you asked. Actually, while Being, these demands would not show up because they reflect a point of view, a testing with force. While Being, the context continues to dismantle relative to relativity itself. That is, increasingly nothing needs to relate to anything, the context of matter is increasingly no longer relevant or perceived as a limitation or even form. The content clouding the reality that Light is projecting the illusion of matter into 'existence' increasingly collapses. When all context dissolves in knowing, our reality is the All/No-thing. In these formless Enlightened states even the asking illustrated above is possible as You do not need form to create form, it appears on request, there is no context. It projects by Light from Oneness, the Truth of the apparition of form. That Is All It Is.

As we awaken, there is a progressive dismantling of context no matter 'where' we are functioning from. While functioning in the dualistic reality, we expect only what is known from past experience. This relates to anything, from the expectation of how a caterpillar forms a butterfly, to the body healing, for example, from the common cold, yes, or diabetes, no, not yet. The story has conclusions as part of its identifications and accepts research as a vehicle to change. Those researching a cure for diabetes are being informed by awareness while utilising their bright minds. Depending on the degree to which knowing is being received clearly or contorted by the ego/mind will determine the outcome. The story will not notice this awareness. Mostly, it only acknowledges left brain knowledge and the application of that, even though that is not the only thing informing the research. Objectivity is not possible in a dualistic reality. The result could be no further change, new knowledge, a pill, or a new awareness of the body's capacity to switch back 'on' what has been triggered 'off' by charge and content.

The context of what is deemed possible continues expanding as we awaken. For example, in our history it was thought that if we walked far enough we would fall off the end of the world. Today, we accept the possibility of living on Mars.

As awareness is increasingly received and perceived, knowing informs the expansion of possibilities. This is not imposed. Suddenly we shift from impotent to potent. In the New World, awareness is received, and context will expand dramatically, increasingly reflecting Infinite possibilities.

Being, we perceive the energy or vibration of how something is showing up and then perceive the energy of our choosing and choose that. There is a knowing that what is asked will unfold, while also letting go, surrendering the how. This letting go occurs naturally. As choice is always reflecting a changing of form and we are not working out the how, the nature of choice is always an asking for the change of form. Even when we make a choice for something to stay the same, its matter is constantly changing and generating to reflect that sameness, thus, this too is asking for the changing of form. Cells are not real, they are a projection. The same content maintains the same projection. Change the content and we create a different projection. In the New World this will be the approach to rebalance our body/mind complexes.

Now let us notice a further dimension to asking and surrendering. It is the knowing that surrendering invites Infinite possibilities that are inconceivable to the ego/mind.

While this all seems passive, it is not. Do not misidentify not needing to work out the how with not perceiving awareness and Being or doing what contributes to your asking unfolding into form. This is active facilitation of creation. There is no personal 'I', We are One with God.

This is reflected in prayers like 'May Your Will Be done', 'Ask in the name of God'. The awareness is still Present, we have lost not only our own potency in the asking, we have forgotten that we are not separate from God. What We have an awareness to choose is God's Will. The key is awareness, not ego/mind thinking. Jesus said, 'I tell you the truth, if you had faith even as small as a mustard seed, you could say to this mountain, 'Move from here to there', and it would move. Nothing would be impossible' (Matthew 17:20 NLT)

The word 'faith' can throw us. It is not the same context as we use today. Today 'faith' is imposed belief within the dualistic reality of the ego/mind. It hits the brick wall of the ego/mind and moving mountains is not possible in that reality. Jesus is referring to knowing. We do not need to fully grasp the Unfathomable Nature of God, the Immeasurable. We do not need to know how that Magnificence orchestrates manifestation. We only need to know Who We Are and in knowing Who We Are, whatever We ask is unto us. Knowing Who We Are is available to us in every form, innate in its fabric Consciousness, even in the smallest fragment of form, as the literal mustard seed. Knowing accesses Infinity. Even a glimpse of knowing as small as a mustard seed accesses Infinity, it Is All unto You. Whichever way we look, we perceive the reflection that knowing projects: Who We Are can move mountains. When we awaken fully to Who We Are in the formless Enlightened states, in an Eternal Moment of Being, with all form and context dissolved in knowing, anything is possible, including moving mountains, if we choose.

Again, I do not want you to believe this, to have faith in this. I want you to know.

We have misidentified prayer within religious practice only, and even then, buying into the impotence and separation of praying 'to' God. When we Be, a humility arises that knows the Magnificence of God, and It includes us. Being never diminishes us. Prayer should never reflect us in a diminished capacity, rather, reflect Our Infinite capacity to 'ask and you will receive'.

'Until now you have not asked for anything in My name. Ask and you will receive, so that your joy may be complete.' (John 16:24 BSB)

Do you doubt the capacity of the body to heal a cut? No, you know. It is not a belief, you don't have faith, you know. It is unwavering despite anything outside of you. Our capacity to choose, to ask and create is also a knowing. Most do not allow themselves to know this. The ego/mind has content that cloaks this knowing and replaces it with a diminished capacity within the dualistic reality. Often any 'accepted' healing capacity is limited to those that have trained and learned to fix problems. This is such a narrow perspective. This is an example of limiting context. Our perceptions are Infinitely broader, as are the possibilities to heal and rebalance.

Let us recontextualise 'healing' in the story as a reflection of Our Potent and Infinite capacities rather than a diminished self in fear because of what is going wrong with us.

Let us step into the bigger picture of Our Life not just this incarnation. Perceive this incarnation as the Isness of Our Life in this moment. There is no away. We Are.

Now notice if there is some form you choose to show up in a different form. Let's make this an exercise.

Exercise Eight

Observe the energy and vibration of how something is currently showing up and then observe how you are choosing it to show up. Write, draw or document this choice in your journal, capturing the vibration of the change in form you are asking for. Again, observe it like a case study rather than 'going down the rabbit hole' of judgement. That is a different vibration altogether and that is what will be reflected back to you.

Be willing to receive all the information, be as detailed and inclusive as you can. Be willing to receive everything, no exceptions, no exclusions including 'the good, the bad and the ugly' as labelled by your ego/mind.

I say to receive everything because often we cut off noticing information because we automatically go into judgement of ourselves that it should have been different or that we should have done it better, etc. In protecting ourselves from our own judgement we don't allow ourselves to receive the information. Judgement is detrimental to the form changing to reflect our cognitive asking. It can perpetuate the same form showing up rather than allowing transformation. If you are willing to look at everything, without judgement of you, you have freed yourself from the identifications locking that form in place. You have risen above the form. This is a kindness for you that is known in Being.

As part of this information you are receiving, notice also whether you have made the choice to change the form or whether you are observing the choice. The vibration of each is totally different. Fear is often present when we observe a potential choice. Do not be afraid. You are only making a choice. You are not doing anything else in this moment and you certainly don't need to worry about how the choice will come to Be. Often our fear that something is not possible stops us from choosing. We have already decided it is not possible. This is content of the ego/mind and is reflected in what is created as the Universe has no point of view, it will project the net vibration of your asking. Fear is another filter to your awareness. The ego/mind uses fear to keep you contained in its prison. It is a lie of the ego/mind to keep you impotent, unless you are in physical danger and then it is knowing (triggering fight/flight) and a totally different type of fear. The acronym is really true: ;False Evidence Appearing Real'. The ego/mind wants you to stay within its confines. It will even turn excitement into fear, and you will feel like something is blocking you. No, it is the ego/mind stopping you from creating, from changing status quo. Free yourself and the brick wall of your prison dissolves in a Divine Love for and as You.

If you are not willing in this moment to step into making a choice that you would like to make, that is the choice you are making. Rather than continuing to observe the choice from afar (a definite separation and diminishment of you), choose to not choose it in this moment. Recognise the potency of that. Recognise your choice as not making that choice in this moment. You choose for you. This does not diminish you. Document in your journal, in whichever way you choose, any awareness you perceive in relation to this. For me, success is making the process more conscious. I often say 'let's put everything on the table and look at it all with eyes wide open'. No secrets from yourself. That is freedom. That is also the vulnerability of Being. Be willing to be vulnerable and charge does not generate.

For any choice you are making, if you would like to articulate your choice in a prayer, do so. Utilise the potency of 'Amen' or 'Aum' or the vibration that Is.

Take a moment now to reflect on the Isness of form. Creation is the reflecting back of choices, whether conscious or unconscious. In this moment it Is. There is no linearity even though that is how we may receive it in the mind. I remember Richard Bartlett, founder of Matrix Energetics (Dr. Richard Bartlett D.C., 1992), saying 'It is what it is until it isn't'. I want you to know that you can take the reins of Your Life and It can Be what you choose. Do not go passively, be vigilant; notice the choices you make in every moment. Continue to make the choices you are making in every moment. It will feel like stepping into the energy of the choice and in each moment you make the same choice anew. You will vibrate as your choice. This active vigilance and choosing is itself of a high vibration and of itself transmutes charge, it is very potent.

As you vibrate as your choice, what you are noticing, what you are being vigilant of, is the Being and/or doing required in this moment to facilitate the unfolding of your asking. 'Is there anything to Be or do now?' 'Now?' 'Now?' It is only ever in this moment. This is how the unfolding of your asking works. God's got it. You will perceive any Being or doing required of you, the aspect of Divinity You Are. 'Keep your lamps burning' (Luke 12:35 NIV) otherwise you will not perceive the information. This is what is required. Otherwise the diminishment of you, the stepping back, the separation, shows up again as you 'leave it to God'. That doesn't work. It changes the vibration and that vibration will be reflected back to you in what is created.

Keep space in your journal to record awareness you receive and perceive in relation to your asking. This is any Being or doing. Record the content of any doing informed by awareness. Capture the vibration or energy of any Being as much as you can. You may ask here: 'How do I know if it is awareness or my ego/mind?' I have been asked this many times.

Awareness arises instantaneously, that first piece of information. There is no mental processing. It may not all be funnelled down to be cognitive, it is a knowing. Also, awareness has no point of view or charge. It is information perceived. If there is any charge or you have an opinion, position, attachment, ownership or point of view about that piece of information, it is not awareness or is no longer awareness (contorted by the ego/mind making it personal to your perspective). As you continue to practice observing the receiving and perceiving of information, the vibration of form/no form, including the reality you are functioning from (non-dualistic or dualistic reality), you will strengthen your muscle to know for yourself. I don't want you to have to go and see someone else to perceive awareness for you. That may be useful in the short-term as a crutch, but that is all. I want you to perceive clearly your awareness, as no one will ever Be like You and Oneness awaits you Being You.

If you Be and/or do based on what you authentically receive and perceive as awareness, and it did not work for you, notice the information, receive it all, allow it to contribute to your knowing. Be kind to you. Do not stop, keep noticing. Notice if you made any assumptions on that information, for example, the context of the information or the outcome, whether you processed it in any way through the ego/mind, whether you second guessed your knowing, or whether you were attached to what you perceived as the outcome of the awareness. Sometimes awareness presents in a visual to provide a bundle of information. It is tempting to become attached to that visual as a literal outcome. Awareness is not about clairvoyance, which is another skill altogether, it is always about more of You showing up.

A common practice is to receive awareness and then immediately relate it, reference it within the ego/mind. Until we are Being and using the mind as a tool, our ego/minds take charge and create charge with the input. Practice noticing if this occurs. Retrieve the information as it was before creating a charge with it, before making it significant.

The more you practice, the more you hone your capacity to differentiate knowing from thinking, and the more potently You Be.

Record in your journal what awareness you do act on and/or Be. Record any changes in form, any additional awareness and remain vigilant, while also being caring to you. You are an integral part of creation. Know it. Record what you are creating.

We are using one choice in this exercise. We are making multiple choices in every moment. There is no need to hold those choices, including responsibilities which in the story we have a tendency to carry on our shoulders. We vibrate as the choices we make. In the moment, perceive awareness relating to the unfolding of any choice and potently choose any action or Being. This is not overwhelming, unlike the intensity of charge within the ego/mind. We are Infinite and have Infinite capacities and capacity. One piece of awareness can inform you of which choice(s) it is facilitating, when, where, its interaction with others, other things, events, other Being and doing. This is all within the Eternal Moment of perceiving awareness in no time/space. You may not funnel all this information down to be totally cognitive, yet you know.

Now I ask that you go back to everything that you have recorded, drawn, written in your journal for this exercise and surrender it all to God, allow it all to flow beyond into Infinity. In every moment, let go your choices to change form, there is no need to hold it and do not hold it, let it go while still vibrating your choice. Let go everything you have reflected including the choice to not choose something you would like to choose, if that showed up for you. Choose in every moment and surrender it in every moment, surrender it into Oneness of which you are not separate. Do not diminish you in this process. This is not the vibration of praying 'to' God. This is not a handing over and delegating 'to' God. That is separation. Continue to vibrate as your choices. Be the Oneness You Are, Be beyond the ego/mind to the Infinity You Are.

Let go your asking into The Isness which is God, like a wave folding back into the Ocean. It is This Isness (both Manifested and Unmanifested) that unfolds the how, that unfolds the Inconceivably

Vast Innumerable interactions of Consciousness in form and No-Thingness accessed to create your asking. It requires no force, projecting with total ease within the vehicle called Light. When all context is collapsed, it is instantaneously form in no time/space.

Surrendering choice is innate in Being. It reflects the knowing of Oneness, of no separation. David Hawkins spoke of this practice of surrendering everything to God as it arises (Hawkins, 2003). Even as a Right Action, this practice reminds us of the Vastness beyond the ego/mind. In Access Consciousness, Gary Douglas speaks of Being question (Douglas, 1991). This is the same as surrendering. This is the same as the bowing of our heads or prostrating when praying. What we are 'doing' is a Right Action of mimicking not having all the answers to work out 'how' to create our choice. We are bypassing both the conscious and unconscious content of the ego/mind that thinks it has all the answers. When we Be, surrender is a Nature. We innately know that We do not hold the asking. We let it go into Oneness and await vigilantly for awareness informing our unique contribution (any Being and/or doing) that is required to unfold our asking.

How can the limited capacity of the ego/mind compare to the Synchronised Magnificence of All/No-Thing interacting to create your asking? You are a part of that Magnificence. If You ask, It Is reflected to You because You asked. You will receive the awareness of any Being and/or doing required of you to facilitate the creation of your asking.

When we think we have the answers, it is always from the ego/mind. In Being, we know there is no such thing as a finite answer to anything. We remain open and invite Infinite possibilities.

Step out of the dualistic reality, into Your Magnificence. Choose and surrender it all to God. Be One with This. Now what do you perceive? Do you notice how integral you are to creation? Does this change what you are choosing? What will you choose now?

Note to Practitioners

I am specifically addressing practitioners in this section because I very often see a diminishment of self with practitioners, particularly in the alternative therapies arena. Feel free, however, to allow this discussion to inform any action chosen consciously or unconsciously.

The story at the macro level does not commonly receive practitioners that do not meet the identifications within the story, and what often presents is a perpetual need of the ego/mind to prove its worth. This, together with the misidentification of being of service and the Right Action of humility, shows up as a need to give all of yourself to the client to 'help them'.

If there is any level of diminishment of you, if you are giving 'all of you' to your client, if you are taking on their issues and problems because you want to prove you can make a difference, the ego/mind is in charge. The ego/mind references the lack of acceptance of you within society, the lack of meeting benchmarks. It does not know Who You Are.

Being never diminishes you as it is known that you can only Be You and that is the gift to the one before you. A diminishment of you in any form to facilitate another is not awareness, it is an ego/mind 'trying' to create identifications of significance, position and importance or acceptance and acknowledgement of healing capacity or trying to mimic selflessness and humility which are often recommended behaviours.

Such recommended behaviours may be from religious and spiritual teachings but if they create ego/mind selflessness and humility such behaviours will generate more ego/mind charge rather than transmuting it. The target is to transmute the personal 'I' and Be You. Such recommended behaviours often dismiss Being You, 'making' you unimportant, and you energetically become invisible. This is not the target.

When we prostrate 'in front' of God, while this may seem selfless and subservient, it is not. When chosen from Being, it is a potent, conscious and empowering choice to Be open to All that Is and 'lay bare' all identifications. Be clear of the difference between crutches adopted to try to mimic Being and actual Being (or even Right Actions). One is imposed, the other Is Who You Are.

When we adopt ego/mind points of view, particularly if adopted as a long-term practice, practitioners can present within varying ranges of duality from ego/mind empowerment to feeling everything in their own bodies and welcoming that as facilitating change to 'being a doormat'. These all contribute to illness showing up for practitioners. As well as being in the effect of the diminishment, the outcome of any facilitation will be lower in vibration.

Fundamentally, it is mimicking what the ego/mind is informing you that 'being a practitioner' looks like in the story, thinking it will facilitate being received as a practitioner at all levels.

Oneness is experienced in a communion with All that Is and that includes You.

Being with a client has no point of view relating to the outcome. Often, I am just as surprised as the client as to what unfolds within a session. How do I know the awareness until it arises? I do not know what words will come out of my mouth until they do. There is no thought processing, only awareness.

When we Be with clients, it as an interaction of Consciousness, where the laser beam of awareness interacts with the client's Consciousness in the non-separation of Oneness. We are bringing attention to this interaction point in Oneness in this moment. Awareness arises unique to this interaction. It is always about more of Who They Are Being in the world and existence. Functioning from Being invites Infinite possibilities. If we are not Being, rather, functioning from the ego/mind, the interaction is more broad-brushed but do not buy as real any diminishment of you. Practice the Right Action of choosing more of Who They Are showing up.

There is no need to anticipate or hypothesise what may be needed. Set up for the session as required, be in the moment of setting up, then let it go, Be. You will access your minds tools as required. You will access Infinity too! It is Delightful, Joyful and You facilitate in Oneness, not in the finiteness of your body/mind complex.

This is when we truly Be Who We Are, facilitating All to return Home. The content of the session may not reflect anything that sounds like this. It may relate to health, relationships or family, it may be mending an injury or dispensing a treatment or putting hands on in any capacity. Any transmutation at a higher vibration is facilitating Being, no matter the language or practice adopted. A smile alone can change someone's life. An open heart, and beyond, a Soul Being with someone, changes forever the vibration of content carried by another. Never forget the simplicity of Infinite resources available to and for all.

Expectations of the client, including codes of conduct within the story, remain relevant at the level of story. Awareness knows and embraces it all. All is addressed as you surrender to awareness.

Functioning from Being is also true caring, not only for clients but for you. When we function from the ego/mind, this is a Right Action which we adopt for clients but often not for ourselves.

The vibration of true caring projects a beautiful allowance and honouring of what is.

Awareness is received and perceived about the situation or client and true caring arises naturally with no point of view or attachment to the outcome. For some, it may be facilitating the transition from a current incarnation. Being knows any caring requirements within the story and awareness informs what will arise as true caring. The vibration is very high. This innately Presents in the interaction of Consciousness with a client.

While functioning from the ego/mind, be willing to receive the true caring and nurturing of you both when you are working with clients and when away from clients. This includes the non-diminishment of you referred to above. It may also include boundaries in how you function as a practitioner, the setup of your work space, the seeking out of facilitation yourself, gathering and debriefing with colleagues, and allowing space in your environment. In essence, you could create your own Kit Bag for the true caring of you. A Kit Bag that resonates like You would innately be true caring for you.

Exercise Nine

Here is a quick and nurturing exercise that invites the true caring of you.

Sit comfortably yet still alert on a chair and ask that all the content that you have taken on from a client, or anyone else, be released and let go from your body. There is no need to hold it. Surrender it into Oneness.

Know that God has your back and their back. God has all our backs. You don't need to hold anything before, during or after a session or take on anything for anyone else. You do not need to force an outcome or prove your worth.

The gift You are is Your Presence. Being You in the world changes matter, and the world will never be the same. Thank you.

Repeat this practice over and over until it is innate in you and you Be it. Allow it to inform your knowing. You are a facilitator of creation. Let go the trying that is unsustainable and Be You.

Seven

LET GO AND LET GOD

I WISH TO ACKNOWLEDGE THE wisdom and teachings of Paramahansa Yogananda. His Love and relentless quest for all of us to return Home, awakened my knowing. Seeking stopped and much yearning dissipated into a Divine Love beyond measure.

I let go and let God and realised that all the effort and journeying towards 'some thing' concealed Who I Was. God had my back and 'was' my back.

When you awaken enough to know even a glimpse of this, You will perceive your knowing. You will let go the holding, the needing, the search and Radiate Your Divinity and know You are not separate. When you no longer look for the answers in the finite dualistic reality and open yourself to Infinity, the Magnificence begins to Shine from and as Who You Are.

Surrendering to This is more truly Being Home. I use an analogy of the puppy who wandered off from Mother, exploring the world and thinking that existence is the finite world it experiences, then finds Home when again in Her Embrace, receiving warmth, love and nurturing. The sigh of relief comes from the letting go. You do not have to wait to Be at the Mother's Bosom to let go, let go now, there is no away, and the relief of Home will Be Yours, You will 'see'

Mother and know. Stop trying and surrender to a Love so Divine that You will feel like You could burst.

This is the freedom you are seeking. This is what you are yearning. There is no need to hold anything. There isn't anything else.

I have heard it said that a future You, the Enlightened You is leading you to Enlightenment. This is truth but maybe not the way you think. The fully Enlightened You is no longer a 'You', You are Home in Oneness and beyond Oneness, remerged as the Unmanifested. There is no 'you' (the first stage of Enlightenment) and there is no 'You' (the final stage of Enlightenment). It is the All/No-thing that is guiding you, from which you are not separate, you have never been separate. So, it is everything that Is and everything that Isn't that is guiding you Home. There are no separate parts. It knows It is incomplete without you. It lacks without you. That Is Who You Are. All that is lacking is you knowing This.

Enlightened Ones return to reflect this knowing. This is why they, the great prophets, angels and even deity take form, this is why nature Is. This is how Oneness reveals Itself in form. Look around you, everything that Is and 'everything' that Isn't exists for you to know this. Open your eyes, open all the senses, open to awareness, to the vibration of Being and you will know that everything Is for you to know Who You Are.

Who You Are always Is, whether in form (existence, including incarnations) or non-form (non-existence). This Is, no need for a future anything. There is no evolving, only transmuting what cloaks you from knowing this, from allowing You to Be.

Enlightenment, therefore, refers to the degree to which the cloak has been transmuted. When the ego/mind 'flat-lines', what David Hawkins calls the only true death (Hawkins, 2003), there is no longer a 'you', and when even the individuation of the Soul returns to the Source of its projection, 'You' remerge in and as the All/No-thing.

The significance of all our cloaks, our Michelin Man suits, is what does not give us access to know Who We Are. You Are more Radiant than the sun, more Magnificent than the most beautiful sights that nature reflects back to you. The reflection of Who We Are is free. We buy the stuff manufactured to mimic this, we try to own it, we try to find the most obscure, the most precious. It is all misidentification of our true yearning, thinking that what we grasp defines who we are. This pales in the Glow of Divinity, of Who We Are.

Awakening from the dream of the dualistic reality occurs in an Eternal Moment. 'Before' this Moment, awakening unfolds progressively as we continue to transmute what remains cloaking us from Who We Are. This is the toggling between dualistic and non-dualistic realities, from Being and functioning from the ego/mind. Eventually, for everyone, there is an Eternal Moment when all the karma that cloaks You is no more.

For most the progressive unfoldment commences when we begin to realise that the ego/mind does not have all the answers. We drop the need to be right or wrong, and this is replaced with allowance of all positions and points of view. This is the letting go and letting God before awakening. This is opening yourself to Infinity, not just the finiteness of the ego/mind. You create space, allowing awareness to be received and perceived without contortion. You will increasingly Be in the Joy and Love of All That Is. When interacting with others, You will receive and perceive beyond the cloak worn and experience the Radiance of their Souls. You will increasingly commune with your body and Be with the non-separation of Oneness.

As we continue allowing Consciousness to Be, while we continue toggling between Being and functioning from the ego/mind, an increasing degree of Presence is maintained as an Isness. This expands the more we choose to transmute the karma that cloaks Who We Are. Despite the ego/mind still having charge, awareness is being received and is not resisted or contorted. It may still retrieve content, yet we are able to distinguish thoughts from awareness. This is why practicing to build the muscle of observation, noticing vibration and reassuring the ego/mind, facilitates our awakening. Notice however, that often when we get close to dropping the charge of the ego/mind, the ego/mind comes out in full force. It behaves like a cornered animal, fighting to maintain its position as 'captain of the ship'. We are seeing this at the macro level at the moment. Do not be distracted by this. Continue to be kind and caring to you. You are awakening beyond its confines. No matter how the awakening unfolds, when more is chosen, space, the experience of Consciousness, invites Who You Are to Be.

In an Eternal Moment, when this experience of Being shows up fully as an Isness, death of the ego/mind occurs. Do not look back, hold God in your 'sights', let go and let God. You are not alone, You are in God's embrace and 'you' are no longer. What you thought was your life is no more as You experience the collapse of the veil, an 'exploding out in all directions' experiencing Infinite Life. This is the first stage of Enlightenment.

You may choose to remain in the world or not, either way, You have no position or point of view. Your Will is God's Will, the non-separation Is. If You choose to Be in the world, You are free of identifications. You may continue to utilise identifications for functional purposes or not. The distinction is the no attachment to or significance on identifications. For example, You may be addressed by your name and continue to utilise that name to facilitate communication with others. You may continue to purchase and wear clothing, yet one piece of clothing is no more significant than another. You are not influenced by expectations in the story. You choose in the moment, informed by awareness.

You Present as Your Essential Nature, the Unique aspect of Divinity that is You. Your Spirit Radiates. The cloak that hid Your Light has been transmuted. Resistance is no more as You allow Life to Be.

You reflect humility, love, joy, vulnerability, authenticity, intimacy, beauty, honouring: Presence. It is known as the reflection of God, there is no personal 'I'.

Purpose is known singularly for all to know Who They Are and return Home. This reflects another Nature that shows up, devotion to God.

While devotion to God is very often a recommended behaviour that is also a Right Action, it arises naturally and with deep surrender as an Isness when awakened to Who You Are.

When you know that Everything 'Is' to Return Home, this Be Comes your singular focus. In a very literal sense, you are devoted to this purpose. It arises naturally and is experienced with a great ease in Oneness. It is not imposed or separate like the Right Action of devotion to God. It Is like everything You Be and do is for God and Is God, the aspect of Divinity You Are.

The vibration of Your devotion to God creates a letting go and letting God that Presents as an Inconceivably Beautiful Nurtured Release within Oneness. No further 'death' is possible and You will now forever experience Being in God's embrace whether in form/no form, existence/non-existence.

While this is inconceivable to even the mind, let go and let God, receive what I say and allow knowing to arise rather than logic. This Is the relief of Home, You Are to Be and/or do God's Will as 'you' are no more. Your Will is simultaneously God's Will. Your awareness Is the Expression of Divine Will and You facilitate that creation.

The veil is lifted and You 'see' God in and as everything, and this is perceived in a vibration of Absolute Divine Love. It is known that All are to Return Home, and every Being and doing facilitates this, whether You are incarnate or not. Every thought, every action, every idea, every Being, every Breath is for all to know. As You are no longer separate, You feel the same pang in your heart and Soul as God when You look around You and others are not Home.

In the story, both at the micro and macro level, we see examples often of people justifying behaviour in the name of God or declaring actions as reflecting the Will of God. I am not here to judge right or wrong, I am saying, check the clues. The Will of God will only ever show up as a Divine Love for all with a singular purpose of Oneness. The content may be specific to the identifications and story presenting, yet reflecting back to Its simplicity and Its vibration, it is always about coming back to God for all. If there is any position, significance, exclusion, judgement, vested interest, attachment to the outcome, right or wrong, it is not God's Will, it is an ego/mind justifying its will by labelling it God's Will.

If we notice the vibration of the action, this will give you the information. If the vibration of the action is anything other than a Divine Love for and as All, then it is not God's Will. Information about the vibration is useful as we can avoid any judgement or position on the content of the behaviour. For example, a behaviour in one culture may be deemed inappropriate in another. The vibration of the behaviour will inform you more truly than noticing content that may be clouded and contorted by ego/mind position and point of view.

When Enlightened, it is known that all roads lead to God. There is no away. Being in Oneness with God, You perceive the awareness that Presents and choose to Be and/or do from awareness in any moment. No expectation, no past reference points, no right or wrong, total ease, excluding no-thing and no one, knowing We Are All One. The Right Actions and recommended behaviours that may have facilitated awakening are not required. They may arise in awareness to Be and/or do in any moment, now reflecting Your Essential Nature.

Everything is experienced as connected. You perceive the Divinity within all things, with a capacity to 'look' past the cloak and know Who Is before You. The Beauty is Immense. Even what may be judged as trivial and mundane, like the action of spreading peanut butter on toast, can Be experienced as an Exquisiteness of Divinity within Oneness that Is.

Functioning from this non-dualistic reality as Who You Are remains with some context. You Are the individuation of Oneness projected as Your Soul, experienced as an Isness of such Divine Love and Joy.

The form of any individuation, by definition, has context. Awareness arises within the context. Any asking reflects the vibration of remaining context, thus, creating is within the scope of contextual potentialities from Infinite possibilities. While this has limitation, its Vastness is beyond measure. Let me illustrate with a comparative example. The scope of asking from the ego/mind is like a grain of sand that needs to be manufactured. The scope of asking by the Soul is like a million trillion grains of sand that will unfold as You asked in Divine Synchronicity with the Universe/Oneness working out the how. The scope of asking when there is no individuation (the final stage of Enlightenment) is like the apparition in form of any amount of sand at Will with a mere 'thought'/attention, a fleeting Reflection of attention. No unfolding required. The context of form is no more, the illusion of form is lifted, everything is a projection of Light.

While we Be the aspect of Divinity we Be, whether incarnate or not, whatever realm or reality we frequent, there is no position. There is no judgement that asking is limited to contextual potentialities from Infinite possibilities. It is an Isness. The letting go and letting God unfolds as Life. The laser beam focus to choose from awareness is a Nature, knowing that All Is as It Is. The singular focus is for all to Be Home.

As we continue to awaken, we continue to transmute even context. Similar to the increasing degree of Presence while still functioning from the ego/mind, there is an increasing collapse of context in and as Your Life. We continue to awaken beyond form and the knowing that all form is an illusion, a projection of Light reflecting content, increasingly Be Comes an Isness.

The potency and scope of creation increases as context increasingly transmutes. There have been examples throughout history of those who have awakened to Who They Are and incarnated to show us Who We Are. They have illustrated varying capacities including capacities to eat poison with no ill effect, not eating food and living off the Breath, stigmata, and other physical feats such as coming back into a body after 'death', and a body remaining in state after 'death' (Rinpoche, 1992) (Yogananda, 2016). The context of our physical body and its limitations are bypassed in Divinity. The purpose remains the same, to show us Who We Are.

In the past such Beings maintained secrecy and isolation. As the New World expands this will no longer be necessary. We will embrace and value awakening rather than the gaining of identifications. We will invite those awakened to share openly what they know. For those sharing, it is never personal, always to facilitate all to realise Who They Are.

As this all unfolds, the scope of context even within the dualistic reality will broaden significantly. The narrow identifications of the old dualistic reality will seem so confined.

Eventually for all, even the context of existence dissolves. This is with Pure and Infinite Devotion to God, the Ultimate surrendering to God. Not only giving Your Life to God, You let go Your existence to God. The individuated Soul is no more, You have returned to the Infinite Diamond Infinitely Radiating and You remerge in the All/Nothing. This is beyond words. The All/Nothing is Unfathomable and Inconceivable. It Is truly 'where' Nothing is lacking and All is unto 'You'. This is the Supreme Freedom of God. Nothing matters or is matter, it doesn't matter, yet can Be matter with an instant attention to Be matter. Creation is within Infinite Possibilities. This is Our Origin, this is from where Home Itself is projected utilising the vibration of Aum.

Those fully awakened, the prophets and saints who originated our religions are no longer individuated. The form is no more, remerged in Oneness and beyond as the All/Nothing. We maintain conflict and division in the dualistic reality even with the one identification of religion, yet, the Sources of those religions are merged in Divinity.

The All/Nothing is the One Source, the Unmanifested God. If you call on 'those' awakened to facilitate you, form is reprojected from this One Source into a form recognised by you. It will be a form within the context of your reality, what is meaningful to you. Any level of form may be reprojected, for example, rematerialisation, visions, being perceived through awareness, creating thought and emotions, reflecting in nature, through another human being. They may literally glow in the Light of Divinity, reprojecting within form from the Infinite Diamond of Manifested God. This is the resurrection of Jesus and others that return after 'death' to show us Who We Are. This is not a fable, this is literally Who We Are. Resurrection or, if that word label has too much charge for you, rematerialisation, relocation, being in multiple places, Omnipresence, are how Enlightened

Ones Present not separate from God when called upon. 'They' will continue to return. The job is not done.

This Is. This Is Who You Are. What you are collapsing is what hides This from you. Behind the veil you think is who you are Is This. It is the cloak you are shedding, that is all.

Chapter

Eight

DEATH OR IS IT?

THE DREAM OF THE dualistic reality places most of the significance of life, and the definition of what life is, on what happens to you between your birth and your death. In this reality, who you are begins to be defined at birth, starting with when and where you are born and the family you are born into. Who you are continues to be defined as what you do between then and the time you die.

The clock is ticking as you need to accomplish your dreams, your bucket list, and create your legacy. You need to leave some lasting impression of who you are, or rather, who you were. If you can't do it for yourself, others may try and do it for you. It is deemed that you end when you die. Anything else beyond this, most likely, is still a belief, another imposed point of view.

The focus is on the doing, which creates identification. This is insatiable and will never be enough. If you attain something, it needs to be maintained for fear of losing identity or, position.

The force required to maintain being forever famous, forever young, leaving a forever legacy, forever belonging, forever grieving and forever known is exhausting.

This is such an unkindness to us all.

It will only take a couple of generations before all this content is forgotten in the world. The grave-sites will not be visited; the names will not be recognised.

If you choose to reincarnate, you may not even remember you, you are a different you but not a different You.

The dualistic reality misidentifies the yearning of Home as gaining identifications which are familiar. You will never Be the costume You are wearing, the play You are acting in, or even the theatre company You are with.

The purpose of an incarnation is to know Who You Are that is wearing the costume.

Do you even remember all the names you have been, all the stories you have been in? You have been famous, infamous, rich, poor, hungry, male, female, you died a child, died old. These are the stages of your incarnations, they are not Who You Are.

Let go of the race between birth and death. This is not Your Life, this is one incarnation.

Even if you are not cognitive of it, it is with great celebration in Oneness that You incarnated into your current body/mind complex. How awesome to experience You animating a physical body? That alone is a gift to us all. Your birth is known in Oneness to Be an Expression of Divinity, not just your birthday.

As you grow and expand in the world, what if there is nothing you need to do? Would that ease you? Take the pressure off. Your awareness can inform your choices rather than the frantic right or wrong race of imposed and fixed points of view and judgement, often contradictory, depending on where you find yourself.

What if, even for those that incarnate for a short time, we receive and perceive the Eternal Moments of Being that are not recognised in the dualistic reality? What if, rather than needing to be remembered in the story, we receive the Beauty and Magnificence of Presence in each and every moment as a contribution to All? What if that contribution does not stop? What if, rather than holding on to the past, we allow our loved ones to contribute to what we choose to create?

If we 'look' past the cloak, we are all Radiant. Our legacy is our contribution to the expansion of Consciousness on the planet and within existence. Our legacy is the contribution of Our Whole Life, not the content of one incarnation. You are much more Infinite than one incarnation. Your contribution continues beyond an incarnation.

This Is. This is innately what we are Being and doing.

Do not use the measures of the dualistic reality. Know beyond the density of judgement, You Are an invaluable contribution to awakening Consciousness in the world and in existence.

How does this look?

It is with simplicity. Instead of trying so hard to be noticed, it is the simplicity and warmth you feel deep inside when you Be and/or do random acts of kindness; when you rush to someone's aid without needing to; when you pick up rubbish without needing to; when we all drop our identifications after a tragic event and help in whichever way we can.

These are the glimpses of Who We Are. This is glimpsing Oneness. If this feeling in your heart is a glimpse, imagine that times Infinity: That Is Who You Are.

It is these contributions of Being You and doing from Being You that changes the planet and existence, that expand Consciousness and awakens all. Nothing goes unnoticed, even a kind thought not expressed is noticed. It is not which brand of handbag or which car or how much money. These are distractions, however, even these, gifted from the heart can be a contribution. It is not the 'getting' but the open and unconditional gifting that is the contribution. Why 'get' one by one fuelled by force when in gifting you receive It All, now that is Power. Opening your heart is the gateway to the Soul, glimpsing Who You Are and there is no turning back.

Everything is noticed and nothing is forgotten. You are never forgotten. Oneness lacks without You and Oneness awaits the Expression of You within Consciousness. This you have misidentified in the story, as if the greatest fear is being forgotten or that you never existed. This can never happen. You are inseparable from

Oneness, and even when You 'remerge' with the All/Nothing there is a Completeness because of You.

The finite will never last and will always take great effort and force to sustain and maintain. The Infinite takes no effort, it Is Your Essential Nature.

The Soul will choose when this lifetime is to be transitioned from. The contraction of this lifetime begins. In the Oneness that Is, all is considered in this choosing, including knowing in no time/space.

When we transition from an incarnation, it is not the end. You don't even miss a beat. Your Life continues, reflecting Divinity continues, there is no away. You have dropped your physical body and this too will transform within Oneness.

The glory of this transition is often not recognised in the story. There is awareness remaining in some of the rituals and rites of passage undertaken within the story. I have observed that often this awareness is adopted as belief and a hope that it is true. If we only knew the truth, it would free us from a lot of the grief. If we could only perceive the wealth of 'goings on' prior to and during transitions, then the story would have no hesitation in acknowledging that the end of an incarnation is not the end of life.

No matter whether a transition period is long or not at all, that is, a sudden and unexpected passing, the Soul is always in charge. This may not be cognitive.

When the choice is made, the vibration of the reality within which that Soul is functioning changes. Mostly, it rises higher and the veil of this reality begins to lift. The person transitioning and immediate family members may also experience the lifting of the veil between realms and receive and perceive information relating to the transition. Those who can perceive the information, will be able to notice information of any 'action' required of them (if any) to facilitate the transition. They may also receive information on who is waiting for the person passing. Often 'action' means merely bringing your attention to what is required and in these vibrations of no time/space, it is done.

I have found that noticing this information and facilitating transitions is not only an honour, it eases the grief when you can 'see' where the Soul is transitioning to and all those waiting expectantly for the transition to occur.

I have seen mums, dads, grandparents, siblings, pets, angels and Divine Glows (almost formless) waiting. I have called on long lost brothers and others, if immediate family was not available. I have seen them cross back into our reality, being in the room with them as they prepare to transition. I have recently seen a determined and loving mother cross into this reality, rolling up her sleeves, ready to work, with an attitude 'Leave this to me, this is my son, I know what to do'. I have seen a bunch of siblings turn up, chatting away, it wasn't possible to get a word in.

Close to the moment of 'death' the veil between the worlds is lifted. The person passing will converse openly with loved ones. Know that they will be in and out of the physical body. They will function both in this reality and beyond, similar to when incarnating. This can occur from a few days before passing or even longer for others.

Also, know that the Soul will choose whether they prefer to pass on their own or if they are happy for loved ones to be around. They are often out-of-body and know the conversations. They know if someone is coming, they may not pass until they say goodbye. They may communicate with loved ones to come, planting a thought in their minds that is received 'out of the blue'. They may also communicate their feelings to them. If they don't want anyone present, they will not pass and may wait until you leave or go to the bathroom. I know of one instance when the Soul was so keen to pass but wanted to be alone. When his loved one said goodbye to go home for the night, the Soul passed when she walked out the door. She felt regret for not staying longer, however, he would not have passed. He would have felt relief, 'Oh, I'm alone, great, all done, time to go'.

When there is a hesitation in passing over, that is, there is a lack of peace with the transition even when it seems imminent, following your awareness to perceive any Being and/or doing can be a huge contribution to the process. For example, they may need closure on something, asking for forgiveness, they may need to be acknowledged or to acknowledge you (even if energetically as they may not be able to speak), they may need to be alone, they may need you to ask for someone over the other side to step forward or they may simply need reassurance that everything is OK and it is OK for them to go.

One thing I know that will facilitate transition is to give permission for the one before you to leave. Let them go and let God. What a gift to our loved ones to 'let them go', more identifications dissolved in pure love.

Immediately after passing a period of reflection begins. They will visit those they love and places familiar in the incarnation. The rituals of funerals and even prayer after 40 days are examples of some of the awareness still informing our stories. Crossing over, if it is successful, will occur during or at the end of this period. It may also occur immediately on passing. Letting them go allows that transition. Any holding on can lock in an attachment. When they do transition, know that they continue to Be with you. After a period of healing and adjustment to their new environment, they can facilitate what is happening for you, if they choose.

Increasingly, we will perceive this information and Be in allowance of the glory that truly unfolds in our transition. It really is Magnificent. Yes, we will miss their physical presence, however, in letting them go, we will experience an honouring most profound for our contribution to a glorious event within Their Life.

So, where do we go? Where do we transition to?

There isn't another place. Everything is Oneness. We transition to a different vibration. Innately we know and often look up when reflecting on a loved one. It is not another place 'up there in heaven', it is a higher vibration, so we look up to glimpse it. This is a knowing, which our ego/minds misidentify as another place.

When we pass, if karma is still cloaking us, this will contribute to the net vibration and, hence, where we will now function from. We 'go' to a reality that matches our net vibration.

I perceive four fundamental realms, each with varying vibrational resonances, like a bandwidth of vibration.

We could be in a particular fundamental realm and function at a relatively higher vibration. It is not dissimilar to this reality where we are all functioning from varying vibrational frequencies. Some people are functioning at very dense frequencies, while others may be Radiating Light.

Additionally, wherever you frequent, you may still be functioning from a dualistic reality. While you continue to buy into polarity, reflecting the content of any karma, you will continue to function within a dualistic reality, even without a body. Like I said, we don't miss a beat. The target of transmuting karma and knowing Who You Are remains.

The four realms I perceive are:

☐ Crossed over and in a realm almost formless;

☐ Crossed over and in a realm of more form;

☐ Not successfully crossed over and in a realm of confusion and doubt; and

☐ Not successfully crossed over and in a realm attached to the incarnation.

There is a clear process of crossing over and transitioning successfully or not. When I perceive information about someone who has passed, one of the first pieces of information is whether they have successfully crossed over. This is a relief and facilitates an ease for the Soul. Crossing over is transitioning out of this reality and an incarnation, you are no longer functioning in this reality. Crossing over allows a greater freedom of non-attachment and possibility to heal and further transmute karma, and it is astoundingly beautiful too!

Let me describe them in reverse order.

Not successfully crossed over and in a realm attached to the incarnation

The fourth realm is very close to the form of this reality. It is a dualistic reality, with Souls heavily cloaked in form by identifications from their incarnation. When someone passes, if there remains any unfinished business or an injustice, they can remain attached to this reality. This occurs with war and atrocities. This can occur if someone has been murdered and the case is unresolved or injustice remains; if a partner dies and feeling inseparable, stays with their 'other half' in this reality. This can occur if family do not let loved ones go and at their passing literally pull them back or hold on to them, desperately wanting them to stay. The Soul sees it all and in confusion stays only to be locked into the incarnation.

These are the Souls that may be noticed in old buildings or in their previous homes, in the jails or hospitals where they were at the time of passing. They may be attached to land where previous battles, atrocities, homes or buildings or other injustices took place. While new buildings may be there, it does not change the attachment.

Graveyards are not necessarily reflecting Souls that frequent this realm. Our physical remains are a beacon for us back into this reality after we have crossed over. This can be useful when facilitating those still in this reality. As an aside, candlelight is another such beacon. Lighting a candle for our loved ones is awareness still in the story. It lights the way for them to 'see' us and Be with us.

When something remains unresolved, it can lock the Soul to an incarnation. Many of these Souls don't even know they have passed and experience the frustration of wanting to take action and find they cannot effectively do that. They often don't realise they no longer have a body.

It saddens me when I see television programs that look to capture the visual of these Souls inhabiting locations they are attached to all for the purpose of entertainment. Time is irrelevant here. They can be in this realm for thousands of years. Even for those murdered, if the case is unresolved, do not lock the Soul in with the content of the murder; do not hold the Soul in this reality. They will be able to present to you with much more ease if they cross over. If you hold on to loved ones and they choose to stay attached to this reality, time may go by and you may yourself pass and cross over only to realise that the loved one you held on to is still stuck in this reality. They are in a perpetual 'mouse wheel' looking to resolve their situation. It is all such unkindness.

While these Souls remain attached to identification, they cannot know Who They Are. Free them. We are Infinite Beings and we can guide them out of attachment and facilitate their crossing over. In the no time/space of these realms and utilising our awareness, it really does not take effort. Literally ask what is required here, allow those on the other side to facilitate. Don't worry if you think you are using your imagination, label it so and keep using your imagination. There is no away in Oneness. Imagination creates.

If you do choose to facilitate Souls stuck in this realm, an initial awareness may be to communicate to them that they have actually passed away, and that they can now cross over if they choose. Nurturing and reassurance is required, not fear of ghosts. Reassure them that they can be more productive in resolving anything outstanding after they cross over. Reassure them that they will feel much more ease once they cross over and they will most likely reunite with loved ones. In this realm of no time/space, this 'action' shows up as soon as you bring your attention to choosing to share the awareness. Don't use this prescriptively, these are suggestions and what has arisen from my awareness when I have facilitated Souls crossing over. Follow your awareness or imaginings. The clue is that it will be about what can facilitate more of Who They Are to Be.

I also wish to suggest that when Souls are attached, for example, to your home and other buildings or land, be in the question of whether or not that works for you. Sometimes Souls do not choose to cross over and the situation may require you to declare how you are choosing this to appear. For example, you may declare that they are not to disturb your children at night time (Souls perceive who can receive them the most clearly and attempt to communicate to them and children are very receptive). You may declare that they are to keep the noise volume low or disturbances to a minimum or only during the day. You could also give them boundaries around the areas they can be such as the garden or corridor or out of the house. Talk to them as you would anyone else incarnated that you are sharing your space with. They can hear you; they just don't have a body. Let the Soul know that you are the current custodian and if they are not choosing to cross over, you are now in charge. Be assertive, not aggressive, you choose how this shows up.

Not successfully crossed over and in a realm of confusion and doubt

The third realm is probably similar to what the Catholic Church calls Purgatory. What I perceive as the reason for being stuck there and not crossing over successfully, is not the same as what I learnt when I was a child. They are not judged for their unacceptable behaviour by someone or something outside of them. They are not judged for not doing something. No, these Souls are still cloaked in much content and charge and judge themselves profoundly based on that content. They feel unworthy of crossing over. The content that forms this judgement is often based on measuring themselves against the recommended behaviours advocated by religion. The very thing that the recommended behaviours tries to avoid facilitates Souls getting trapped in this limbo. Recommended behaviours that have conditions that if not complied with you will 'go to hell' create that very thing if bought as real, creating fear and self-judgement that lock it in as deserving.

At the time of passing there is a self-judgement of unworthiness and of not getting it 'right'. It is this cloud that locks them into this realm. They have reached a conclusion of determining that they have not succeeded and it has an energy of such harshness towards themselves. This is always against the benchmarks of the ego/mind and is not Who They Are. They cannot access Who They Are because they have decided they are wrong.

I remember being told that those who commit suicide go 'here'. This is not truth for me. The only reason someone who commits suicide frequents this realm is when the 'fog' of content that contributed to what is deemed a necessity to commit suicide is the same vibration of 'fog' that locks them in this realm. The vibration is a match. It is not the content, the means of 'dying', that predetermines in any way that they will frequent this realm; it is the self-judgement of failure. There are no categories of good or bad 'deaths', the net vibration is the information, not the content. I have equally perceived suicides where Souls crossed over with much ease.

Having said this, not all of those who judge themselves a failure fail to cross over successfully and frequent this realm. I perceive it as a specific vibration of turmoil, internal anguish and self-determined confinement. This holds a tremendous charge. Those who have a less charged judgement of failure will most likely cross over successfully, cloaked with their judgement of failure, no different to every other judgement and identification.

I have also heard that those not baptised go 'here'. That is also not truth for me. Oneness includes everything and there is nothing we need to do. Baptism is a beautiful ritual and rite of passage that recognises and acknowledges God as an integral aspect of Who We Are. Even this may have been lost in the story. Baptism is not a prerequisite to crossing over. You may equally Be Immersed in nature, in physical activity, when cooking, when feeding someone else or even yourself. There is no away. The vibration is the information, not any prescriptive doing, which often has been contorted by ego/mind. Practice noticing the information, You will know. For me, when I scan for information relating to crossing over generally and this realm specifically, whether a Soul is baptised does not show up as relevant information. What is relevant is the level of Presence of God in their life (however that Presents) reflecting the degree to which they have shed what cloaks them from Who They Are.

This realm is like a perpetual judgement of oneself as not good enough. It is a self-punishment. There is a mirroring of the self-determined vibration of confusion, frustration and lack of clarity. Awareness is not received and nothing is perceived with ease.

If the individual chose to cross over they could and would. They don't choose it because they don't think or believe they deserve to.

Existing in the vibrations of this realm can be quite tormenting. The polar extreme of this dualistic reality is what is sometimes labelled 'hell'. At all vibrational ranges within this realm, getting clear enough to get past the state they find themselves in is challenging. Across the spectrum of vibration within this realm it all feels like a 'place' between worlds, a limbo. It is the intensity and density of vibration that varies.

Similar to all Souls who have not successfully crossed over, facilitation by others provides a greater ease and is a huge contribution to crossing over. Again, we are all in this together. While some remain stuck, we are all the lesser. Oneness awaits for all to know Who They Are.

I now wish to broadcast throughout existence:

'You deserve to Be free of the content that clouds you from knowing how Magnificent You Are. Your self-judgement is a lie. You cannot see that, we can. It is not Who You Are. Cross over and receive Love. You think love needs to be earned. No, this is another lie. This Love loves you as you are, as It Loves everyone and everything. This Love knows Who You Are and we are all the lesser without you.

Don't be stuck in a judgement that is not real. Fly. Be You. It is safe and It awaits you. We cannot Be Who We Are without you. Oneness cannot Radiate fully without You.

Choose to cross and we will summon the angels and the saints to escort you over. We are all the lesser without you.'

Once we begin to realise that Oneness includes everything, we will not limit even our perspective of life as an incarnation. Our Love can Radiate beyond the physical to the unseen of which we are never separate.

If we do cross over successfully, there are two fundamental realms that we can cross over into. The first is denser in vibration and is 'where' most transition to while carrying karma that cloaks Who They Are. The other is Angelic in Nature and quite formless. Those not carrying karma or have little karma left cloaking Them can frequent this realm. They may also come and go into whichever vibration they choose. Even after we pass, there is only one purpose: to know Who We Are.

Let us look at these two realms individually.

Crossed over and in a realm of more form

When most transition from an incarnation, they cross over into a realm that I perceive still has a lot of form, even though we do not generally perceive it when incarnate.

While we tend to describe it as 'there', it, like all realms and dimensions, is a vibrational bandwidth. It presents in form not dissimilar to our reality, yet at a higher vibration. We look up to 'see' and 'talk' to our loved ones.

There is no away and this vibrational bandwidth can Be anywhere and most certainly is at vibrational resonances on this planet, our cosmos, our universe and other universes. It can Be where we are yet to discover.

From my personal experiences with my father, we have been together in various 'locations' on the planet. Where he mostly frequents is the village he was born in his last incarnation. When he showed me around together with my dear cat who has also departed, I noted physical landmarks, in particular a local church. When I returned to this reality, I found out that church burned down 200 years ago. Well, it is still standing in the higher realms and my father tends the fields nearby with my cat chasing whatever moves!

The process of crossing over to this realm can be immediate or can be after a period of reflection on the incarnation being transitioned from. You may go backwards and forwards between this reality and this realm as you transition after passing, similar to before passing over, obviously now having permanently dropped the physical body. Even if you have successfully crossed over and completed the transition, you may choose to return to these denser vibrations either to continue reflection, or after 'moving on' as somewhere you choose to be as you settle into functioning from this realm. Often, we also choose to return to facilitate for our loved ones.

Karma, or the identifications that cloud you from Who You Are, will present in this realm. The cloak that buffers you from Who You Are does not magically disappear when you pass. You are not Enlightened when you drop a physical incarnation. It is all One Life.

Your karma at the moment you transition is reflected in a vibrational signature. The process of passing can transmute your karma, as may what occurred to result in your passing. This is also why some traditions advocate not physically touching a body at the time of 'death' as it can short-circuit a Soul's choice to transmute karma by pulling them back to attachment.

You will function in a dualistic reality if you continue to buy as real the fixed points of view and polarities such as what is right and what is wrong. Thus, even at this vibrational bandwidth, identification can show up as polarity, even without the physical presentations of the ego/mind, and you will function from that perspective.

Others who have passed, cloaked in their identifications will present in this realm. You will be reunited with those you have known in this and any incarnation. This incarnation will be forefront in your identifications so you will present reflecting that appearance and those characteristics.

Others you have known that are no longer cloaked in karma or have little karma and frequent the next realm, may take form familiar to you and meet you 'there'.

Any of these Beings may have been present at your passing, awaiting your transition. One or more may have been the specific Beings whom you were handed over to from this reality, a practice I have noticed consistently. You are received with love and excited expectancy.

Despite karma still cloaking you, crossing over to this realm is a joyous coming together and can be experienced as Infinite projections of Light of boundless beauty, love, ease and joy.

How you present will normalise, becoming an appearance that may not be your physical age at the time of passing. It seems to reflect a wellness, no more ageing. There is no time/space and this apparition seems to remain static. For example, my father presents in his fifties even though he passed at seventy-nine. His brother presents at about thirty, even though he passed at age five.

When we scan for information on loved ones who have passed, this is how they will appear, together with information that distinguishes them for you, confirmation that you have 'reached' the Being you are intending to connect with.

I have noticed that immediately after crossing over there is a process of healing, of rebalancing. During this initial healing process, and when tasked with 'jobs', you are not available to those that may attempt to perceive you in this reality. This is why at the time of another's passing, those it's thought 'should' be present to either escort them over or bear witness to their passing, may not be available. Others may need to be called on to facilitate the transition. Not having someone present to hand over to can be a reason why someone does not pass over, even though 'death' seems imminent.

The healing that takes place seems to be at specific vibrational resonances, and can be summed up as being like an energy hospital. There is no time/space or any prescriptiveness around this. In the case of my father, I could not perceive him after his transition was complete for a period of six months from time measured in this reality, yet I knew what was occurring.

After this process, we seem to free up and Be and/or do as we choose. Again, all Being and doing is for you to continue to transmute karma and know Who You Are. There is no away. While there is more ease in this realm, distractions can continue to filter perceiving awareness, particularly if you are functioning from a dualistic reality. Without the physical limitations, there is ease of movement, only a glimpse of attention to a thought and it is so. While time is no longer a factor in these realms, experiences of thought, emotions and feelings remain, as does the invitation and opportunities to 'drop your identifications' and continue to contribute to getting back to You.

This does not exclude those in this reality. Our loved ones who have crossed over delight in facilitating for us. They may even become cognitive of being part of Oneness facilitating us Being more of Who We Are. If I was to sum up their capacities and match the knowing into words, it is 'to facilitate a smoother running of things' in this reality. They can orchestrate events, connections or ease in what is happening in your life. Can you feel their delight? It is a joy for them. It transmutes their karma (even though they don't necessarily choose it for that reason) and is a feeling of love connecting the realities. Often they facilitate because they can 'see' so much clearer now and have much less content than when incarnated. They are still carrying identifications, yet the cloak is less dense and knowing is received and perceived with much greater clarity. It can 'make up' for opportunities lost when incarnate.

Other evidence that they are present with you is when they send birds, coins, butterflies, sounds, familiar smells and fragrances. At the level of vibration they are functioning from, they can ask and the matter takes form. You will have a knowing that it came from them. It will pop into your head, probably as a question. Don't doubt. Know what you know. You don't have to share it, others may not be able to receive it or may judge you as imagining things or, at best, a coincidence.

Our loved ones do not need to be Enlightened to facilitate this. They will, however, still be influenced by karma and context. It is a similar capacity to us asking or praying for form to show up as chosen. In the realm they are frequenting, there is less framework, including thinking, which would limit, or rather, distort creation from what is chosen.

In this realm we do 'jobs'. While my perception is that they are allocated, which implies a separation, in the Oneness of All That Is, we are not separate. 'Allocated' is more like a reflection or projection of how Our Essential Nature Presents and what we are tasked with is a vibrational match. It is chosen with ease. It is a Natural Right Action to facilitate existence. There is an allowance and Isness more Present than in this reality. This realm at the macro level is not as unconscious as this reality.

No matter where we are in existence, the purpose remains the same: to know Who We Are, return to Oneness and 'remerge' in the All/No-thing.

Crossed over and in a realm almost formless

This brings us to the other realm that Is when we cross over. This realm is much more formless while also being a bandwidth of vibration. The more karma is transmuted, the less form presents. We frequent this realm when we have transmuted most or all karma. The dualistic reality is not bought as real. I am using words which have been more than transcended in this realm. This is a realm of Unfathomable Beauty, projected in Light. This realm Is Home not clouded in any content and as we Present more formlessly, Its clarity Radiates more Magnificently. Imagine the most beautiful and exquisite sunsets across the planet over all time and space and all showing up together in one moment, Radiating a Vision of Perfection. Now multiply that by Infinity and you begin to glimpse the reflecting Glow of Manifested Oneness. This realm reflects this Manifestation. It Is from 'where' All arises in form and to 'where' It returns. This Is Mother's Bosom. There is little or no content. There is Being, not separate from anything.

Recently, a dear friend of mine passed away and when I perceived her I noticed a Magnificent Golden Glow. I knew It was 'her'. I noticed 'she' had crossed instantaneously after passing (in no time/ space). When I later met her in the realm of more form (we were meeting another friend who had passed over), she projected into a form recognised as her previous incarnation.

For those in this realm with some karma remaining, it will not be much. Who They Are will Present with a thin veil. This filter will continue to transmute until they awaken fully to Who They Are. All content is known to be that, just content. They are able to Be and/or do in any realm or reality. Attention is on facilitating others to know Who They Are. No significance is placed on remaining karma as it is known that it will transmute while in the embrace of this realm.

If they do choose to reincarnate, they will most likely remember Who They Are or, if they don't, will equally choose a stage to facilitate others to know Who They Are, no matter what language or doing is used to facilitate that.

I do not perceive 'doing' in this realm, it Is. There is no sense of linearity, including moments and Being in the moment. Existence has transcended to Isness. Transmutation continues as context is transcended. Context of identification continues to dissolve in Divine Love so Brilliant and Warm.

The highest vibration of this bandwidth is Aum vibration from which all form is projected. No context here. Those that have not only awakened to Who They Are but have also transcended context, vibrate at this resonance. The Radiance of the Facet of the Diamond has returned to Its' Source, the Infinite, Exquisite Diamond Itself. In the Glow of The Diamond all content is no more, the Facet is Blinded in The Light, the Soul is no longer individuated. This Is Manifested Oneness.

Those who have transcended karma do not require existence. We now 'reach' the Unfathomable, the Unmanifested. Transcending context is Freedom of Knowing, beyond Manifested Home, beyond existence. Non-existence may Be. I cannot describe no context as to describe anything is to use context.

Enlightened Ones, prophets, the angels and the saints, all energies of Light with no content can re-project in Light and reform in response to our asking to know Who We Are, there isn't anything else. This is a possibility if chosen by those Enlightened beyond context. This is real and reflects Who We Are. There is never a personal 'I' as Enlightened Ones return to show us the way Home. We are All This and will All return to Manifested Oneness and beyond to the Unmanifested.

HEAVEN AND HELL

Let us end this chapter reflecting on the word labels 'heaven' and 'hell'.

Within the story these word labels are utilised to establish a benchmark for our overall behaviour within a lifetime. The knowing of the vibrations that these word labels may represent is mostly misidentified into a judgement tool for behaviour. They are also discussed as places we go when we die. If we were 'good' and adopted recommended behaviour, we will go to 'heaven'. If we were 'bad' or 'evil' we cannot avoid 'going to hell'.

During a lifetime these deemed polar opposites are used to steer us towards 'good', to avoid Judgement Day and the fear of God casting us to 'hell' or welcoming us to 'heaven'. It maintains a disempowered position that someone outside of us, even God, will be judging us.

While often it is determined in the story that religions within our societies are the closest custodians to 'knowing' what 'the final judgement of us' will be, the inconsistencies of recommended behaviours across societies and religious institutions that guide that 'knowing' gives us a clue that what is adopted in the story is not absolute truth.

There is a profound misidentification that those that are religious are closer to God and know more how God would judge us. While there are a great many religious who have shed the ego/mind cloak, there are a great many who have not, rather, have expanded their cloak of content. Again, the vibration gives you the information and to have a blanket acceptance of any advocacy is disempowering.

We have lost knowing. What may have begun as Right Actions targeted at Being Who We Are, became imposed points of view and often imposed authority given to those outside of us to judge us 'right' or 'wrong'.

My knowing is that the word labels reflect an attempt at matching the vibrations of the realms we frequent, even when incarnate. There is no away. 'Heaven' can be a polar opposite within a dualistic reality, however, more truly, it is a non-dualistic reality and the vibration of Being You and Beyond when all context dissolves. 'Hell' is the vibrational range at the polar end of a dualistic reality of extreme self-judgement and self-imposed torment based on the tremendous charge on content worn. Deep within the Soul is Shining brightly, access is lost by the cloak of that content.

The net vibration of our karma is what is projected when we are incarnate and when we transition from an incarnation. It is as it is in any moment. Thus, there is no future 'heaven' or future 'hell'. It is as it is in this moment whatever reality we frequent. Equally, the content that projects that 'Isness' can also be transmuted in any moment.

The story limits 'heaven' to the realms we frequent when we successfully cross over. This is an aspect of 'heaven' as the realms project at higher vibrations. This aspect still reflects within a dualistic reality when karma remains cloaking us from Who We Are. 'Heaven' is not a place. Due to the higher vibration of these realms we will experience them as 'heaven', they are incredibly beautiful. 'Heaven' is not only this. It Is the non-duality when we Be. Being raises us to a vibration non-dualistic in Nature of Exquisite DeLight and Radiance and Love that is 'Truly Heaven' beyond any karma. It Is as we awaken to Who We Are. 'Heaven' can therefore also be expressed as the increasing expansion and reflection of Our Essential Nature as we awaken to Who We Are. Our experiences Become more and more Magnificent, Radiating Love, Joy, Beauty, Peace, Stillness: Home. 'Heaven' is the reflection and projection of Who We Are. When We fully awaken, there is a reality of Heaven beyond even this context, it Is Unfathomable.

We experience the varying resonances of the vibration of 'heaven' from dualistic to non-dualistic as we live our One Life (incarnate or not). 'Heaven on earth' is when we function within these vibrations and when we Be Who We Are, when we Be in nature, in sacred ceremony, in space, in beauty, in Oneness, when we lose ourselves while in sport, cooking, creating art, being still, dancing, making or being 'in' music, any doing.

'Hell' is also not limited to the extreme polar opposite in the dualistic reality when we do not successfully cross over and remain in confusion. It can equally be experienced while incarnated. It is vibration, not a place.

In our torment, when we adopt every benchmark we have 'failed at', every thought that 'condemned us', every intention to 'destroy ourselves', we create a 'hell'. We remain wearing it when we drop an incarnation. At the macro level, a matrix of energy is maintained mirroring the content bought as real by Souls cloaked in this content.

This can all be dismantled. There is no away and utilising vibrations that rise above the issue will transmute it. Love will dismantle it. We are all in this together, and while some remain cloaked in a karma that deems they are unworthy, we are all the lesser and Oneness is incomplete.

In the non-dualistic reality of Oneness, there is no 'hell'. It is a product of duality. Oneness reflects Our Essential Natures, Our Being, and we can label the experience of these vibrations 'Heaven'.

I do want to illustrate further my awareness on 'hell' using an example. Our history has a great many examples of individuals whose behaviours resulted in countless atrocities to individual human beings and human kind. The ego/mind content had such tremendous charge that, like 'Lost Souls', the awareness of their Souls did not filter through into their thoughts, intentions or actions.

Part of dealing with such behaviours is deemed assurance that these individuals would unavoidably 'go to hell'. There would be many shouts to 'go to hell'. There arises a need to create a separation of the 'good' from the 'bad'. However, this and any judgement outside of the 'perpetrators' does not determine whether they will 'go to hell'. If we do not deem our behaviour as a tormenting of self, as an inescapable confusion and self-punishing 'whipping of self', we would not 'go to hell'. We may successfully cross over. Consciousness does not have a point of view about it. It is known we are not our behaviour and it is known when we are cloaked from reflecting Being. What is still present is the Michelin Man suit, karma. No one can escape karma with a high opinion of themselves. With all of us cloaked in karma, the only difference is the diverse buffers we all wear, and that is between you and God, for truly that is what separates 'you' from 'You', a Spark of Divinity.

The story will continue to judge the behaviours as atrocities to human kind. Do not be distracted by feeling a sense of satisfaction in thinking that, at least, they will 'go to hell'. Receive and perceive the awareness from what occurred rather than any guessing of unavoidable punishment. This more truly is the purpose of bearing witness to story. Allow it to inform our awakening. Incarnations sacrificed are such profound contributions to the expansion of Consciousness. If we all as potent Beings step into our awareness and function in the world from Who We Are, we would never again be swept up in another's unconsciousness, in the rantings of another's ego/mind. We would not sign up for it, follow it, allow it.

We are seeing a movement towards this now. This is the evidence of Consciousness expanding on the planet. It has expanded sufficiently that a new reality is emerging. I call it a New World. In the New World, following ego/mind will not 'cut it' anymore. Our hearts and Souls will guide us and this will not include 'hanging out to dry' the perpetrators. We can receive them but not choose it. They are not their behaviours and while there will be systems of justice in whichever society they frequent, caring and honouring should never be replaced with exclusion and separation, casting adrift a Soul who is not separate from Who We Are.

Take the reins of your life. Do not succumb to any determination outside of you, wherever you frequent. Free yourself and what will show up is a knowing that we are all in this together. Call forth all who are tormented and confused and lead them out of their 'hell' to Who They Are. Until we all return Home, a vibration of Absolute Joy, Love and Comfort, our job is not done. There isn't anything else.

Nine

NEW WORLD

I̲ᴛ ɪs ɪɴɴᴀᴛᴇ ɪɴ and as Who We Are to expand our knowing. While this may be thought in the story to be an expansion of knowledge in and for the story, the true yearning to know is to know Who We Are and return Home.

Since we have existed, the yearning to return to Oneness is what has been driving us all.

Seeking more in the story is not the target, yet that too contributes to expanding our knowing.

When we choose incarnation, that quest for knowing is within the context of the world, including this planet. The context of what constitutes 'the world' itself expands as knowing expands.

When we reflect on history, we see understanding and the human brain expanding in capacity in direct correlation with more knowing and knowledge. What we also notice is that knowing became personal. We input knowing into the ego/mind and the ego/mind then became 'captain of the ship' as it thought it knew better. Competition was born. We shifted from harmony, balance and Oneness as the target, to separation, a fixed point of view, imbalance and the expansion of the personal position.

Our expansion of knowledge has increased both Consciousness and unconsciousness.

We have shifted from very limited, small and isolated worlds to a global community. We have moved from indigenous knowing reflecting harmony and balance (no charge) at both the micro and macro level (no matter how small that world was), to personal position, knowledge and an establishment of separation and win/lose.

The one constant within the story is the seeking of more and while the ego/mind clouds the true target of 'more', Our Souls continue to guide us Home. Even though we continue to think that the road is the destination, that our identifications are the 'more' we are seeking, Our Souls continue to know that all roads lead to Oneness, to God.

Since we have existed, the yearning to return to Oneness is what has been driving us all to 'more'. 'More' is more expansion of Consciousness. There isn't anything else. Since existence and on this planet since its creation, those awakened to this knowing have come to show us the way Home.

Now is the time on this planet that we can 'see' the contribution of all in the expansion of Consciousness.

Even 10 years ago, anyone choosing to Be Themselves needed to exclude Themselves from the stage or limit their participation to stages that could receive them, such as religious and devotional settings and isolated groups and communities. Thanks to all, including you, this is no longer a necessity. You can Be You in suburbia or anywhere You choose to frequent.

Consciousness is illuminating the planet. As we continue to awaken to Who We Are, even toggling between Being and functioning from the ego/mind, Consciousness is increasingly reflected in our reality.

You may think that we need to change how the dualistic reality functions, to make it more equal, to heal it. This has been occurring to an extent, as has a reaction to this, which I call 'the Cornered Animal Syndrome'. However, something else began showing up that was not limited to the context of that dualistic reality. What I noticed was beyond this, literally.

I perceived a New World. A New World functioning in both duality and non-duality and functioning at much higher vibrations than the dualistic reality it is now embracing. I perceived a tipping point in January 2016 when Consciousness had expanded sufficiently on the planet that a New World actuated.

We are now in a transitioning period. This is a period where there is an overlapping of realities. While the New World is embracing and transmuting the old dualistic reality, those still functioning in that dualistic reality do not know it exists. They continue to function in the dream.

Within the New World, the target in the story is to awaken to Who We Are and Oneness. It is known that there is no away. The target is no longer hidden under the cloak of the ego/mind. The ego/mind at the macro level has itself awakened sufficiently to no longer resist awareness. We are transitioning to the macro ego/mind receiving and perceiving awareness with no contortion. This will arise fully as the duality within the New World also transmutes to non-duality.

With the target of the New World being Oneness in the story, this alone contributes to transmuting density within the old dualistic reality, now embraced by expanded Consciousness, noticeable by all who bring their attention there. We do not need to heal the old dualistic reality, we rise above in vibration and the issues will never be the same again.

Those functioning within the old dualistic reality will continue to try to heal it. The no charge which is our knowing is being received in that world as 'equality' at best. Equality is never achievable as equality is not balance; it is a fixed point of view that certain benchmarks need to be the same. This is a vibration within the old dualistic reality that if reached in specific situations is unsustainable because it is forced positioning, not a natural balancing of the charge.

Embracing diversity was another clue for me that something shifted; there was a reflecting of openness rather than a fixed point of view.

What I also noticed was that there were a lot of shifts unfolding and they were of a different class, a different vibrational range. They rose above the previous fixed points of view of how something had to be. What in the past were words of demand, now presented as an invitation to embrace all. This reflects the transition that has already begun. In the old dualistic reality, the classic 'for' and 'against' positions were still being maintained and in another world was an energy of inclusivity and love for all, no matter what the position or how they showed up. The narrow context created by identifications was dissolving.

The conversations being shared were at higher vibrations than the issues being discussed and debated. When awareness was spoken, a change occurred in no time/space, and it rippled through Oneness. Facilitated by a model of Oneness in the physical story, the internet, it rippled through, communicated instantaneously, mirroring the no time/space of awareness.

There is no coincidence in the unfolding of Inspiration in our world and in existence. You chose to incarnate now to actively and physically participate and facilitate the unfolding of a New World. Thank you.

The transition is now in 'full swing'. While it may present as confusion as to what is going on, don't worry, something much more powerful and potent is emerging.

Part of the confusion is the transition from identifications as our foundation to Consciousness being our foundation. God's got our back, however, we do not perceive it clearly yet. What we are noticing is that the foundations which were constant and safe now feel unstable, as if they may not hold for long. For those choosing to no longer function in the dualistic reality, do not try to force any maintenance of those foundations, let go and let God and transition with kindness to you as you realise the lie that you didn't need the foundation, You are an aspect of Divinity with no needs, only Magnificence and Radiance Presenting as You Are. You will notice You can 'fly'. You will notice there is nothing You need to Be and/or do, only choice. What freedom to express, Be, Who You Are.

Be reassured by a different 'coming to arms' that is emerging. While the 'cornered' ego/mind may still seek 'arm" literally, a great many are embracing their arms in inclusion and communion. We are literally Becoming a Common Unity, a hologram of Oneness. Every Being reflects the Whole.

The internet itself a reflection of Oneness, is facilitating us all to Oneness. It provides access and connection in virtually no time/space. Yes, it reflects Consciousness and unconsciousness, even the facilitating of further unconsciousness. Be willing to 'see' it all. If you can receive it all, we step into our capacity and ability to respond (true responsibility). This also is part of the transitioning to more Consciousness.

As this emerges, rather than maintaining separation, we are discussing what maintaining status quo looks like and not being counted looks like. We are coming together and noticing that if we aren't in this together, an awakening will not unfold into reality, even though the story may still call this 'solving problems'. There is now a tangible realisation that we all count and are being asked to stand up in the story and be counted, no matter how that looks. Oneness knows that, the story in the New World is awakening to that.

Even an industry that in the past provided an escape within the dualistic reality, is now beginning to advocate the allowance of all being their authentic selves rather than needing to look a certain way. Hollywood, previously received solely as entertainment and fulfilling fantasy, is awakening beyond its own identifications to embrace the potency of bearing witness to story, of reflecting and literally projecting awareness for all to see. The all that turned to this industry for an escape are now being guided out of identifications by a means that is received, 'looked up to' and 'aspired to' by the ego/mind. Consciousness is imbuing what the ego/mind utilises and, what was a crutch for survival, is now further facilitating a transition out of duality.

We can observe Consciousness practices and awareness being taught, energy medicine being taught and being considered as we look to the future of medicine. Consciousness and Being You is even being referenced in marketing and advertising as targets, it is selling products even in the dualistic reality.

We are beginning to receive each other without needing to look any particular way. Also, things we turned a 'blind eye' to in the past because of compliance to identifications, are no longer being tolerated when the heart and Soul know something else. We are cognitively recognising a shift from thinking to feeling. We are opening our hearts. This is a strengthening of the muscle of observation which leads us to the doorway of the Soul and perception of awareness.

In the story, one of the key forms that has been holding the space for this is 'good will', a Right Action of wanting the best for each and every one of us. Anything that is functioning within the dualistic reality can be subject to ego/mind, and religious, spiritual and charitable organisations are no different. Yet, it is they, who, in the story, have held the most visible 'flag' for God. Beyond any judgement or contortion is Love, Divine Love, from which they originated. They have 'held the fort' for Consciousness on the planet to catch up, whether they allowed themselves to know that or not. No 'forts' or structures are required now, even the economy of religion is no longer needed. We will even transition from the differences in form and return to the heart of religion, back to the origin of Divine Love and Oneness. The Common Unity of churches will be part of our global Common Unity.

Recommended behaviours will be replaced by choices made from the heart and, as we transition to Who We Are, from Our Souls, expressed in the language of awareness, reflecting Our Essential Natures. Even the crutch of the Ten Commandments, which could only take us to the brick wall of the ego/mind, will no longer be required. It has serviced its purpose: to facilitate the expansion of Consciousness until we know. In the New World we go beyond belief and faith and Be our knowing. We know that the non-duality that arises from heart and Soul is what Being together is and what brings us all to Oneness.

In this transitioning phase, a release of what has been held will occur. This may misidentify religious, spiritual and charitable organisations and teachings as being irrelevant. Quite the opposite is true, the need for these is collapsing and will be replaced by choice. Oneness will be known as no away. Ease will replace any unsustainable force to hold a structure in place. Let go and let God. The job is done, holding is done. Enjoy Being with God and reflect that Joy, that is the invitation to others. Religious or spiritual practice and charity will reflect from Our Essential Natures. We will all choose what resonates as Who We Are. The rigidity of these frameworks will be dismantled, and the Love of God will Radiate even brighter. We will no longer choose from 'fear of God', we will Radiate the 'Joy of God'.

So, what is required now?

There is nothing we need to do. Being Who We Are is already instituting Oneness. Everything we have all ever Been and done since existence has facilitated this 'now' to Be.

You have chosen to be here on the planet at this time. Some are choosing to leave and contribute in a different form whilst not incarnating. Others are contributing at the vibrations they frequent. We are all in this together.

My awareness leads me to ask that we all begin to institute within the New World, not the old dualistic reality. We can perceive the energy and vibration of the New World and choose to create there.

Instituting your reality within the New World also has the effect of tricking ego/mind still in place, as the ego/mind has no reference points on what to expect, how to judge or any criteria for how it should show up within this World. The context changes immediately. The reference points of the old dualistic reality will always hit a brick wall. In the New World duality, the ego/mind is more open to receive awareness. This is not only functioning at higher vibrations and consequently transmuting further content, it also introduces new, more expansive identifications that have a broader scope of 'acceptability'. This is part of the new crutches that are emerging as we transition out of duality in the New World and eventually out of all identifications as our foundations. The New World duality is transitory; it is known it will phase out. We are rising above it and will step into an allowance of all, not just 'acceptance' which retains judgement as its framework.

If you do choose to institute in the New World, you can cognitively choose to institute your body/mind complex in the New World from this moment. Choose it and let go. You do not hold the choice, you vibrate as your choices and this reflects those choices in every moment.

You cannot, however, choose for someone else. You cannot bring someone 'over' to the New World. Actually, there is no 'over', it is a different vibrational range that is embracing the old dualistic reality. It is a reality that has Presented from the expansion of Consciousness. Depending on the vibration that someone is functioning from, will determine whether they can even receive and perceive the New World. It is like the analogy I used in Chapter Two of the ball within the ball. Someone functioning from the dense reality of a ball within a ball does not know that there is anything beyond their own reality. This can only occur when the framework (charge on identifications) collapses and they experience an expansion of their reality.

As the New World continues to expand in Consciousness, as duality is transitioned out of, the old dualistic reality will be nurtured and transformed, the same as our physical bodies are transformed when we no longer incarnate within them.

While we continue to wear any cloak of karma, instituting in the New World will transmute karma much more potently than in the old dualistic reality. As awareness is received and perceived and becomes the fundamental language of the New World, Infinite resources will be more readily accessible.

At both the micro and macro levels in the New World, context is already dissolving. Even in this transitioning period, we are already seeing the merging of cultures and nationalities and nations. We are embracing all, as well as communing even our DNA into Oneness. I perceive the collapse of even the polarity of male/female, not only from a behavioural perspective, but from the physical way our body/mind complexes will be. All matter will transition to be less dense. It is all part of the collapse of identifications as our foundations. As we Be Who We Are, and even as we toggle between Being and the ego/mind, context continually dissolves and matter changes. Change the content and charge and the form projects differently. Rise above the matter and a permanent and material change, vibrating higher, will Present.

A kindness to ourselves arises naturally as we allow this all to unfold. It is the difference between grasping at competing identifications and Being in allowance of the Magnificent Diversity with which we each Be in the world and in existence.

We can also choose to incarnate within the New World. We can cognitively choose to incarnate into a physical body within the New World and, increasingly as this occurs, the Infinite capacities we Be will truly come to the fore, both in our Inspiration and our physical capacities. We will not be limited to receiving energy from outside ourselves such as food and water. What is currently deemed impossible or miraculous or fantasised about as superhero capabilities, will Become commonplace, while also Being acknowledged and honoured as what it reflects: Being Who We Are, an aspect of Divinity.

Instituting our Consciousness practices, energy medicine and in fact all 'systems' within the New World, will also facilitate their expansion.

I have noticed that while modalities and practices remain being generated and created within the old dualistic reality, their expansion is limited and often hits the same brick wall, limiting possibility. I know that many of those facilitating these 'systems' have been wondering why they are no longer flourishing, and why it seems like such hard work to 'keep things going' or for those adopting their guidance to get past ego/mind reality. It is because they are yet to receive and perceive the awareness of the New World and have been utilising unsustainable force to maintain presence in the old dualistic reality which continues to resist and react to them. Awareness is informing them to institute in the New World.

Instituting in the New World frees limitation and anything is possible. These 'systems' were present in the old dualistic reality to Radiate Light in the 'darkness', now they too can rise above and be created in a world that can not only receive them but also welcome them, and invite them to inform potentialities and possibilities for all, both at the micro and macro level.

The New World now has its own life force, its own 'hum' in existence. It is only limited by what we do not choose. We will find that the Laws of the old world are no longer relevant in the New World. 'Ask and you shall receive' will Be known as what Is rather than the hope it is in the old dualistic reality.

We are there. Anything is possible. The New World thrives with all Being Who They Are. How matter will present will be lighter in vibration and density (that is, how it physically looks).

It is where we will increasingly Be functioning from our Infiniteness. There will no longer be judgement of right and wrong, rather allowance and acknowledgement and Being Our Authentic Selves. The old world does not value Our Unique Self, Our Essential Nature, it values the cloaks of identifications we are wearing. In the New World, the cloaks of identifications will be received as obstacles to Self. The New World is about dropping identifications rather than adding and valuing identifications.

Diversity in the New World is not only being in allowance of how someone shows up, that is, the cloak they are wearing (and the limit of possibility in the old dualistic reality), it celebrates You Being You no matter how you show up. It rises above the cloak to bear witness to Our Souls, showing up as Our Essential Natures. That is truly embracing diversity and that is the target within the New World.

As we welcome a shift from identification to embracing all in the diversity with which they Present, we further drop the charge on identification and reflect the same DeLight as when we observe the diversity of nature and the cosmos. We will return to Be a part of that Beauty, no longer separated by significance and superiority.

Our hearts will initially be the guides, leading to the target, Our Souls, no charge and no point of view, only choices born of awareness.

We will find the piece of the puzzle of Oneness that reflects Our Being and Be that in the world, in the New World. Initially, it is the following of our hearts in all that we Be and do, even work. Work will Be how we choose to live our life rather than what we 'have to do' to get funds to live. The target is following the awareness of Our Souls, Presenting in the world as Our Unique aspect of Divinity, of God, Our Essential Nature, Our Spirit.

We will also perceive a pang in our hearts and Souls when others remain cloaked from knowing Who They Are.

In the New World, 'systems' will adopt a win/win and community approach. Our Common Unity is really what our New World is. As a global community, there will no longer be a right and wrong but an allowance of difference and coming to a Common Unity. We will function from our Authenticity of Being, reflecting this in the world. Getting more identifications, including holding on to personal position and gain, is received as a distraction. Functioning from ego/mind, and particularly ego/mind empowerment, becomes 'the elephant in the room'. Its denser vibration relative to the ease and joy of Authenticity of Self, of Being, is no longer aspired to or chosen either to mimic or to embrace in our lives.

The values and significance we placed on identifications will be transitioned out of as we continue to transmute duality within the New World. This may initially present as new identifications that reflect a greater degree of embracing or defending of all.

Countries will have respect and honouring for one another and will acknowledge and celebrate the Beauty of the diversity of Divinity they each reflect. Judgement of how something presents will be no more. We will perceive the vibration and choose or not choose. You could choose cream, tabouleh or spaghetti bolognese. It doesn't matter, all is available as we choose to create the kaleidoscope of our lives. We will choose which elements and ingredients we would like in and as our life, without attachment, only choice. We will paint the picture of our life with a joyful and childlike wonder of what is possible.

Inspiration has facilitated the coming to Be of the New World. What is possible now with an allowance of awareness is beyond measure. Inspiration will continue to expand, no longer from behind any cloak. It will continue reflecting and projecting our Divinity, accessing Infinity.

We will make even more incredible advances in technology, health, sciences, well-being, and life in general. Advances experienced in the last 50 years will pale in its reflection. We will transition out of linearity to a means of expansion not experienced before. We will go vastly beyond our current capacity to articulate the Inconceivable Nature of what Is as our own very Nature reflects that same Infiniteness. The more we Be Who We Are, the more we access Infinity. Nothing will be perceived as separate from Oneness and this will ripple through as knowing into knowledge as we access and utilise Infinity to function and Be in the New World.

Our brains will also evolve to this non-linear functionality, where input and output is not linear, rather reflecting a vast and Infinite capacity to receive and perceive Oneness in no time/space. We will also experience Oneness in our physical bodies at vibrations higher than form within the old dualistic reality. We will transition to no karma and no context with our physicality, not separate from form or no form. There will be no limitations on physicality. All is unto us.

In the New World, we will generate rather than repair, physical boundaries no longer need to apply. There will be no separate categories, rather Oneness, true wholistic existence. In the dualistic reality, Inspiration and awareness was generally not acknowledged or strongly opposed as informing anything, even though it was Present and informed knowing and knowledge. The dualistic reality trusted only objectivity which never was and can never be. In the dualistic reality, perspective always clouds objectivity.

Fixed solutions will be no more, rather, we will have an Infinite bandwidth of possibilities informed by awareness, utilising our minds as tools and addressing what is uniquely presenting before us. Whether it is the exchange of goods and services, health, justice, managing a country or traffic, schools, holidays, it is Infinite possibility that will be sought to achieve balance as required, both at micro and macro levels.

I am sure we will soon tap into the Infinite energy of Who We Are to commune together sustainably rather than strip the planet of finite resources. We will commune in the Magnificence of nature rather than cut it up into chunks to sell. We will transition from resources like oil, coal, gas, and wood which are unsustainable or cannot be sustained without force, to resources which are in Infinite supply. The target is maintaining balance and no charge, no karma loaded on the planet. We are currently informing our choices with awareness as we develop fuel options from such gifts as the sun and air and movement in general (another presentation of transition to the New World). This is a glimpse and minute fraction of what is possible when we harness in harmony the Infinite capacity of Consciousness. This will collapse the foundation of the global economy as it now stands. Transition is possible. It is only greed, the product of identification, that does not 'see' anything else.

The target is no longer wealth and position. The target is more Consciousness.

Personal gain and wealth will have a different energy. In the past it was all about identification, rich or poor and the innumerable presentations of those identifications. Like all identifications, this will be transmuted in the New World as we transition out of duality. What if the pressure of needing to achieve identifications is not present? What would you choose? How would wealth show up? What would money be?

In the New World, there is allowance of all things and no-things, including how we as Beings are in the world. The New World will not judge someone that is rich as being more significant than someone who is poor. They are identifications. We will perceive the level to which they are Being Themselves or not, and even this is not judged, it Is an Isness. Our hearts and Souls will receive and perceive everyone and everything. It is what it is and judgement is futile and would not arise.

Take the pressure off and Be. In the New World, richness is Being. Being in nature, with family and friends, in church or temple, with air, with laughter, with tears, at work, anywhere, and Being and/

or doing anything or no-thing. Wealth is your 'cup' being filled by Being and/or doing what resonates like You.

You will know the contribution you are cognitively choosing, and the New World and existence knows too. Separation is obsolete. Everything is a 'twang' in Oneness, no-thing is unnoticed. This has always been the case energetically and vibrationally, now in the New World it will be known in the story.

What we choose in the New World is known to contribute to the target of the expansion of Consciousness and for all of us, incarnate or not, to know Who We Are and return Home. In the New World, this is the target in the story, no longer hidden behind cloaks of content and charge. We have awakened sufficiently to know this.

The fulfilment we experience from participating in any way and to any degree (in the no time/space of awareness) in the expansion of Consciousness further dissipates the insatiable yearning for more, as we recognise we have Been and/or done for and in Oneness. All yearning dissipates when We Are Home. The insatiable nature of yearning eases when we know we are contributing to and facilitating Oneness. This is not another imposed point of view, it arises as truth for each of us as the veil of content transmutes.

If when you Be and/or do you generate cash and assets, then you generate cash and assets. You have chosen the scenery without attachment or significance. You free yourself to enjoy the abundance of your life. What gives you the freedom? Not the 'wealth' but the contentment of contributing to and facilitating Consciousness. 'My cup runneth over' (Psalm 23:5 KJB).

You may choose to utilise your 'wealth' however you choose. Informed by awareness it will continue to provide contentment and joy. Collecting more 'nuts', for the sake of collecting more 'nuts' or showing them off, now seems nonsensical.

If Being and/or doing does not generate cash and assets, look around, if you have chosen from awareness you will equally be wealthy and abundant in other forms. The abundance and contentment is derived from choices from awareness, from the vibration you generate, rather than any significance placed on the end result. The projected form is different, that is all.

So what is money then?

Money is a convenient means of exchanging energy. If I give you a bag of potatoes, can you give me some of that beautiful broccoli you grew? A piece of paper is much lighter to carry, especially if you would like lots of broccoli.

I am not sure if there has ever been a time on this planet when money was not contorted by the ego/mind. It seems to have always been clouded by personal positioning and identification requiring more grasping. It was deemed so significant and again the road became the destination. The identification took hold. It was a measure of success or failure.

In the New World, as we transition out of duality, we can transition back to money being an exchange of and for energy. Rather than perceiving money as an outcome, money can be utilised as a method of acknowledgment and honouring for the goods and/or services for which we are gratefully exchanging it for, and for which we have expended energy to generate. Additionally, the context of what we are choosing to 'acquire' will change from collecting more identifications, 'getting', to an energy of gifting and receiving from our hearts and Souls, being in joy of what we choose as the stage of our life.

In the transition to the New World, some systems of bartering have arisen. If they arise out of protest or exclusion, they will not be sustainable (an example of the ego/mind contorting awareness again). If they arise out of the clarity of exchanging 'this' energy for 'that', then the simplicity will reflect the same purpose of money and contribute to facilitating 'money' being perceived as what it is. Again, the vibration will give you the information.

There is no away in Oneness. Money itself reflects energy generated no different to a chair, or cake, or listening to someone, or a book made from Being and/or doing or Being with no doing. Money is a word label we use for a piece of paper that has been given generic denominations that we use to vibrationally match the energy we have generated and which we use for exchanging that form of energy generated into something else, rather than Being and/or doing another energy exchange. Interestingly, if the exchange of energy is not vibrationally matched, even in the old dualistic reality, we innately generate further charge to achieve balance. This charge can be in the form of anger and resentment if 'we have been short-changed'. A money exchange, if chosen, would match the energy. In Being, there may not be an Infinite energy money exchange as there is a mutual exchange from Being. There may be an exchange of money that vibrationally and mutually is perceived as a match for the energy exchange.

The fact that money is made at the macro level, usually by a government, does not change its nature. Establishing money as a commodity and a finite economy lost its purpose. It was no longer a facilitation for the exchange of energy generated, which is Infinite in nature, is became finite and a measure within polarity. We equally lost access to awareness when we made chunks of finite resources the same as finite 'money'. They are not exchanges of energy, they are pieces of the planet and their supply is not sustainable.

Buying into the measures of duality, we created value in the finite. The rarer the more valuable, the 'have to have', even manmade items were created to create rarity or 'must haves'. Our ego/minds excelled at creating identifications to set us apart from everyone else, all for the sake of identification and the pecking order of duality. It is all worthless in the context of reflecting Being, except for its contribution to awakening you to the lie that this 'wealth' is not real. True wealth is the contentment of Being You.

Why is a rare diamond more valuable than the sun's Magnificent rays reflecting on the dew resting on a leaf after rain? Only the identifications of significance and position make it so, only holding on to the finite makes it so. You don't have to have it, possess it, to Be with it and enjoy (in Joy) it. You are not separate from All that Is. It will rain again.

Trying to possess the most rare is perpetuating the illusion of identification. Celebrate and Be with the Beauty of Infinite Diversity projecting all around us, available to all, reflecting Oneness and Our Natures, Who We Are.

It is not separate and no different to the Infinite Love we experience when we bypass or dismantle the ego/mind and identifications. Our hearts open, we access Our Souls in Infinite energy. This 'fills our cup', not with finite wealth that is never enough, but with Infinite wealth which ceases yearning.

In the New World, we will flip what 'value' is. 'Value' will no longer be measured inversely as the rarer or harder to attain identification. What will be received as greater in value is the Infinite, the Infinite Nature, Infinite resource, Infinite capacity, a balanced and no charge resource arising with ease, not force.

Even the internet at the macro level, and our computers and phones at the micro level, are already placing value in Infinite data accessibility and downloads. There are no coincidences. This mirrors the receiving and perceiving of awareness from Infinite resources, from Consciousness. Our Inspiration and awareness will inform how we access this Infinity to thrive in balance on the planet.

It is said that you can't take your 'wealth' with you. This is because deemed 'wealth' in the old dualistic reality is not real. True wealth You do 'take' with You as it reflects You and Is You, incarnate or not.

As we transition in the New World, we will choose with greater awareness the ingredients we use to produce products. We will no longer monopolise for personal position or mutate nature to squeeze an extra dollar. We will choose sustainable resources, transitioning to Infinite resources, and those resources that maintain balance at both the micro and macro level. Sustainability is maintaining balance and no charge on the planet, not from force but with an ease like the wind blowing.

If energy does not flow like the wind, it becomes stagnant. This is true in all existence including our physical bodies, our lives, the planet and money. Holding on to money creates stagnancy, not wealth.

Exchanging energy generated is our future economy. The point of difference with our current economy is that we can transition to a system in which we exchange diverse forms of energy that may be not even be tangible. We will no longer play the demand and supply game for finite resources. The focus will be on matching the energy for the exchange, knowing that we are not separate and there is no significance on personal position, rather, the no charge of balance. Our awareness informs this, it is not imposed, and it certainly is not forced.

When this comes to Be, all is sustainable in the clarity of awareness. All choice is from awareness and energy is the movement of awareness to create. Exchange that!

I am not saying that everyone who has cash and assets needs to share and use it for others that don't have. This is the same judgement that makes 'wealth' significant. Be Who You Are and allow your Essential Nature to Be in the world, to inform choice, whether in the old duality or in the New World.

As we continue to blend beautifully in our Common Unity, we will all Illuminate as Who We Are, no matter 'where' we frequent.

Being is not passive. It is consciously chosen and Presents with ease. It is a flow like the wind. We access our awareness in that 'wind'. This is what I recognised in a song. It was a hope that is now to be known by all. It was always there and Is for all of us to know. Do not settle until you know. Even if your ego/mind gives up on your knowing, Your Soul never will. Oneness will never forget about you and experiences Your Presence as part of All There Is even when you are yet to experience Your Self.

You Are Magnificent beyond description. You Are known in Oneness and we all await your return Home. Everything is for this purpose. There isn't anything else.

'Knock, and He'll open the door

Vanish, and He'll make you shine like the sun

Fall, and He'll raise you to the heavens

Become nothing, and He'll turn you into everything.'

Rumi

Glossary

Term	Definition
All/No-thing	Beyond Manifestation and the Manifested God, Oneness, is All/No-thing which is beyond context and often described as the Unmanifested, Unfathomable, Unnameable and the Inconceivable. We are not separate from All/No-thing yet cannot conceive of it while cloaked in an ego/mind or attached to existence. We re-merge with the All/No-thing when Enlightened beyond our Souls, beyond existence. While, describing it creates a limitation with the use of context, This Is the Ultimate Freedom of God.
Amen	Potent declaration to change form, declaring that whatever we are asking be returned to before form, to the 'Aum' vibration, and returned to us in the form of our asking.
Apparent	In truth, we are a projection of Light from Oneness, and while form appears real, it is not. At times, I refer to this as 'apparent', like an apparition.

Aum	'Aum' is the origin of existence. It is the Word of God and God Manifested. It is a vibration that maintains its 'Hum' in all form and from which all form originates. From the 'Aum' vibration Consciousness forms, and with the fabric of Consciousness, all form comes to Be.
Awareness	Awareness is the language of the Soul. It is our knowing, uniquely expressed as You in the characteristics of Your Essential Nature. It arises naturally when in the moment or when ego/mind content is not buffering the receiving and perceiving of awareness.
Being	Being is the natural state of the Soul. It shows up as Your Essential Nature. When we awaken to Who We Are, Being is an Isness. While we remain functioning from the ego/mind, we can experience moments of Being. You have no position or point of view in Being, only choice. Being is in no time/space.
Breath	Breath is the rhythm of 'Aum', of God in our Life. It is present when incarnate or not. When we incarnate, the breath rhythm present when not incarnate communes with the body/mind complex. As the body/mind complex develops it changes form into a physical rhythm and then a physical breath. It is a road to God and communing in Oneness. In Life, it expresses as Inspiration. It informs the ideas and advances in the world, all for the expansion of Consciousness within the world and existence.
Buffer	When I perceive the charge on content held by the ego/mind and bought as real, it presents as an energetic buffer to Who We Are showing up in the world and in existence.

	This buffer is literally creating the separation, the shielding, of our authentic Self. Without the buffer we would be awakened to Who We Are.
Charge	It is not the volume of content within the ego/mind that buffers Who We Are from Being in the world, it is all the charge we have on that content that is the obstacle. The charge on that content is all the judgement, significance, expectations, conclusions, position and points of view we have. If we did not have a position on the content of the ego/mind, we would be free to Be and choose in any moment.
Common Unity	It is not the separation that all our identifications have created that is Who We Are. In the world, we define ourselves by these identifications. We will always struggle to embrace all, even when we label it as embracing diversity, when the very structure of what we are measuring with values identifications and the distinction of identifications held which is all separation. The reason for everything is to know Self and Be, and this is our Common Unity, this is what will truly embrace all, as beneath any identification is Who We Are and we are all here for all to awaken to this. This is our Common Unity that will never be destroyed. It is Oneness of which no-one is separate.
Communion	Communion is the state of no separation. It can Be when we slip into Being in particular experiences or when Enlightened as an Isness with no separation, no separate parts. The experience is 'feeling' merged and when you perceive around you there is no beginning and no end and it includes You. Everything is an Isness of Being.

Conception	An Exquisite Presentation of Divinity as a new form coming to Be, a new reflection of Divinity referenced by the coming together of a mother and a father. Imbued in the new form the 'Hum' of Aum continuing to Be. Conception and incarnation are distinct and vibrationally diverse events in the unfolding of our Presence on the planet.
Consciousness	Consciousness is the form that arises from the 'Aum' vibration. It is the fabric of all form. Consciousness has no content and is experienced as space. It is what holds everything together even though this is a language of separation. Consciousness, experienced as space, is communion. There is no away, and it is all from the fabric of Consciousness.
Content	I define all the identifications we buy as real and adopt as who we are in the story of our lives as the content within our ego/minds. We do not have capacity issues with the volume of content. It is the charge we have on the content that creates separation not only from each other but from Our Selves. When we awaken to the realisation that the content is merely the stage of the current incarnation, we are freed to choose from awareness, with no point of view.
Contextual Potentialities from Infinite Possibilities	When we awaken to Who We Are as an Isness or in the moments of experiencing Being Who We Are, creating remains influenced by the context we maintain as real. Increasingly, this context dissolves and collapses as we awaken further to the realisation that all form is a projection of Light from Oneness. Until this is an Isness, creating is limited to contextual potentiality to

	the extent that context is bought as real. When all context dissolves, Infinite Possibilities can Be in no time/space, if chosen.
Cornered Animal Syndrome	I have noticed that, both at the micro and macro level, when we have transmuted much of the charge of the ego/mind content and we are at the point of receiving awareness without contortion, the ego/mind comes out in full force in an attempt to maintain control. This full force can show up as aggression, confusion, extreme doubt, physical symptoms, actually, it can be anything the ego/mind deems will destabilise you to the foundations it has established for you. I call this reaction the 'Cornered Animal Syndrome'. A similar behaviour can show up at any level of foundation when we are seeking to expand our scope and context of functioning. However, when 'combatting' the receiving of awareness, the ego/mind interprets this as a 'last ditch effort' to maintain control as 'captain of the ship'.
Crutch	A crutch is a tool adopted to facilitate you as you awaken to Who You Are. Labelling a tool as a crutch is useful as it reflects an intention for the use of the tool to be temporary. It also facilitates you taking charge of your life and cognitively choosing the tools you are choosing to facilitate you. A level of Presence exists when a choice is cognitively chosen. Even if behaviours that perpetuate identifications are continued to be chosen, if they are chosen as a crutch until it is no longer required, that is success. This is more of you showing up rather than unconsciously replicating patterns of behaviour based on past reference points.

DeLight	A play on the double meaning of the word, reflecting the Delight at the Divine Nature of what we receive and perceive as well as the truth of all form, a projection of The ('De') Light.
Dualistic reality	When we buy into a reality of identifications and the benchmarking and positioning of those identifications, we establish not only a structure of separation, we also establish a reality of opposites. In order to achieve a benchmark, there must be a relative 'not achieving'. Thus, a reality in which position exists maintains what is right/wrong, good/bad. This is a dualistic reality. The reality created by the ego/mind is by its nature dualistic. It maintains control with all the positioning and point of view along the spectrum of conformity and rebellion, with a few establishing new benchmarks to either comply to or rebel against.
	The existence of form is bought as dualistic by the ego/mind even though it can be experienced in Oneness, as the projection it is and thus can be perceived as non-dualistic in nature.
Ego/mind	The ego/mind is a bundle of information stored vibrationally at a denser vibrational range than the Soul yet it is linked to the Soul. This bundle of information contains every identification you have ever bought as real since you have existed, the vast majority of which originates from outside of you, from what you have been told to adopt as 'you'. When you deem something to be real, you assign a level of charge to it and relate each piece of information to every other piece of information. This occurs both cognitively and unconsciously and reflects in any moment what your perspective is.

	When we incarnate, the ego/mind as it is in any moment is reflected in our physicality, in how our brain develops and functions and in how we respond and show up in the world. Within any incarnation, we add to this library of information including judgments, expectations, conclusions and correlations. The target of transmuting the charge on this content is not known until we transmute this content sufficiently that the awareness of the Soul informs that the 'you' created by the ego/mind content is not really who you are. The ego/mind will continue to define who you are in the world even creating a confinement of the possibilities and potentialities you will function from. It is literally what is buffering all of us from Who We Are, the only difference is the different content. The ego/mind at both the micro and macro level will continue to define the different content of 'you'.
Energy	Energy is the beginning of form that also has content. It is made from the fabric Consciousness, projected by Light (the 'doing' word of Consciousness) and reflects the characteristics intended for that energy. The content is the characteristics of the energy. It is the beginning of differentiation within Oneness.
Enlightenment	Enlightenment literally means 'to remove the dimness and blindness, to shed light upon' (Etymonline.com). When we transmute the charge on all the identifications within the ego/mind that we have bought as real, we have shed the light of awareness on a reality we thought was who we are but it is not. We experience our only true death, the 'flat-lining' of the charge and the

	death of the ego/mind. We Be Who We Are as the individuation of the Soul, as an Isness in the no time/space of Being, a reality non-dualistic in nature. We have returned Home to Oneness, to the Manifested God. Everything is known as non-separate and You experience the joy, ease, love, beauty that Is. In whatever reality You frequent, You radiate Presence reflected as Your Essential Nature. This reality does maintain context within existence and even this progressively collapses and dissolves until You awaken fully beyond the individuation of even Your Soul. You return to Source and You no longer exist individuated, 'You' re-merge into the All/No-thing. While describing this reflects context, no context exists and 'We' are at the Unfathomable, Inconceivable where the All/No-thing is unto 'Us' and 'Is' Us. This is the Supreme Freedom that awaits us all, the All/Nothing that is God.
Essential Nature	Your Essential Nature is the Nature of Your Soul that arises when Being You. It is the characteristics of how You show up when You Be and can be described more like archetypes than personality traits. Personality traits are the product of the ego/mind and are layers buffering You. Your Essential Nature Presents in the world and in existence when the charge of the ego/mind has 'flat-lined' as an Isness (Enlightenment) or in the moments you experience Being Who You Are. Your Essential Nature can also be described as Your Spirit. The Unique Breath of God imbuing Inspiration into your Being and doing.

	While You exist, You will reflect Your Unique Essential Nature, Your Unique Spirit. No-one will Present like You in the world or in existence ever.
Eternal Moment	An 'Eternal Moment' are word labels attempting to reflect the no time/space of Being where a single moment measured in a dualistic reality can be experienced as a no-beginning and never-ending moment. A magnitude of awareness may be received and perceived, and while not necessarily funneled down into cognitive words and knowledge, it is known. The 'background' to an Eternal Moment is communion and a recognised familiarity which is Home.
Existence	Existence is the creation of form, and existence is with the 'Aum' vibration. This is the Manifested. The 'Aum' vibration, the Source of all form is the Manifested God. From this vibration forming existence arises all form, including the existence of Who We Are as an apparent individuation of this Oneness.
God	The Infiniteness, Eternalness, Allness and No-Thingness and the Potency, Beauty and Absolute Love that Is the Manifested God and the Unmanifested God truly is Inconceivable, Unfathomable, Immeasurable and Indescribable. To describe is to utilise context. How can you describe the Source of All that Is 'before' It Is and as It Isn't? How do you describe the Source of all you would describe? The aspects of God that we can observe reflect the Manifested God, Oneness. It is the Infinitely Loving, Nurturing Isness that reflects the vibrations of form and the fabric of all existence.

	It is mind-boggling to even contemplate a Presence so vast and yet so Loving and Magnificent and not separate from anything. God Is Our Home. There isn't anything else. The play of light and shadow is to remember Who We Are, an individuation of this Source, and once remembered return to It's embrace.
Healing	Healing is rebalancing, coming back to balance, removing the charge that has accumulated which may be presenting as dis-ease. It is not about fixing. Fixing has an attachment to the outcome and this alone limits what is possible as it locks the attention and intention on what is 'wrong'.
	Healing is returning to no charge, guided by awareness.
Heaven	Heaven is the non-dualistic reality when we Be Who We Are and Beyond, when all context dissolves and even the individuation of the Soul returns to Its Source. It is a reality Radiating Exquisite and Infinite Beauty and Love. There is an aspect of heaven that is at the polar-end of a dualistic reality. This is what is often experienced when we successfully cross over and we remain cloaked in ego/mind content. Depending on the vibration of that content in any moment, you may experience the higher vibrations of heaven. Heaven is a vibrational range, not a place. We can also experience heaven while incarnated, when we Be Who We Are in any moment. Often this can occur when we are doing something

	that resonates like Who We Are and we slip into Being. This is heaven on earth.
Hell	Hell is the vibrational range at the polar-end of a dualistic reality created by extreme self-judgement and self-imposed torment due to the tremendous charge on content worn. It is as it is in any moment, transmutation of charge will change the vibration worn.
	Hell is not a place we go if we failed to meet expectations of the ego/mind at either a micro or macro level. It is a self-imposed torment and it can be experienced even when incarnated.
	Hell can be observed at a macro level as a matrix of energy mirroring the self-judgement of all those creating this dualistic reality. Hell is not the polar-opposite of heaven. There is an experiencing of an aspect of heaven at the opposite end of a dualistic reality but this 'heaven' is a minute fraction of what heaven fully is. Heaven is more truly non-dualistic in nature.
Home	Home is God. Home is both Manifested Oneness and the All/No-thing of the Unmanifested. It is from whence we all individuated, and all yearning is to return Home to the Mother's Bosom where all yearning dissipates, all is unto You and You Are in a Divine Love and Joy beyond measure.
Identifications	Identifications are anything that you have ever identified with, that you ever created your identity with, that is important to you and/or you deem as being you or a part of you in the environment of any lifetime. Identifications are both cognitive and unconscious. It includes all the identifications you unconsciously adopted as who you are.

	Identifications are stored in the ego/mind and how you show up in the world or in existence in any moment is a direct reflection of the charge on this content. The content is charged to the extend that the identifications are significant to you, even unconsciously significant. Their role is to differentiate you and thus even their role creates charge as it encourages the creation and maintenance of separation, an imposed buffer from Who You Are. When we 'flat-line' on the charge, we may still function utilising identifications but there is no significance to any of it.
Incarnation	The 'coming into flesh' of Your Soul, an individuation of Oneness, into a body/mind complex already conceived. The timing of incarnation varies in each Presentation. The Soul inhabits the heart torsion field and remains merged until the choice to transition is made by the Soul.
Individuation	I use the term 'individuation' to reflect an apparent separation into a Unique aspect of Oneness projected as Your Soul. When we observe You, as Your Soul, we notice the Unique Essential Nature of the Soul, yet it is not separated. It is like we are looking at a Radiating Ray of Light from Oneness and we can then observe an individuated Soul as that Ray of Light. Everything that we experience as separate is individuated, an apparent separation from Oneness. Separation is an illusion. It is our ego/minds that have expectations and conclude what we are observing, deems separation as real and solidifies and isolates the form.

Infinite	Infinite means without end, limitlessness. When we reflect on Divinity, Infinite also reflects an Immeasurable and Incalculable Nature with no beginning and no end.
	When used as an adjective to describe such expressions as Infinite capacities, Infinite Resources and Infinite Possibilities, it reflects the same qualities. The capacities are endless and without limit, the resources inexhaustible and the possibilities boundless and beyond any scope or context.
	This is truly Who We Are and is fully Present when we collapse the individuation and re-merge in the All/No-thing.
Inspiration	Inspiration is God in action. It is awareness informing new ideas and new information Sourced from our non-separation from that Oneness and reflected literally as the Breath within our physicality.
	The 'Hum' of creation is Present whether in form or no form. When we incarnate, that 'Hum', that rhythm, transforms into physical breathing. As we breathe Life, we continue reflecting that Inspiration into the world. Whichever way we look, in form or no form, Inspiration is informing our expansion of Consciousness on the planet and in existence. Science and spirituality, there is no conflict. Awareness has been informing inspiring results always, yet the ego/mind can not acknowledge this. The ego/mind is limited to what it contains as content, including referencing existing knowledge. It does not even consider that all knowledge was at first awareness and knowing that has been input into the ego/

	mind. The ego/mind creates a separation and personal position that 'owns' knowledge. That is a lie. Receiving and perceiving awareness is known not to be personal, with a beautiful allowance of expressing that knowing through each of Our Essential Natures.
Isness	Isness reflects a no time/space non-dualistic reality where form or no form is what it is. There is no judgment, expectation or conclusion. There is no referencing to 'try and work out' what an ego/mind would deem the form or no form to be.
	Isness also reflects allowance of what is and the ease that arises with allowance. There is no need for the form or no form to be anything other than what it is. Awareness and choice arises naturally, without needs or any contortion, only choice.
Karma	Karma is all the charged content that buffers You from showing up in the world and in existence. Karma is your Michelin Man suit.
	Karma is as it is in any moment, reflecting the net vibration of all charged content, and it remains cloaking you whether you are incarnate or not.
	Karma is generated whenever 'you' have not followed the awareness of 'You' and it adds to what karma has already been generated, unless it is transmuted.
	Information on karma is stored in a vibrational signature.

Karmic and Contextual Potentialities from Infinite Possibilities	When we choose to create, what is reflected back to us mirrors the net vibration of the asking. When functioning from the ego/mind, all our identifications, both conscious and unconscious, influence the net vibration of any asking. Consequently, what we think we are asking is not necessarily what is received and perceived by Oneness as what we are actually asking. The Universe does not have a point of view about it. It will reflect back the net vibration of all the content relating to the asking. This content is karma and it includes any contextual framework we think is realistic to expect. What is created is limited within the scope of karma carried as charged content, including the context 'believed' to be realistic. Infinite possibilities are available, yet with the karma and the narrowing of context within that karma, we limit what is possible. The Universe doesn't try and work out what you meant. It is vibration and will mirror the vibration. Thus, while functioning from the ego/mind, we limit ourselves to karmic and contextual potentialities from Infinite possibilities.
Kit Bag	A Kit Bag is full of tools and techniques, chosen by you, that either perpetuate identifications or, ideally, facilitate the transmuting of charge on identifications. A Kit Bag is itself a tool and crutch until it is no longer required. Being cognitive of using a Kit Bag maintains a level of Presence, even if we are perpetuating identifications.

	Items in a Kit Bag that perpetuate identifications are items that maintain the status quo of what is significant to you. Predominantly, we choose actions unconsciously, and bringing attention to what we do in a day to perpetuate our position and points of view begins observation and cognitive awareness. Items in a Kit Bag that target the transmutation of identifications are any tools or techniques that function at vibrations higher than the issue or charged content. The most useful is a Kit Bag that vibrates like You, like Who You Are. This is of such high vibration that it will transmute what is buffering 'you' from 'You'. You may even slip into Being while utilising or accessing a tool within your Kit Bag. When we Be Who We Are, there is no need for a Kit Bag. The crutch of the Kit Bag is no longer required. Choice is informed by awareness. A Kit Bag is very useful when functioning from the ego/mind.
Knowing	Knowing is the information received and perceived when we function as Who We Are. It is awareness expressed through the Soul, reflecting Our Essential Nature, the Unique Aspect of Divinity we Be. Knowing does not need to be funneled down to be cognitive. It can be received and perceived quite formlessly, yet we know what our knowing is. We have no position or significance on that knowing. When we Be, we can bring our attention to any interaction of Consciousness within Oneness and receive and perceive our knowing. Knowing

	is not personal, it is a reflection of Oneness, uniquely expressing through You.
Life	With the observing of Our individuated Soul from Oneness, we can observe our existence and our Life 'begins'. When we buy into the separation of this individuation, into our existence, the yearning to return Home to Our Source arises. Incarnations are chosen as a means to know Self, they are not distinct lives. We have one Life played out in innumerable incarnations and not incarnations. It is our ego/minds that create further separation and categorising of a lifetime as our 'life'.
Light	Light is made from the fabric Consciousness. It is a transported, a channel, a vehicle of communication. As a vehicle, of itself, it has no content. It projects the content of any form reflecting and projecting apparent individuation. It is like the 'doing' word of Consciousness.
Lost Soul	A Lost Soul is someone who has so much charge on the content of their ego/mind that none of the awareness of their Soul filters through. They do not even receive the awareness to be input and contorted by the ego/mind. They function solely from what is stored in their ego/mind. Such individuals can be functioning at either end of the polarity spectrum. They can be dogged with no flexibility in thinking, deeming what they know is the only valid and correct position. They do not think any other point of view is worth considering. At the other end of the spectrum are those Lost Souls that are imprisoned by their thinking. One thought can become inescapably

	persistent and insistent. They predominantly withdraw from the world or seek relief from a fantasy or altered reality.
Manifested	The manifested is existence, that which is form. The origin of the manifested is the 'Aum' vibration from which all form arises, this is the Manifested God.
Manifested God	The Manifested God is the Oneness of existence, the rippling of the 'Aum' vibration as what Is. As we expand Consciousness on the planet, our awareness increasingly informs the articulation of the Magnificence of the Manifested God, Oneness. In truth, it can never fully be captured as its Nature is Eternal and Infinite, with no beginning and no end, reflecting a Divine Love that dissipates all yearning and which awaits all to know Who They Are and return Home.
Matter	Matter is form. With the 'Aum' vibration we have the origin of existence and form and matter. From the 'Aum' vibration Consciousness arises, and from Consciousness, energy with content is created when attention is given to create. As we create, the ripple effect from the 'Aum' vibration appears to condense into energy, molecule, atoms, etc. Matter at these apparent condensed, dense vibrations, is able to be received by the five senses.
Michelin Man suit	All the content and charge of the ego/mind creates a buffering that energetically shows up as wearing a cloak. When I perceive it, it shows up as a Michelin Man suit. It isn't Who You Are, it hides the Magnificence of You, yet you and the world will judge the Michelin Man suit as who you are. It is a lie.

New World	A New World is instituting. I perceived a tipping point in January 2016 when a New World, with its own 'Hum' came to Be.
	The New World is functioning in both a dualistic and non-dualistic reality at higher vibrations that the old dualistic reality.
	The target of the New World is for all to function from awareness and Be Who They Are. The target is for all to awaken.
	As we transition to this, there is an allowance of awareness and diversity of how we all show up in the world. In the old dualistic reality, awareness was generally not received or misidentified as personal knowledge.
	The New World is embracing the old world, and as we transition to Being, that old world will transition also. It is happening already. I have dedicated a chapter to the New World. Allow your awareness to arise and Be that in the New World, institute in the New World. This is what the world has been waiting for. We are all in this together.
No charge	When information does not illicit a reactive response, position or point of view.
	When functioning in a non-dualistic reality, no charge arises naturally.
	No charge can also be described as no further karma as You are functioning from awareness in that moment. While we remain functioning from the ego/mind, the target is to transmute the charge on identifications, including how that charge presents in our physicality, until there is no charge, a 'flat-lining' on the content.

No content	When I refer to anything having 'no content' I am referring to a form or not form void of identifications, including thoughts and emotions that would otherwise buffer the pure nature of that form or not form. The energy that creates any form may be present but without any buffering, more like a nature. There is also the 'no content' of Consciousness and Light where there is not even the content of energy as a differentiation of form. When we function from a non-dualistic reality, when we Be, we are void of content because of the lack of attachment, position or point of view. Everything arises in the moment and it is what it is. Choices are made or not made. There is no holding on to anything. Holding on reflects content.
Non-dualistic	When we function from Being, we no longer measure form in terms of identifications. Form is what it is and is received and perceived with no processing to determine where it 'fits' on the spectrum of conformity, rebellion or reform. There is no point of view. Form is then observed as non-dualistic. Further, while even light and shadow (the reflection of form itself) appear dualistic in nature, when Being, Oneness is experienced as an Isness beyond the apparent form that is observable. This is what is meant by non-dualistic whether in form or no form.
Non-dualistic reality	A non-dualistic reality is a reality where we function from Isness not separate from Oneness. Individuated projections of form are known to be not separate and knowing continues to inform this.

	There is no benchmarking, positioning or points of view that create duality or polarity. Choices are made from knowing with a singular focus for all to return Home
Non-existence	Non-existence is the Unmanifested. It is the All/No-thing before form. When we awaken to Who We Are, we function from a non-dualistic reality of Our Soul, an individuation of Oneness, reflecting an aspect of Divinity. When we awaken fully Beyond even the Soul, we return to Oneness and surrender with Absolute Devotion to God. 'You' are no more and there is a re-merging with the All/No-thing of non-existence. There is no point of view or position, that is the product of a dualistic reality. There is a deep surrender, the giving of Self to God with Unfathomable Love for God. It is from non-existence that Enlightened Ones re-project when called on. They are no longer individuated yet will Present in a form recognisable to the Soul asking for facilitation. The story has such charged point of view differentiating particular prophets and saints and religious leaders who are Enlightened. In truth, they all re-project from the same Source, the unique differentiation is to reflect something meaningful to the dear Loved one requesting guidance. They do not differentiate. The story creates the separation and conflict. It is a lie.

Non-separation	Non-separation reflects communion of everything that Is and everything that Isn't. It is experienced as 'no away'. Whatever we experience, perceive, observe, Be or do is never separate from Oneness, and Beyond Oneness, the Unmanifested God. You are never alone. While form appears separate, it is an illusion created by the ego/mind.
Oneness	Oneness is the Manifested God. Everything that exists is non-separate and is a aspect of Oneness. 'Aum' ripples through Oneness and the fabric Consciousness 'condenses' from 'Aum' enabling the projection of all forms from the creation of Light to energy to form that can be received by the five senses. When we receive and perceive beyond the five senses, we know that nothing is separate, and all is Oneness. We experience the Isness of Oneness It is only when we observe form in isolation using the five senses, and input that observation within the ego/mind, that we experience our separation from Oneness. Separation is an illusion. Oneness is existence. Oneness is the manifested. When we experience from the functioning of the ego/mind, we do not experience Oneness. We experience the separation and significance on that separation that is the very structure of the ego/mind. When we awaken to know Who We Are as Our Souls, we awaken to Oneness, we experience Oneness yet do not experience it fully while any context remains reflecting any separation. When we awaken fully Beyond Our Souls, Oneness is experienced fully..

Perception	Perception is the information you receive and perceive from Oneness and Beyond via Your Soul (When we awaken fully, we would not call it perception, it is an 'Isness' that is Beyond words). Perception is not clouded or filtered by any content of the ego/mind. When awakened to Who We Are, this is an Isness. When we have moments of experiencing Being, we receive the perceptions of the Soul in that moment as awareness, the language of the Soul.
Perspective	Your perspective is your unique experiencing of every moment. This is determined by all the identifications and charge on content stored within the ego/mind. Everything you experience is filtered and coloured by this content, resulting in your unique perspective.
	It is as it is in any moment. When the charge on content changes, your perspective changes. The target is to transmute the charge on this content until your perspective and Your perception provide the same information. This can also be called Enlightenment.
	This changing of perspective gives the illusion that we are evolving. We are not evolving, Who We Are Is. It is the cloak we are wearing that we are shedding.
	While functioning from the ego/mind, your perception will continue to be input into the ego/mind (except for Lost Souls) and contorted to create your perspective.

Polarised reality	A polarised reality is another word label for a dualistic reality where we function from an ego/mind and measure all identifications against a spectrum of conforming, rebelling or reforming, that is, right or wrong, good or bad or new benchmarks for right or wrong, good or bad. We experience our reality against those identifications, including experiencing a dualistic and separate nature of form itself.
Polarity	Polarity reflects the measure of opposites utilised within a dualistic reality to determine who we are and whether we are meeting identifications or not. Judgments, expectations and conclusions are established as what is right and what is wrong, what is good and what is bad. It is the establishment of the spectrum of measurement of success or failure. Different societies and groups establish different criteria for all of these measures. This is functioning from polarity.
Potentialities	Potentialities are what is possible within a framework or structure that is bought as real and which limits Infinite possibilities. When functioning from the ego/mind, all the charged content and identifications, including what is deemed realistic, creates the framework and structure that limits Infinite possibilities to potentialities. When awakened to Who We Are, we are limited to the extent that context is still in place. When we awaken fully, potentialities are Infinite possibilities. No framework or structure exists to limit anything. All is possible.

Presence	Presence is when the Infinite and Divine Self shows up in the world and in existence. It is a Radiance of Being. Presence is a vibration without content clouding it. It has the Nature of Our Essential Natures while We exist. While identifications may be in play for functional reasons, there is no charge or attachment to them. Common characteristics of this Nature for all are exuberance, intimacy, vulnerability, authenticity, Divine Love, irresistibility, non-attachment, gratitude, allowance, beauty, humility, caring, generosity, honouring, joy and devotion to God.
Presentation	When I use 'Presentation', I am highlighting the reflecting and projecting of Magnificence and Divinity as it Shines in any moment. Noticing Infinite Nature can facilitate observing when we filter that Nature with content.
Projection	I utilise the word 'projection' as a reminder that all form is a projection of Light from Oneness. While form appears real, it is not. It is our ego/minds and the context we limit ourselves to that solidifies form.
Re-merge	I used this word label to capture the returning to a non-separation rather than 'arrive at' or 'joining with'.
Re-Present	In hyphenating 'Represent', I wish to highlight the Infinite and Divine Nature of Presenting and Being Present in any moment. I am also highlighting 're', a reflecting and projecting anew, reflecting and projecting again and again.

Re-Project	I have used 're-project' to reflect the truth that everything is a projection of Light from Oneness. Those fully awakened Beyond Soul are not, and thus create the illusion of separation when choosing to re-project an image of 'themselves' as recognised by those seeking facilitation. Even Souls frequenting the higher realms and presenting more formlessly can re-project into a form they are recognised as, when chosen.
Right Action	Right Actions are actions we choose which mimic what would arise naturally when we Be Who We Are. Despite the ego/mind still in place, Right Actions facilitate the transmutation of charge as they function at a higher vibration similar to Being. They may also facilitate slipping into Being and you glimpse the joy and contentment of Being Who You Are. While we remain functioning from the ego/ mind, Right Actions and anything that resonates like You are what will 'fill your cup' and replenish you when you are drained within a dualistic reality, other actions provided only temporary relief.
'self'	When I refer to 'self', I am referring to the 'self' created by all the charged content of the ego/ mind. It is all the identifications you are wearing and that show up as 'you' in the world and in existence.
'Self'	When I refer to 'Self', I am referring to Your Soul, an aspect of Divinity individuated from Oneness.

Separation	Separation is the illusion of non-communion with Oneness. While functioning from the ego/mind, separation is experiencing everything we receive from the 5 senses and even from awareness (which is input and contorted by the ego/mind) as isolated observations. We may choose to join common threads or experiences together, yet this is not communion, this is the summing of parts, the summing of separation. Another way of describing separation is by observing something and if you can experience the beginning and the end, the finiteness of the 'some thing', you are experiencing separation. The wholistic communion of all is not experienced.
Soul	The Soul is the apparent individuation of Oneness reflected and projected by Light. The Soul incarnates a body/mind complex and is Infinite in nature. Its language is awareness and its only content is its Unique Essential Nature. The Soul reflects our One Life and is an Isness when incarnated and when not incarnated. When we awaken fully, the individuation returns to Source and the allowance of non-existence arises with ease and Divine surrender.
Soul mate	A Soul mate is someone who's Soul has a high degree of similar vibrational resonance to Your Soul's vibrational resonance. There are Souls whom we have Soul connections with from previous lifetimes and while frequenting other realms, however, these Souls are not Soul mates. They are more like the familiarity of family members.

Space	Space is the experience of Consciousness with no content. Consciousness has no content and when we Be in any moment, void of content, we experience the fabric of all form, Consciousness, and it is experienced as space.
Spirit	Your Spirit is Your Essential Nature. Your Spirit also comes with Breath, reflecting the rhythm of 'Aum' and transforming into a physical breathing on incarnation. It is Our Spirit, not separate from any other Divine aspect of Who We Are, that reflects Inspiration in the world and in existence. It has and will continue contributing to the expansion of Consciousness on the planet. It is God in action.
Stage	When we function from the ego/mind, we deem that all the identifications we have is who we are. I know that this is not who we are. All of these identifications create the stage upon which we are playing out a lifetime. Often, we have multiple stages, for example, a home stage, a work stage and a friend stage. By discussing our environments as the stage(s) of a lifetime, I hope to facilitate an observation that our environments can be a choice rather than an assumption that it is who we are. Thus, if you choose to change the environment you are not 'losing' you, you are merely making another choice, choosing another stage. With regard to Who We Are as a Soul, the stage is irrelevant, it is only a different choice.

Transformation	Transformation is the changing of form into another form. This change can be to a form more formless. In existence, everything is as it is and when transformed there is a new Isness. There is no death, only a changing of form. Even when we collapse the individuation of Self, being in allowance of non-existence, form and no form is as it is. Context dissolves yet there is no fretting or unease, there is total allowance of what is.
Transmutation	Transmutation is also transformation with an additional focus on removing charge on content. The word label, for me, was an energetic match to reflect the reduction, removing or 'flat-lining' of charge on content within the ego/mind.
Unique Potentiality	Unique potentiality is the potentiality that is presenting for you in any moment as a product of the identifications and charged content you are wearing and functioning from.
Universe	The Universe is another word label for Oneness, the Manifested God. In the story of the world, the term is restricted to all of 'space' and everything in it. I utilise the term much more expansively, Infinitely more expansively, to include not only form that can be observed by the five senses, even form we have not yet discovered, I include all of manifested reality, the origin of manifested reality, the Manifested God. If I was to illustrate, what the story defines as the Universe is a speck of dust compared to the Magnificence and Infiniteness and Eternalness of the Manifested God from which the story's Universe arises. The story's universe is a stage we play in.

Unmanifested	Beyond the manifested is the unmanifested. This is not a polarity within a dualistic reality. The manifested and unmanifested are more truly experienced in a non-dualistic reality. The unmanifested is before form and before the 'Aum' vibration of the Manifested God.
Unmanifested God	The Unmanifested God is the All/No-thing Beyond existence. It is beyond reference or context and is Unfathomable, Inconceivable and Unnameable. It is Before. It is from which All arises, yet this reflects context and has already limited the Indescribable Isness and Not Isness of the Unmanifested. There is No-thing Beyond God. There is No-thing Before God.
Vibration	All form can be perceived as the energy it reflects. Equally, this energy can be perceived at the level of vibration, that is, the unique pulsating of information reflecting that form. The less content within the form or rather, the more formless, the higher the vibration. When there is a lot of content, and/or when there is charge on content, including the point of view of the separation of that form, we can observe a greater density of form. When form condenses to such density, it can be received by the physical senses.
Vibrational resonance	The vibrational resonance of something is the specific vibration at which it frequents.
Vibrational signature	The vibrational signature is a storing of information at the level of vibration as it is in any moment. This is how information relating to karma and even information projecting Who You Are is stored throughout Our One Life.

| Who You Are | Throughout the book, I refer to 'Who You Are' with a capitalisation of each word. I found it useful to parallel who you think you are based on the perspective of the ego/mind, both at the micro and macro level, with Who You Are, an individuation of Oneness with a Divine and Infinite Nature, Your Soul.
By referencing what the ego/mind perpetually 'tries' to reinforce, we facilitate the awakening to awareness that informs that Who You Are is far more than a list of identifications. |

References

Bruce H. Lipton, P. (2005). *The Biology of Belief: Unleashing the Power of Consciousness, Matter and Miracles.* Santa Rosa, CA 95404: Mountain of Love/Elite Books.

CatholicAnswers. (2011, August 5). *What exactly does amen mean?* Retrieved from Catholic Answers: https://www.catholic.com/index.php/qa/what-exactly-does-amen-mean

Douglas, G. (1991). *Gary Douglas, Founder.* Retrieved from Access Consciousness: https://www.accessconsciousness.com

Dr. Richard Bartlett D.C., N. (1992). *Our teachers.* Retrieved from Matrix Energetics: http://www.matrixenergetics.com

Dylan, B. (1962). Blowin' in the Wind [Recorded by B. Dylan].

Etymonline.com. (n.d.). Retrieved from Etymonline.com: https://www.etymonline.com/word/enlighten

Hawkins, D. D. (2003, April 5). The Highest Level of Enlightenment: Tap the Database of Consciousness for Total Self-Realization. Niles, IL, USA.

Jonsson, M. J. (n.d.). *Articles: The Field of the Heart.* Retrieved from Matrix Energetics: https://www.matrixenergetics.com/pdfs/the_field_of_the_heart.pdf

Moore, K. L. (1988). *Essentials of Human Embryology.* Toronto: B.C. : Decker Inc.

Rinpoche, S. (1992). *The Tibetan Book of Living and Dying.* Harper Collins.

Setterfield. (2017). *God's Firmament & the Earthquake [part one].* Retrieved from AstrologyCom.com: https://www.astrologycom. com/godsfirmament1.html

Setterfield. (2017). *Zero Point Energy.* Retrieved from Zero Point Energy: http://www.setterfield.org/zpe.htm

Tesla, N. (2017). *Zero Point Energy.* Retrieved from Wikipedia: https://en.wikipedia.org/wiki/Zero-point_energy

Tolle, E. (2004). *The Power of Now: A Guide to Spiritual Enlightenment.* Vancouver, B.C: Namaste Pub.

Various. (2018). *Near-death experience.* Retrieved from Wikipedia: https://en.wikipedia.org/wiki/Near-death_experience

Veltheim, D. J. (2013). *The BodyTalk System: Principles of Consciousness Manual.* Sarasota,Florida: International BodyTalk Association Inc.

Wachowski, A. W. (Director). (1999). *The Matrix* [Motion Picture].

Weir, P. (Director). (2006). *The Truman Show* [Motion Picture].

Wilcock, D. (2006). *Kozyrev: Aether, Time and Torsion.* Retrieved from Divine Cosmos: https://www.divinecosmos.com/start-here/ articles/334-kozyrev-aether-time-and-torsion

Yogananda, P. (2016). *Autobiography of a Yogi.* London: Arcturus Publishing Ltd.

CPSIA information can be obtained
at www.ICGtesting.com
Printed in the USA
FFHW021932150819
54326810-60002FF